BI 3598700 8

D1145606

Beauty and Education

Routledge International Studies in the Philosophy of Education

Beauty and Education

Joe Winston

Routledge
Taylor & Francis Group

NEW YORK AND LONDON

BIRMINGHAM CITY UNIVERSITY LIBRARY

First published 2010
by Routledge
711 Third Avenue, New York, NY 10017

Simultaneously published in the UK
by Routledge
2 Park Square, Milton Park, Abingdon, Oxon, OX14 4RN

Routledge is an imprint of the Taylor & Francis Group, an informa business

First issued in paperback 2011

© 2010 Taylor & Francis

Typeset in Sabon by IBT Global.

All rights reserved. No part of this book may be reprinted or reproduced or utilised in any form or by any electronic, mechanical, or other means, now known or hereafter invented, including photocopying and recording, or in any information storage or retrieval system, without permission in writing from the publishers.

Trademark Notice: Product or corporate names may be trademarks or registered trademarks, and are used only for identification and explanation without intent to infringe.

Library of Congress Cataloging in Publication Data
Winston, Joe.
    Beauty and education / by Joe Winston.
        p. cm. — (Routledge international studies in the philosophy of education)
    Includes bibliographical references and index.
    1. Education—Philosophy.   2. Aesthetics—Philosophy. I. Title.
    LB14.7.W56 2010
    370.1—dc22
    2009038556

ISBN10: 0-415-99490-X (hbk)
ISBN10: 0-415-89664-9 (pbk)

ISBN13: 978-0-415-99490-3 (hbk)
ISBN10: 978-0-415-89664-1 (pbk)

This book is dedicated to the memory of my mother, Mary Catherine Winston, and my father, John Joseph Winston.

'The annihilation of beauty would leave us with an unbearable world, as the annihilation of good would leave us with a world in which a fully human life would be unliveable'.

Arthur C. Danto, 'The Abuse of Beauty'.

'Spirit of BEAUTY, that dost consecrate
With thine own hues all thou dost shine upon
Of human thought or form – where art thou gone?'

Percy Bysshe Shelley, 'Hymn to Intellectual Beauty'.

Contents

Figures

Acknowledgments

First and foremost, I would like to thank Colette Conroy, Mike Fleming, Fred Inglis and Miles Tandy for their invaluable comments on draft chapters of this book. My thanks also extend to Juliet Fry, Mary Pereira, Peter Reid and Gill Winston, all highly gifted teachers whose exemplary practice I draw from in examples that pepper the book. Thanks, too, to the educational team of the Royal Shakespeare Company—Rachel Gartside, Ginny Grainger, Helen Phipps and Jacqui O'Hanlon—whose work is referred to specifically in Chapters 5 and 7. Finally, I would like to thank my editors, Ben Holtzman and Jennifer Morrow, for responding patiently and efficiently to all my many queries.

Parts of the book have been aired in previous publications:

'Beauty, Goodness and Education', *The Journal of Moral Education*, vol.35, no.3 (September 2006). Copyright Taylor and Francis.

'"An Option for Art but Not an Option for Life": Beauty as an Educational Imperative', *Journal of Aesthetic Education*, vol.42, no.3, (Fall 2008). Copyright 2008 by the Board of Trustees of the University of Illinois. Used with permission of the University of Illinois Press.

'Drama and Beauty: Inspiring the Desire to Learn', in *IDEA 2007 Dialogues: The Notes, the Keys, Our Youth and Their Voices: Hong Kong Drama/Theatre and Education Forum & IDEA2007 World Congress-Hong Kong*. Published by Hong Kong Drama/Theatre and Education Forum (TEFO) and International Association of Theatre Critics (Hong Kong, 2008). Used with permission of IDEA and TEFO.

The child's poem in Chapter 5 was first published in my book *Drama and English at the Heart of the Curriculum*, London: David Fulton Press, (2004) with permission from the author. David Fulton Press is part of the Taylor and Francis group.

The extracts from Kit Wright's poem *The Magic Box* are printed with the permission of Penguin Books, UK.

The image of the Parthenon floor plan in Chapter 2 is taken from the Web site http://www.greeklandscapes.com/greece/acropolis/parthenon-picture.html where it states that it is not subject to copyright.

Titian's *Sacred and Profane Love* is printed with the permission of the Archivio Fotografico Soprintendenza per il Patrimonio Storico, Artistico ed Etnoantropologico e per il Polo Museale della città di Roma.

Jacques Louis David's *Portrait of Madame Récamier* is printed courtesy of the Musée du Louvre, Paris.

Pablo Picasso's *Les Demoiselles d'Avignon* is printed with the permission of the Estate of Pablo Picasso and the Artists Rights Society (ARS), New York.

Otto Dix's *Die Skatspieler* is printed with the permission of Die Bildagentur für Kunst, Kultur und Geschichte, Berlin.

The photos in Chapter 4 are of *The Emerald Cave*, a production mounted by The Play House, Birmingham, UK, printed with permission.

The child's painting in Chapter 5 is printed with the permission of its owner.

The image in Chapter 6 is printed with the permission of Wolframscience at www.stephenwolfram.com.

1   Seeking Beauty in Education

WHY IS BEAUTY SLEEPING?

A few years ago, when I first became interested in the topic of beauty and education, my colleagues were somewhat bemused. Their responses ranged from polite silence, to critical disbelief, to laughter. One colleague looked me up and down commenting that, for someone with an interest in beauty, he would never have guessed from the way I dressed. My dress sense aside, their responses are hardly surprising; beauty appears to be on no one's educational agenda. Whether in the detail of curriculum documentation, national strategy papers or educational research reports, you will look long and hard to find any reference to beauty. Even in arguments for the educational value of the arts, words such as culture, creativity, quality and excellence are common, but beauty is entirely absent[1]. John Holden has gone so far as to suggest that using the concept of beauty in any debate about the cultural value of the arts is nowadays 'an embarrassment at best, contemptible at worst'[2]. If beauty is sleeping, few educationalists are trying to awaken her, and the vast majority seem happy to forget about her altogether.

A recent debate held in London in March 2009 provides a useful starting point to help account for this neglect[3]. Speaking on behalf of the motion 'Britain has become indifferent to beauty', the philosopher Roger Scruton displayed an image of Botticelli's *Venus* alongside a photograph of the fashion model Kate Moss. Scruton's intention was to demonstrate the innate beauty of the former compared with the crass commercialism of the latter, arguing for the aesthetic and moral superiority of established art works over the crude products of contemporary culture. The design critic Stephen Bayley, on the other hand, speaking against the motion, embraced a more inclusive vision, presenting people's everyday search for beauty in fashionable clothes shops and contemporary design as a valid and energetic pursuit rather than an activity that merited our scorn. He ridiculed Scruton for his inability to recognise and welcome the beauty of the Venus *and* the beauty of Kate Moss. The problem for education, however, is that there are longstanding, ideological arguments that seem to present teachers with moral and political reasons for distrusting the beauty of both.

Beauty may well be very much alive outside of schools, but it is ethically difficult for teachers to ignore the way it is packaged and commodified by marketing experts to shape and exploit the desires and aspirations of young people. A quick glance through a telephone directory or a short visit to the newsagents is enough to signal a strong contemporary identification of the word 'beauty' with fashion and, in particular, cosmetics—products to beautify hair, nails, skin, face—noticeably evident in popular magazines aimed at teenage girls and young women. Young men, on the other hand, are presented with beauty in the form of female bodies, flaunted semi-pornographically in laddish magazines and in the metallic gleam of high performance cars and motorcycles. Glossy images of footballers, film stars and fashion models such as Kate Moss elide glitz and glamour with beauty and desire, and the promise of endless sunshine (and parties) on a beach in Mallorca or the Caribbean completes the picture. Underneath the surface glamour are dreams that blur wealth with well-being and consumerism with happiness, dreams that are anathema to any sober educational vision and particularly damaging, we are told, to the welfare and happiness of young people from disadvantaged backgrounds[4]. Elektra's condemnation of Helen of Troy would appear to be relevant still: 'Oh, what a vileness human beauty is, Corroding, corrupting everything it touches'[5].

Whether this corruption of beauty should lead educationalists to ignore it altogether, or whether their very negligence has exacerbated its corruption as a cultural value, remains a moot point. However, progressive voices have been equally critical of anyone who proposes, like Roger Scruton, that high art can act as a remedy for the debased values of commercial culture. Feminists, in particular, have been highly suspicious of beauty and its representation in the historical context of visual art as well as the contemporary world of fashion photography, arguing that both serve to obscure and reproduce the politics of gender. The traditional embodiment of beauty in the figure of the female nude they see as identifying beauty in its highest form with the servicing of male pleasure. The images of high art cannot, therefore, be so readily separated from the values of the fashion and cosmetics industries as all are guilty of peddling impossible images of perfection to women, perpetuating what Naomi Wolf famously called *The Beauty Myth*. In her book of the same name, she claimed that the cult of beauty ensnared girls and women, causing low self-image, depression and eating disorders[6]. She thus presented beauty itself as a political trap, one that operates profoundly against female interests.

The idea that beauty within the field of cultural production serves covert political interests has been particularly influential within the academy, from where it has permeated into the teaching profession. The idea that there exist universal examples of beauty which merit inclusion in a canon of great works of art has been challenged not only by feminists but also by scholars from within the fields of post-colonialism and disability studies and, most famously, by the work of French sociologist Pierre Bourdieu[7]. In brief, Bourdieu argued that an appreciation of beauty and an education in 'good taste' were sources of cultural capital, bestowing the signs of social distinction upon those who could benefit from them. Basing his study on the Parisian middle classes, he claimed that their artistic tastes—tastes which Roger Scruton would wholly approve of—were not the result of disinterested aesthetic pleasure but closely related to their desire for social distinction. The canon, he concluded, framed within an education system that told the stories and served the interests of a dominant class, worked against the interests of the lower classes by excluding them from participating in aesthetic pleasures they were nonetheless taught to regard as superior to their own.

From within such a critical clamour, with the politics of gender, race, class, the body and post-colonialism making their voices heard so stridently, many artists and teachers have looked back for inspiration to the aesthetics of German playwright, Bertolt Brecht[8]. He, too, saw beauty as seductive and consolatory, an emotional narcotic that put people's moral reasoning to sleep. Art, for him, should be overtly political, intent on awakening people's consciousness to the realities of political repression; its purpose was to change attitudes and not offer the shallow consolations of beauty. His theory—what he called the *Verfremdungseffekt*, usually translated into English as the 'alienation effect'—was offered as an anti-aesthetic, its aim being to shock and unsettle. Thus *rupture* rather than *rapture* was proposed as the key aesthetic determinant for any work of art committed to the furtherance of social justice. Small wonder, then, that Brecht still holds great currency in cultural and educational institutions among those artists and teachers committed to the furtherance of social justice; small wonder, too, that beauty as a concept has been so muted, arousing active hostility as well as passive disinterest in the field of education.

An introductory chapter should raise the issues it intends to examine throughout the book rather than attempt to resolve them. Yet there is one obvious aspect of beauty that such cultural and political debates have tended to ignore and that cannot be wished away; that is, its very ubiquity as a value in areas of human experience beyond the worlds of art and fashion, an ubiquity that marks it out as of central importance to our lives. Germaine Greer's contribution to the March debate began squarely from this position, arguing that the general elation and excitement caused by the recent visitation of spring was evidence that an innate love of beauty was a feature of our shared humanity. 'Our spirits rose, our optimism rose with it, because beauty doesn't exist outside us, beauty is a concept we have within us and we search for it all the time. We search for it in our daily lives . . . We have it at our back door, we have it on our lips'[9].

Seventy years ago, the philosopher R. G Collingwood made a similar point—that ordinary people use the word beautiful all of the time and know what they mean when they do: 'The word beauty, wherever and however it is used, connotes that in things by virtue of which we love them, admire them or desire them'[10]. Despite the criticisms it has had to endure from cultural and educational theorists, beauty has continuously held currency in the conversation of common experience. Whether used to describe a human or animal form, a male or female body; a sweet sounding, popular melody or a moment of breathtaking quality in a game of sport; whether used by a kindergarten teacher to praise a child's drawing or a mother to describe her daughter's new dress; in praise of a balmy, sunny evening or a particularly striking sunset—ordinary people use the word effortlessly, aligning language to world in a manner that communicates perfectly well how unexceptionally human it is to love and value beauty.

The very ubiquity of beauty in our cultural lives is sufficient evidence for us to regard it as a necessary human value. As with all such values, it will be shaped and influenced by the culture, or cultures, we live in; and one of the key socio-cultural roles of schools has always been to help shape the attitudes and values of young people. We might disapprove as teachers of how the beauty industry constructs and promotes particular images of beauty, but it is able to do this through the very human desire to be loved and admired and through the close connection that we instinctively make between love and beauty. To paraphrase Sappho, beauty is what we fall in love with[11]. We might hazard, too, that it is entirely appropriate for young people to admire and want to be admired, to love and wish to be loved. In which case, rather than to ignore beauty, schools might consider one of their important roles as being to introduce young people to human achievements and cultural activities that are worth falling in love with and to provide them with constructive opportunities to be loved and admired for reasons other than the style of their hair, the shape of their bodies and the brand of their trainers. Good schools may claim that they are already doing this, but if a concept of beauty can help drive and guide this endeavour then it would be negligent for them to ignore it.

THE UNCERTAINTIES OF BEAUTY, THE 'CERTAINTIES' OF EDUCATION: AN EXAMPLE

As beauty is a common human value, it is unsurprising that academics have in recent years begun to take it seriously once again, re-evaluating its place in our private and public lives[12]. Since the events of 9/11 this process has become more urgent as we face a political need to seek out those values we share in common as well as understand the political realities that mark us out as different. Janet Wolff's recent book *The Aesthetics of Uncertainty* can be seen as a significant contribution here. Wolff, herself a feminist philosopher and art specialist, recognises the critical contributions of feminism to the political debate on beauty but nonetheless defends a 'return to beauty'[13]. Whereas arguing that the discourse of beauty will always need to be socially located and historically contextualised—hence uncertain—she does not perceive aesthetic and progressive political values as mutually exclusive. Although she argues that any canonical choices need to be determined ethically through 'reflexive deliberation in the context of communities of interpretation'[14], she implies that beauty cannot be reduced to arguments of social interest and political oppression, as neither its apprehension nor its value can ever be entirely explained away by them.

If uncertainty is presented as an *ethical* virtue by Wolff, Germaine Greer sees it as an *aesthetic* virtue, an inherent quality to all experiences of beauty as they inevitably exist inside time. 'Remember the uncertainty of an April day', she writes, 'more beautiful for us because it is so uncertain'[15]. The current politics of education seem to hold little space for the virtues of uncertainty, however. Its discourse is one of exhortation and urgency, in which the confident assertions of managerialism spin endlessly around their own enshrined axes of certainty, expressed in language as unlovely as it is unremitting. The vocabulary of pre-determined objectives, performance indicators, measurable assessment criteria and visible levels of attainment are now so entrenched in the lexicon of teaching that the utilitarian values that underpin them pass unnoticed and unchallenged by the vast majority of teachers. Occasionally, however, the rhetoric of educational policy makers and their acolytes over-reaches itself, and the absurdity of their metaphors exposes the hubris at the heart of their visions. At such times, their certainties reveal themselves as vacuous.

An example can be found in the rhetoric surrounding one of the flagship educational policies of the current UK government, that of *personalised learning*. As conceptualised and promoted in the writings of Charles Leadbeater, personalisation aims to place the differentiated needs of individual learners at the heart of how schools operate[16]. A number of academic papers have criticised its argument as confused and ambiguous[17]; none of these have been written by David Hargreaves, however, who has been one of its most influential exponents. Working for the government-sponsored Specialist Schools and Academies Trust, Hargreaves has produced a series of pamphlets that promote personalised learning as 'a new educational imaginary' that will finally move schools from a structure developed for the nineteenth century to one more fitting for the twenty-first. In them he has theorised and refined the ways in which schools can restructure themselves in order to deliver the agenda of personalised learning, key to which are constructs he calls the *nine gateways* and the *four deeps*[18]. The nine gateways consist of a variety of thematic issues such as learning to learn, organisation, new technologies and student voice, each of which can be considered as an entry point to increasing the personalisation of learning. The gateways, we are informed, interconnect (or interact) and can be clustered into four groupings or 'deeps'—deep learning, deep experience, deep support and deep leadership[19]. 'Each cluster', we are told, 'compresses its constituent gateways so they form overlapping or interactive wholes . . . This is critical if the gateways are not to become silos insulated from one another'[20].

The desire to improve educational provision for all children is genuine and committed enough but is so buoyed along in its vision of radical restructuring and future transformation that it remains ignorant of the comedy being played out by the conceptual neologisms it has concocted. Hargreaves' terminology presents us unwittingly with a parody of a mythical, quasi-religious quest into an exciting, visionary future[21]. We enter a world of wonder in which, if we are not watchful, gateways can transform into silos and where numbers are highly significant. There are nine gateways, just as there are (or were) nine planets in the solar system and nine black riders in *Lord of the Rings*; there were four humours, four elements, four horsemen of the Apocalypse, now there are four deeps. If the use of deep as a noun is odd, the use of gateways as a metaphor becomes tortuous, especially if, as we are told, they are interactive. How can gateways interact with one another unless they form some kind of revolving door? In which case, whoever enters through one of these gateways quite literally will not know whether they are coming or going. This is more than mere flippancy on my part; as Nowottny has told us, if the metaphor is flawed, then so is the thinking behind it[22].

New language such as this is intended to open up new ways for teachers to understand and act upon the world of schooling. The problem is that it can all too readily have a deadening effect on thinking, resulting in new ways of talking about education but little else. Take, for example, a paper written in 2006 entitled 'Towards a Personalised Educational Landscape' by Peter Humphries, chair of a group calling itself 'Personalised Education Now'[23]. As well as displaying a taste for his own linguistic inventiveness, coining the term 'edversity' (for educational diversity), he takes the metaphor of personalised learning as a quest and transmutes it to that of a trekking holiday. Students become 'PEL travellers' who can take up 'packaged or bespoke learning journeys' and embark on a 'process of co-constructed learning travel'; teachers and mentors become 'travel agents and guides' backed up by 'intelligent ICT agents(cies)'; digital technologies will 'support navigation and signpost the way with guidance and just-in-time learning' and so on. The conclusion is typically unrestrained in its blithe, utopian imaginings: 'A PEL would accumulate societal learning capital having a profound positive generational impact. It would advance social cohesion and inclusion, active democracy and other qualitative aspects of our lives and communities'. Walter Nash has commented wryly on the way such professional jargonising can become a substitute for thought: 'You can shuffle the words and cut the phrases to the admiration of all and your brain need not once be up and running'[24].

This obsession with newness—of language, of theory—reflects the kind of Modernist rhetoric that, because of its progressive agenda, has long captured the attention and the energies of those who theorise education; and, as we shall see in the next chapter, the rhetoric of Modernism is openly hostile to the idea of beauty. There are, indeed, radical proposals in personalised learning that chime with the central tenet of Modernism, namely, the power of reason to make the world a better place by starting again. That schools should form networks so that students can move between them, thus choosing from a broader range of curriculum offerings; that the centrality of the classroom should disappear in favour of more flexible groupings; that the teacher be just one of a network of adults including mentors, teaching assistants, artists, technicians and child support workers of various kinds, responsible for the delivery of an educational programme at home and in work places as well as in schools. Although such proposals might on the surface appear exciting, equitable and rational, there are nonetheless dangers in such attempts to sever links between the profession of education and its historical practices. Robert Hughes has summed them up admirably when writing of the Modernist myth that cast the artist as *precursor*. He is worth quoting at length, if for the word 'artist' we substitute the word 'teacher':

> The cult of the precursor means that you substitute a prospective, and therefore an imaginary, relation between present and future for the tangible and perceptible relationship between past and present. Slow as it may seem, the process by which the past feeds into the present does at least work in favour of the living artist: it gives him or her a solidity, a location, whereas the role of the precursor, pushed to its limits, turns the artist into a historical expedient whose role is less to be than to assist in the labour of becoming. He or she is gripped in a parenthesis between the dead past and the unborn future, and this role has haunted modernist culture for the last century[25].

Despite the seductive nature of some of its emotive appeal, personalised learning is arguably the latest in a series of projects to reform education that follow a rational, managerial, technical model, concentrating on system changes and structures to increase effectiveness. Within such programmes, teachers are, indeed, *historical expedients* rather than inheritors of a social practice with its own history. Their own passions, interests, hopes, dreams are irrelevant, their role being reduced to that of *assistants* rather than autonomous professionals, with educational practice a process of stern and worthy drudgery, a *'labour* of becoming'. The *solidity* and sense of *location* teachers need can only be made tangible through a 'perceptible relationship between the past and the present', not an 'imaginary relation between present and future' as it is in this link between past and present that they can discover and refine their values, values rooted in a historical practice[26]. Like artists, teachers inherit more than they invent and make use of techniques, systems and structures to service rather than determine their values.

STRUCTURE AND PURPOSE OF THE BOOK

Personalisation is a new concept that can only yet be described as a vague aspiration and not as a value, one whose logical and empirical base is open to challenge and whose conclusions, as Campbell et al. point out, are still only a theoretical set of propositions[27]. Beauty, on the other hand, is undisputedly a human value, and a historical investigation into its conceptual history will illuminate how and why this is the case, how its worth as a value has come to be clouded in western thought and what its rediscovery might offer today's educators. In pursuing this investigation, I intend to avoid the broad, visionary sweep that characterises those educationalists whom I have criticised for evangelising the future rather than illuminating the present. I do not propose that a return to beauty will solve pressing problems such as pupil disaffection, social fragmentation or the current crisis of global market capitalism. And yet I hope to show that beauty does, indeed, speak to these and other important issues modestly, through specific examples, in gentle but insistent tones that we can learn from if only we give it our attention.

Two important premises of this book, then, are that we learn best how to imagine the future by looking closely at history and that the concept of beauty can inform what teachers do in progressive ways, whilst avoiding the kind of revisionist zeal that warps rather than liberates their imaginations. Consequently, much of the book's intellectual journey is historical in nature with its examples drawn from existing, not imagined, practices. I begin in Chapter 2 with an investigation into how the confusion of understandings and attitudes towards beauty that exist within education can be enlightened by an inquiry into three traditions of thought—Platonism, the Kantian Enlightenment and Modernism. It is impossible to consider the nature of how we learn through beauty without attending once again to those theories of learning that put an emphasis on experience rather than the accumulation of skills. This I attend to in Chapter 3, which also includes a consideration of chance and uncertainty in education and how this can be related to the fragility of beauty. In Chapter 4 I attempt to argue that an education in beauty can, indeed, be aligned with an education in goodness—and here I deliberately choose 'good' as my key word to complement the more fashionable 'ethical'. Such an argument reclaims education as an intrinsically moral rather than a merely technical endeavour and establishes the relevance of beauty across the curriculum, in subjects other than the arts. It also leads us to consider a vocabulary of homely virtues, as relevant to pedagogy as they are absent from how it is currently theorised. I return to the arts in Chapter 5 in order to look critically at the current attention to creativity and examine closely three examples—two of children's work and one of pedagogy—in which I argue that the concept of beauty provides a more satisfactory basis for evaluation than does the current lexicon of creativity. In Chapter 6 I attend exclusively to how beauty might inform teaching and learning in science and mathematics. This is more than a conscious attempt to counter balance my own personal proclivity for the arts but responds to the surprising fact that scientists and mathematicians are likely to use the term 'beauty' far more freely and less self consciously than contemporary teachers of the arts. In Chapter 7 I conclude with a summative consideration of how beauty might be articulated by teachers as a value to underpin their everyday practices.

Wolff's proposal that specific, interpretive communities should determine aesthetic values needs qualifying within the framework of mainstream education, inasmuch as, within any school community, there are less choices open to members than there are for those aesthetic communities she is referring to. Students have very limited choices over which schools they attend, by whom they are taught, who their classmates are and, until the age of sixteen, which subjects they can study. Teachers similarly cannot choose the children they teach and operate within a curriculum which prescribes much of what there is to be taught. No matter how reflexively they negotiate issues of power and how much they involve children in curriculum negotiation, teachers are given authority for a reason and have the responsibility to use it well. This implies that their job is not simply to negotiate and deliberate upon issues of value but also, in some significant ways, to foster particular values that have been culturally inherited and are deemed to be worthwhile. If, as I am proposing, beauty should once again become such a value, this presents a particular challenge to teachers. If a school is committed to democratic values, for example, these must be consciously promoted in practices within and beyond the classroom by teachers who believe in them, not simply talked about and agreed upon in principle. Teachers must be able to point to particular examples and say 'this is what democracy looks like and this is why it is good'. Similarly with beauty—if it is to be regarded as a value in the classroom, it will not be enough for certain paintings or poems to be discussed and their worth negotiated according to sensitively selected criteria; the teacher must of necessity promote and foster certain examples of beauty *as beautiful*, effectively saying to children (although much more subtly than this) 'this is what beauty looks like and this is why it is good'.

The fact remains, however, that none of our understandings of beauty are detached from historical and cultural experience. The examples I put forward in the book are inevitably shaped by my own upbringing, education and professional life. I was born a heterosexual male in a white, working-class, Roman Catholic family; my formative years were spent in Liverpool during the 1960s; I was educated in a grammar school and studied French at university. These facts of my personal history have doubtless led me to respond to particular kinds of beauty. As a schoolteacher, I spent much of my career teaching across the curriculum and working with children between the ages of eight and thirteen; as a teacher educator, I have been fortunate enough to be able to concentrate on my passion, drama and theatre education. These factors, too, explain the examples I choose to amplify my argument, an argument that cannot be made *without* resorting to specific examples. In this I am guided by a memorable phrase from Clifford Geertz, that in order to illustrate how beauty works as education, we will need to look to the tenor of its setting in order to find the sources of its spell[28].

I first voiced publicly the idea that beauty should once again become a central educational concern at an international drama education conference in Hong Kong[29]. The response from many of my British, American and Australian colleagues was not dissimilar to that of my colleagues from the university—a mixture of puzzlement and polite indifference with some critical curiosity. By contrast, the president of PETA, a young people's theatre organisation based in the Philippines, whose work with street children has become internationally celebrated, approached me afterwards, saying with enthusiasm that this argument was a very important one for the children with whom she works, as often they have nothing other than beauty to inspire and give them hope. Hope, as we shall see, is a quality inherent to the experience of beauty; hope, pleasure and the promise of happiness it entails. The argument spoke directly to her experience as an educator. I took great encouragement from this, an encouragement that nourishes me still.

2 The Meanings of Beauty
A Brief History

What do we mean when we call something 'beautiful'? What nuances of value does the word imply? Crispin Sartwell has explored these questions by examining the semantics of the word for beauty in six different languages and cultural traditions[1]. The Sanskrit term *sundara*, for example, carries resonances of holiness, which guides Sartwell into various meditations, from the beauty he finds in the music of Bob Marley to the spirituality of the *Kama Sutra*. The Hebrew term *yapha* he equates with glow and bloom—the beauty of flowers, the beauty of gems. The Japanese concept of *wabi sabi*, on the other hand, with its connotations of humility and imperfection, leads him to reflect among other things upon the culturally specific art of *suiseki*, or the creation of miniature landscapes from stones, and the simple but rough beauty of the blues. Sartwell's project is personal in its tone and fragmentary in its structure, but it is more than a fanciful, quasi-religious tract. If, as Wittgenstein proposed, language defines the limits of our world, then Sartwell articulates a set of expansive, revelatory and cross-cultural concepts for beauty that can enrich our understandings of what it might mean to others and to ourselves.

Such a project is significant for educators as it reminds us that understandings of beauty are embedded in culture; and it can help us gain some conceptual footholds at a time when globalisation is bringing children from an increasing number of cultural and inter-cultural backgrounds into our classrooms. However, the English words 'beauty' and 'beautiful' have themselves accrued and discarded a range of meanings throughout the turbulent development of Western thought. This chapter investigates some of the more important of these. Like Sartwell, my aim is to open up rather than close down possibilities of meaning in the belief that an appreciation of its ambivalent and sometimes contradictory resonances is necessary before we can discuss the relevance of beauty for education with any real coherence. In a short study such as this, such an exercise is of necessity selective and runs the risk of over simplification. I will concentrate therefore upon three traditions of thought and expression—Platonism, the Kantian Enlightenment and Modernism—as these, more than any others, explain why we think of beauty in the ways we do today. They will also help us rediscover different ideas associated with beauty to inform an intelligent consideration of what it has to offer a child's education in the contemporary world.

THE IDEAL AND THE DESIRED: THE PLATONIC AND NEOPLATONIC TRADITIONS.

The word that the ancient Greeks used for beauty—*kalon*—denoted qualities such as fine, pleasing, excellent and admirable within a broad range of contexts. It was not associated primarily with what we today would call the arts—music, art, poetry, drama—and was just as likely to be applied to a person's character, to an idea or to a deed than to a human artefact; both an act of courage and a philosophical argument could be described as beautiful. In this sense, as Paul Kristeller tells us, the Greek concept of beauty 'was never neatly or consistently distinguished from the moral good'[2].

Plato himself had very ambivalent feelings about the arts. His particular form of philosophical idealism postulated that concepts and ideas were more fundamental—and hence more real—than any physical realisation of them could ever be. The beauty of any particular human being, or any particular flower, was temporary and would pass, whereas the *idea* of these forms would last and was hence more real. This led him to disparage imitative arts such as drama and painting for, if an object such as a flower was itself the imperfect shadow of an ideal flower, then any representation of this flower was, in effect, the imitation of an imitation, the shadow of a shadow. Hence beauty, for Plato, was more likely to be found in the natural world than in the arts, in the actual world of human action than in its imitation, but its perfect form could only be found in ideas. And the purest form for the expression of these ideas was mathematics.

In this Plato was greatly influenced by the teachings of Pythagoras. We remember Pythagoras, of course, for his triangles, but his philosophy went much further than theorising the hypotenuse. For him, the universe (or 'cosmos') had an underlying, simple mathematical order, an order which was beautiful and based on proportion, harmony and balance. The more that an object in the real world conforms to this order—harmonious music, for example—the more beautiful we will judge it; for if beauty is the key to nature, then we, too, are part of that nature, and our souls respond to its rules. One of the great legacies of this idea of beauty has been classical architecture, most perfectly realised in the Parthenon. Here the proportions of the building are based upon strict mathematical considerations, intended to bring most pleasure to the eye. The ratio of 9:4, for example, is operative in the vertical and horizontal proportions of the temple and also in the spacing between the columns and their height. A series of complex, rectangular symmetries are evident in its façade, and the floor plan, too, illustrates the harmony in balance, proportion and symmetry that govern the building's design.

The Elgin Marbles

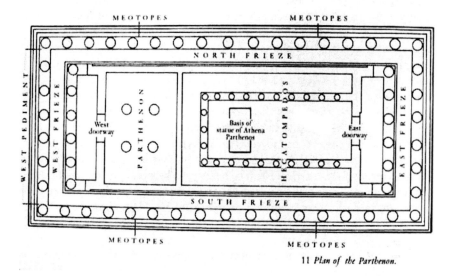

11 *Plan of the Parthenon.*

Figure 2.1   Floor plan of the Parthenon. Image from http://www.greeklandscapes.
com/greece/acropolis/parthenon-picture.html

As a physical and durable realisation of mathematical concepts, Plato held
the beauty of architecture as one of the highest of human achievements. As
he writes in *Philebus*,

> What I understand here by beauty . . . is not what the common man
> generally understands by this term as, for example, the beauty of living
> things and their representation. On the contrary, it is sometimes recti-
> linear . . . and circular, with the surfaces of solid bodies composed by
> means of compasses, the chord, the set square. For these forms are not
> like others, beautiful under certain conditions; they are always beauti-
> ful in themselves.[3]

Plato saw the beauty of mathematics—its logic, its patterns and its
proofs—as present in the dialectical arguments of Socrates, his great
mentor, fashioned as they were to emulate the deductive reasoning of
geometry: 'For geometry will lead the soul to truth and create the spirit of
philosophy'. It is no small wonder that over the entrance to the academy
he founded in Athens he had inscribed the words 'Let none ignorant of
geometry enter here'[4].

Despite its close association with logic and order, Plato's idealism does
not in any sense imply a concept of beauty ascetic in its intentions or coldly
remote from human passions. In fact, in *Phaedrus* and in particular the
Symposium, he relates the experience of beauty intimately to the spirit of

Eros—to passion, desire and the erotic force of human love. As Alexander Nehamas explains, 'Plato and the ancients were not afraid of the risky language of passion because they thought that beauty, even the beauty of lowly objects, can gradually inspire a longing for goodness and truth'[5]. The section of the *Symposium* in which this intimate connection between love, beauty and virtue is explained is in the form of a conversation which Socrates reports having had with a woman, Diotima[6]. Love, she argues, begins with the recognition of beauty in the body of another, and with it comes the desire to possess that body physically. Love sparked by beauty does not, however, stop with the act of physical possession, for it is only natural for us to want to understand the nature of the beauty that has set our desire alight. In Plato's philosophy, any beautiful body is beautiful in so far as it responds to an ideal form of beauty; so lovers, Diotima explains, in seeking to understand their passions, begin to recognise the features their lovers share with other beautiful people. And for Plato these beauties are not only commensurate with the idea of the body as a measure of architectural proportion; in essence, they are beauties of character (or of the soul), derived from the virtues that their lovers embody, more than they are surface features of form. In this sense, falling in love is the beginning of a quest for knowledge. If the lovers follow this quest to its logical ends, they will move through a series of levels, each higher than the previous one; from an attempt to understand the qualities of the soul that make their loved one beautiful, to a desire to learn about the cultural institutions that were able to fashion such beauty and upwards again to discover the knowledge needed to bring such institutions into existence. So, although founded in the erotics of the body, a love of beauty will, for the thinking person, lead into the higher world of philosophy, for 'the lover is turned to the great sea of beauty, and, gazing upon this, he gives birth to many gloriously beautiful ideas and theories, in unstinting love of wisdom'[7]. Very importantly, as Nehamas insists, these higher points of understanding are in no way transcendental, disembodied experiences; for

> though these 'higher' beauties are abstract and seemingly impersonal, they never cease to provoke action and inspire longing . . . The most abstract and intellectual beauty provokes the urge to possess it no less than the most sensual inspires the passion to come to know it better.[8]

In this way, Plato defines the human response to beauty as a dynamic, embodied process, one that unites emotion with cognition, desire with understanding, learning with happiness and fulfilment.

Plato's thoughts on beauty were built upon in the third century of the Christian era by Plotinus, who developed the idea that moral beauty was superior to any of its purely physical manifestations. According to Plotinus, each of us possesses a soul that was once unified with a divine being.

In gaining material form in our bodies, our souls experience a sense of fracture and of loss. If I am confused in my desires and disoriented in my longings that is because my soul is, in his words, 'dragged in every direction by its chains towards whatever it happens to perceive with its senses'[9]. In beauty, however, the soul has the chance to recognise its kinship with the divine. This recognition can be stimulated by physical objects—we might recall Dorothea Brook's response as she gazes at the jewels of her mother in George Eliot's *Middlemarch*: 'How very beautiful these gems are!' she exclaims, 'They look like fragments of heaven'[10]—but Plotinus, like Plato, sees aesthetic qualities as being essentially moral and dynamic in their nature. As John Armstrong explains, 'The beauty of a physical object (for Plotinus) embodies purity, perfection, harmony and order. And these are precisely the qualities that the soul strives to attain in itself. So in the beautiful object we see what we should be'[11]. It is the qualities within these objects that we love rather than the objects themselves, qualities 'more fully realised in beautiful action, in beauty of character or of mind . . . more truly beautiful than any physical thing could be'[12]. It is the moral force behind the experience of beauty, then, which explains why its thrill can both uplift and sadden us at one and the same time; what we recognise in it connects with our deepest longings, longings that have become obscured and obfuscated by the pressures of day-to-day living, a painful fact that beauty can illuminate in our thinking by igniting our emotions.

The ideas of Plotinus had a strong influence on the development of mediaeval Christian philosophy and persisted well into the Renaissance. The writings of Pico della Mirandola in fifteenth-century Florence, for example, and of Ficino, drew heavily from the Neoplatonic tradition and influenced writers such as Erasmus and Thomas More as well as painters such as Botticelli and Titian. Titian's misnamed *Sacred and Profane Love*, for example, as well as being a beautiful picture in itself, can be interpreted as a visual allegory of Plotinus' thinking. It depicts two beautiful young women sitting on a marble fountain, one fully clothed in a gorgeous white dress, the other semi-naked. Both women represent beauty. The clothed (and hence more restrained) figure on the left is human beauty, with the naked (hence more passionate) figure, who holds a lighted flame, representing celestial beauty. That the fountain where they are seated is the fountain of love is indicated by the central presence of Cupid, who gently stirs the water between them. The décor on the fountain itself depicts the more bestial acts of which humans are capable—one man savagely beating another, for example—signifying how the progress from a love of human beauty to a love of the divine does not dispel human passions but purifies them. The allegory is re-enforced in the pastoral background to the right of the celestial beauty, where a peaceful shepherd (who could represent Christ, the Good Shepherd) separates a group of hunters from a pair of lovers, symbolically mediating the animal passions of the one into the purer passions of the other[13].

Figure 2.2   Sacred and Profane Love (c. 1514), Titian. Printed with the permission of the Archivio Fotografico Soprintendenza per il Patrimonio Storico, Artistico ed Etnoantropologico e per il Polo Museale della città di Roma.

This Neoplatonic identification of beauty with love, and of ultimate beauty with divine love, may well strike a chord with Christians even today, but it does not chime so readily with contemporary secular sensibilities. There is a scene in David Lynch's *Blue Velvet* where a female singer in a nightclub performs the song from which the film derives its title. We see a man called Frank in the audience (a brilliant and terrifying performance from Dennis Hopper), someone we already suspect to be a psychopath. As the camera pans closer to him we notice that he is moved to tears by the singing, clutching a piece of blue velvet in his hands like a child as he listens and mouths along to the lyrics. Earlier we have witnessed him perform a bizarre, frightening and abusive sex act on the woman and, as the film's narrative progresses, his behaviour becomes increasingly violent and monstrous, not less so. Any thrill of recognition experienced by Frank at the beauty of the woman and her singing has a post-Sadean, post-Freudian centre that we can all too readily recognise, the potential for beauty to disturb as well as redeem, to inspire acts of rape as well as love.

Despite his apparent remoteness from the concerns of modernity, we can still learn a lot from Plotinus. After all, Frank's actions are *meant* to disturb us and are deliberately portrayed as monstrous and shocking. This is not the world as we would like it to be, and Plotinus recognises the existence of characters such as Frank and judges their warped responses to beauty as those of a soul arrested in its development 'dragged to the exterior and downward into darkness'[14]. In case this seems rather moralistic, a very different example, this time from real life, illustrates how we can use Plotinus to articulate something profound about the vocation of teaching.

In the BBC series *The Choir: Boys Don't Sing*, broadcast in the UK in early 2008, Gareth Malone, a young conductor from the London Philharmonic Orchestra, spent two terms teaching in a tough, boys comprehensive school in Leicester, which had a strong tradition of sports but none at all of singing. His aim was to introduce a culture of choral singing into the school, with the immediate challenge of forming a choir to perform in a national school's festival of choral music later that year. The series followed Malone through the triumphs and setbacks he experienced, concentrating on the efforts of individual boys and on his own mixture of perseverance, expertise, hard work, stubbornness and dogged belief both in himself and in the boys. The series culminated in an exhilarating and moving performance of the Ben E. King song *Stand by Me* at the Royal Albert Hall. One of the most touching stories of the individual boys traced throughout the four programmes centred around thirteen-year-old Imran, whom Malone discovered rapping in the playground with his friends and whose singing voice he immediately recognised as the most talented in the school. Malone's efforts to persuade Imran to join in the choir led to much frustration on his part. Imran's attitude was surly, his behaviour challenging and his attendance unreliable. But Malone did not give up. *Stand by Me* was arranged specifically for Imran and his group to perform a solo version of the chorus of Sean Kingston's *Beautiful Girl* as an integral part of the song. In the event he sang it beautifully and afterwards, his mother in tears, he told her he had done it for her. He was evidently proud of his performance, happy to have overcome his own 'stupidity' (his word), and he praised Malone for continuing to believe in him.

However much this might sound on paper like the sentimental plot of a second-rate Hollywood movie starring Whoopi Goldberg, I know I was not the only person involved in education to be both exhilarated and deeply moved by the story of Imran and Malone's turbulent relationship with him. Plotinus provides us with an explanation as to why that should be. Through the lens of his theory, Imran can be seen as a tough young man, resisting the chance to be part of something beautiful, yet at the same time wanting deeply to be so. All kinds of pressures of identity might have been militating against his participation in the choir—being the eldest son in a one-parent family; being black in a largely white school; seeing a choir as alien to his preferred, popular cultural practices; having framed his identity at the margins rather than at the centre of the school's culture. Yet none of this was making him happy and, having eventually triumphed over these contradictory emotions, he felt the thrill of being part of something beautiful and recognised it as something of great value to himself. As Nehamas reminds us, the Platonic tradition sees in beauty a promise of happiness, something that Imran attained for at least the duration and immediate aftermath of his performance. This is not a moralistic vision, simply a perspective that accords with how many committed teachers respond to challenging children in their charge; that at base there is goodness there—be it talent or intelligence or some other human quality—goodness they refuse to give up on. To see and hear Imran singing at the Royal Albert Hall provoked in me exactly the kind of painful pleasure that Plotinus says beauty can inspire and for much the same reasons that he says it does. It made me wonder how often I had given up on children in my past life as a class teacher; how if I had stuck with them and believed in them as Malone had I might have done them some real service. I then consoled myself by thinking of the times I *had* given challenging young people the chance to shine in performance. Most of all it re-enforced my belief in the transformative power of the arts. My professional soul, if you like, grasping to be re-united with its deepest values, with the teacher I would most want to be, felt at once the thrill and the loss of recognition, a recognition with beauty at its heart. This is the moral force of beauty rejoining goodness, twin values at the heart of Platonic thought.

The Platonic tradition shapes a lot of the thinking in later chapters, and there are several reasons for this. Learning through beauty is here associated with joy, hope and fulfilment, as motivating a quest for understanding based upon our deepest desires. It is built on a tradition of ideas that explicitly does not confine beauty to the arts, but sees it as evident in human action, human character, in the natural world, in ideas, philosophy and the foundational principles of science. In other words, beauty can help us think about values inherent to a wide range of educational concerns; in educational policy, in curriculum subjects, in the kind of society we would like to live in and the kind of people we would like our children to grow into. Its notion of being based in the realm of harmony, balance and proportion is conceptually narrow but can be seen to have moral as well as intellectual weight. It can also serve to frame a subject such as mathematics as inherently *pleasurable*, rather than as the system of disciplined torture that can still characterise its pedagogy in some of today's classrooms. For both Plato and Plotinus, we love beauty as an expression of qualities we admire or yearn for—in other words, it is not dependent upon physical appearance but on how this reflects inner virtues of character. This is what Nehamas means when he describes beauty as 'always manifested in appearance without ever being limited to it'[15]. Nonetheless the implications are complex and might lead us to condemn as morally evil those whom we perceive to be physically ugly. Western history has too many historical examples of this tendency, from the persecution of witches to the demonization of the Jews in Nazi propaganda, for us to dismiss it. For now, we might speculate on the room for conceptual manoeuvre that Nehamas' description provides. What if we could learn to see someone as beautiful by learning to see them differently—not through being preached at but by coming to recognise the potential for beauty within them—through what they think, do, say, write, make or perform? In the Platonic tradition, such recognition is not only a possible but also a necessary condition of the experience of beauty.

THE INVENTION OF AESTHETICS AND KANT'S *CRITIQUE OF JUDGMENT*

The eighteenth-century Enlightenment brought about a major revolution in the history of Western thought through a concerted intellectual effort to systematise and categorise all forms of human knowledge. It was at this time that the sciences and the arts were conceptualised as epistemologically different, the former dependent upon a system of logical thinking, of facts and proofs, the latter as sensuous in nature, founded in pleasure rather than logic and centred principally around the attribute of beauty. *Aesthetics*, the term used to describe this type of knowledge, was first used by the German philosopher Baumgarten, but it was Immanuel Kant in his *Critique of Judgment* who presented the most coherent and influential theory of aesthetic knowledge and the nature of the pleasure at the heart of aesthetic experience.

The key to an understanding of beauty, Kant proposed, would not be found by looking at beautiful objects but by analysing our responses to them. An experience of beauty, he suggested, is dependent upon a set of necessary, inter-related conditions or 'moments', all of which happen in the human mind. First of all, it is a result of what he calls 'harmonious free play' between our capacity for understanding and our capacity for imagining. If our *understanding* relates to our ability to order and make sense of the world, then our *imagination* is the cognitive link between the material world and our human consciousness, as it is the imagination that 'prepares the material of sensation for the reception of concepts'[16]. But when it is in free play with our capacity for understanding, the imaginative process is arrested and prolonged in a pleasurable manner without reaching any conceptual generalisation.

Let us take as an example Jacques-Louis David's *Portrait of Mme Recamier*, painted in 1800 and on display in the Louvre. The subject is a beautiful young woman dressed in a loose-fitting, long white dress of the classical style fashionable at the time. She sits with her legs outstretched on a chaise longue, her right arm poised gracefully over her thigh, and she gazes over her right shoulder at the viewer. Her feet are bare. According to Kant, if I find this painting beautiful I am not, in contemplating her, trying to categorise her in any sense—her hairstyle or dress as particularly fine examples of early Napoleonic fashion, for example. What arrests my attention is her very particularity—perhaps the specific play of light and shadow on her face or how the elegance of her figure and the luminosity of her dress are thrown into relief by the rich green and brown textures of the background. I may well be struck by the eyes that stare confidently from the canvas, seeing in them a sharp intelligence with a hint of vulnerability. Kant describes such a contemplation of beauty as 'disinterested' as it satisfies no other need or appetite of mine; so, for example, if I liked the painting because I found the woman sexually attractive, this would be an *agreeable* experience, not an aesthetic one. Similarly, if I liked it because I admired in Juliet Recamier a feisty, beautiful woman strong enough to resist the amorous advances of Napoleon, then this would be a response motivated by ethical or political rather than aesthetic concerns. In this sense, an experience of beauty is 'purposive without a purpose', by which Kant means that I value it for its own sake, not for any other reason—neither as an illustration of elegant fashion nor as an uplifting reminder of how beauty can defy tyranny, but purely for its beauty *per se*. Finally Kant proposes that any experience of beauty is, in fact, a form of judgment, one that I believe to be correct, even though it is something that I know I could never prove, as matters of taste are not subject to the same logical principles of, say, a geometric theorem or other forms of *scientific* knowledge. I can argue with you as much as I like about the beauty of this particular painting, but the only way I will ever persuade you to agree with me is to get you to *feel* it to be beautiful as I do. Nevertheless, I will feel that I am right to do so.

In many significant ways, then, the Enlightenment theories of aesthetics that culminate in Kant's theory of beauty mark a sharp break with the Neoplatonic tradition by introducing a number of fissures that are absent in the thought of both Plato and Plotinus. First and foremost, Kant separates

Figure 2.3　Portrait of Madame Récamier (1800), Jacques Louis David. Courtesy of the Musée du Louvre, Paris.

beauty from desire and human appetite and, by implication, its experience in art from its experience in nature. The latter is demoted to the merely 'agreeable', relating as it does to the common things that we like and enjoy such as sunshine, good food, a comfortable bed, the smell of apple blossom. 'We call *agreeable* that which GRATIFIES us', writes Kant, '*beautiful* what we just LIKE'[17]. Thus he polarises the gratification of our desires with the purely contemplative pleasures of beauty. This distinction set in motion a cultural process that led to the idea of 'true' beauty being ever more remote from everyday life and hence from the concerns of ordinary people. For Schopenhauer, writing in the middle of the nineteenth century, the chief purpose of beauty was to help us escape from the world of earthly desires, which cause us pain as they unleash passions that can never truly be fulfilled. In the contemplation of beauty we can, if just for a short while, attain 'the bliss and peace of mind of pure knowledge, free from all willing and thus from all individuality and the pain that results therefrom'[18]. In defining aesthetic experience as dispassionate and reflective, oppositional to earthly and bodily desires, Kant and those who followed him also assumed a hierarchical distinction between the fine arts and the popular arts. The latter are meant to distract or entertain us for a short period of time; 'the[ir] whole point is the entertainment of the moment, not any material for future quotation or meditation'. Unlike art works that are beautiful, they are not their own purpose; with 'aesthetic art', the pleasure should not arise out of mere enjoyment but 'must be a pleasure of reflection'[19]. A further and equally significant distinction between Plato and Kant is the latter's removal of a notion of the morally good from any true judgment of beauty. If things are morally valuable, says Kant, they have a useful purpose and therefore operate in a realm distinct from those of aesthetic contemplation and reflection. Beauty does not reside in any extrinsic sense of purpose nor as a feature of objects themselves; instead, it is a judgment located within the human mind that expresses a particular experience of pleasure and that is all. Nehamas neatly summarises Kant's position: 'Aesthetic pleasure is a pleasure we take in things just as they stand before us, without regard to their effects on our sensual, practical, or moral concerns'[20].

AESTHETICISM AND THE LEGACY OF KANT'S IDEAS

The idea that artistic beauty is an end in itself and can be divorced from moral and hence political concerns provided a philosophical underpinning to the nineteenth-century Aesthetic Movement, whose maxim 'Art for Art's sake' still has currency today. Originating in France with the poets Théophile Gautier and Charles Baudelaire, this movement not only accepted but also celebrated Kant's severance of the beautiful from the merely agreeable and, in particular, of aesthetic from moral concerns as enshrined in the Kantian definition of disinterestedness. Baudelaire turned the pursuit of pleasure and sensation into a personal religion, the very subject matter of his life and of his poetry, deliberately seeking out beauty in the kinds of experience guaranteed to outrage the bourgeois sentiments of his day, in places where previously only evil and ugliness had been seen. But in his *Hymne à la Beauté*, he brought a world-weary languor to the celebration of beauty, ironically playing upon the Neoplatonic concept of its supreme form being identifiable with the goodness of God. For Baudelaire, it could just as readily be an ally of the devil, and it really did not matter at all if it was:

> *Que tu viennes du ciel ou de l'enfer, qu'importe,*
> *O Beauté! Monstre énorme, effrayant, ingénue*
> . . .
> *De Satan ou de Dieu, qu'importe? Ange ou Sirène,*
> *Qu'importe, si tu rends—fée aux yeux de velours,*
> *Rythme, parfum, lueur, ô mon unique reine!—*
> *L'univers moins hideux et les instants moins lourds?*[21]

Beauty envisaged in this way is a kind of narcotic, stimulating any or all of our senses, only serving to make the world bearable—less hideous, less boring—and bringing neither hope nor happiness into our lives. For many young artists, Baudelaire came to be seen as a martyr to the aesthetic cause, displaying 'a saintly courage in exploring sin'[22]. Subversive as it was of bourgeois moral codes, however, the movement that he spawned was often apolitical as well as amoral in nature, centring upon individual gratification, the exploration of sensation for the sake of personal pleasure. This was amplified by a deep sense of pessimism towards human affairs in general, an aristocratic disdain for those who devoted their lives to moral, political or economic ends.

The doyen of the Aesthetic Movement that flourished in late nineteenth-century Britain was Walter Pater, the Oxford don who counted Oscar Wilde among his students. In his book *The Renaissance: Studies in Art and Poetry*[23] Pater wrote of individual works and individual artists but saw no moral purpose in the beauty they had created. At the same time as his contemporary, John Ruskin, was urging the Victorian establishment to look to the art of the past as an incentive to improve the society of the present, Pater examined the art of the Renaissance purely in terms of the personal pleasures it could provide for those who knew how to contemplate it and sensitively interpret their own impressions. The key pleasure of beauty as he defined it was to obtain from it as many pulsations as possible, 'to burn always with this hard, gem-like flame'[24]. Such is the essence of decadence, typified, according to William Gaunt, by Pater's later agnostic attachment to high church ritual. 'It does not matter what is said provided it is said beautifully', he is reported as saying[25]. Such quips are typical of the dandy—the mix of wit and aristocratic disdain, of which Oscar Wilde remains the most celebrated example. But it is Pater who first provided us with the cultural stereotype of those who devote their lives to the worship of beauty. In his own day, he was made famous through a satirical caricature that emphasised his particular languor of manner, aloofness of attitude and air of privileged detachment from the world of common affairs[26]. It is no coincidence that such a satirical portrait could be that of the contemporary British art critic, Brian Sewell, as depicted in the BBC comedy series *Dead Ringers*.

From Kant via Pater we can trace the commonly held idea that responding to beauty involves us *only* in acts of contemplative admiration. It does not spur us to action—quite the contrary—and removes us from, rather than brings us closer to, the world in which we live:

> He (Pater) never suggested as Ruskin did that people who were interested in beauty must concern themselves also with such ugly facts as railway trains and factory chimneys and cheap lodging houses. On the contrary, he caused these things to disappear by never referring to them at all. None of the vulgarities of existence must be allowed to disturb the state of contemplation in which 'full and perfect experience' was to be found.[27]

> Those who find beautiful meanings in beautiful things are the cultivated. For these there is hope.
> They are the elect to whom beautiful things mean only Beauty.[28]

Thus did Oscar Wilde famously summarise in his preface to *The Picture of Dorian Gray* the exclusive sense of superiority cultivated by the Aesthetic Movement[29]. It can be seen as the apogee of the Kantian creed of disinterestedness, the extreme if logical conclusion to an idea that drives a wedge between the concerns of beauty and other pressing concerns of personal, social and cultural life.

CAN BEAUTY EVER BE DISINTERESTED? PROBLEMS WITH KANT'S THEORY

Is it at all possible to isolate aesthetic judgments from moral and political concerns in the way that Kant suggested we could and that the Aesthetic Movement attempted to exemplify? John Armstrong believes that it is. He points to Karl Marx Allee in the eastern part of Berlin, built to glorify Stalin and designed primarily to accommodate vast military processions. He suggests that if we concentrate only on the distasteful ideology that stimulated its design we will blind ourselves to the street's genuine aesthetic qualities, its proportions and its style, virtues we can enjoy in and for themselves as they transcend their oppressive political origins[30]. In this sense, he argues, Kant helps clarify a common confusion; people sometimes say that they find something ugly when the ugliness they are referring to is moral rather than aesthetic in nature.

Perhaps we can enjoy a stroll down Karl Marx Allee in the way Armstrong suggests we can, but it is difficult to extend the same principle to Leni Riefenstahl's film *Triumph of the Will*, celebrating as it does Hitler and the Nuremberg Rally of 1934. The singer Bryan Ferry thought he could and openly praised the film in an interview with a German magazine: 'Leni Riefenstahl's films . . . the mass parades and flags—just amazing. Really beautiful'. The outrage caused by his remarks led to a swift apology in which he claimed that they were made 'solely from an art history perspective'[31]. This is a pure Kantian position, and, as Mary Devereux has pointed out, the film does have a moral vision at its heart that it is possible to view as beautiful—the appeal of a benevolent leader, a unified community and a sense of national purpose—themes that are skilfully interwoven with images of smiling, happy children, and of young men and women of striking physical beauty[32]. In the Germany of 1934, recovering from national humiliation and bankruptcy, the appeal might have been irresistible, both morally and aesthetically. Knowing what we do about Nazism today, however, it is difficult for any of us to ignore the inherent racism in these images, or to be anything other than repelled by the displays of Nazi regalia. The formal beauty is more likely to disturb rather than uplift us, precisely because, in this case, it would seem morally wrong for us to try to separate the moral from the aesthetic in our response. As a narrative documentary located in a history we are too well aware of, it is much more difficult to abstract the formal beauty from the political context as we can when we respond to architecture or street designs. Devereux concludes that there are certain types of art—the political and religious, in particular— where the domains of aesthetic and moral values will inextricably overlap. Perhaps more correctly she might have considered how representational or openly referential the particular form of art is, how closely its images reflect a known reality, historically and culturally close to us.

Yet even then it is difficult to envisage how we can ever perceive beauty on its own, as value neutral, detached from other concerns. Alperson and Carroll have analysed this question in relationship to music. Throughout history and across cultures, they argue, people experience music rarely, if ever, as 'music alone':

> Marches, hymns, dirges, love songs, work songs, union songs, social dances, liturgies, anthems, movie music, program music, and advertisements are all aligned with cognitive content whose social and psychological effectiveness they modify and lubricate.[33]

Drama, dance, poetry, literature and art all have the same capacity as music to connect with moral, religious, political and other cultural sentiments. In most cases, the reception of beauty, like music, is seldom if ever as beauty alone.

In much the same way, this very concept of 'disinterestedness' has done damage to beauty as a cultural value for contemporary theorists in the fields of education, sociology and cultural studies who are concerned with issues of social justice and whom we came across in the previous chapter. Although Kant describes the aesthetic experience as disinterested, they argue that the social results are far from disinterested when the aesthetic elite that such a concept spawns does little more than reflect the hierarchies of social class, perpetuated through education and enculturation. Crudely put, aesthetic critics and theorists are never disinterested, never ideologically neutral; those who say they are tacitly serve the interests of high culture and the dominant ideology. This is made much of by those contemporary scholars who theorise through such critical perspectives as feminism, post-colonialism and disability studies. But it is not a new criticism. As early as 1753, almost forty years before the publication of Kant's critique, William Hogarth in *The Analysis of Beauty* was similarly sceptical about disinterestedness as it was then being theorised by aristocratic English philosophers such as Shaftesbury and Hutcheson. (The fact that Kant did not invent the concept of disinterestedness but inherited it from previous philosophers of the Enlightenment is often overlooked by contemporary critics.) Ronald Paulson explains,

> As Hogarth . . . recognized, Shaftesbury's aesthetic disinterestedness had a political underside: the alliance of monarch and church is corrected

by an alliance of disinterested (because property owning, well-off) civic humanist gentlemen; royal patronage of art is corrected by similarly disinterested connoisseurs (the same persons). The only people who can afford to appreciate virtue and beauty are the Whig oligarchs.[34]

We may conclude, then, that to argue for the disinterestedness of beauty is unsustainable; that the appreciation of beauty is seldom detached from other values, be they moral, political or cultural. For teachers, however, this brings beauty into line with every other educational value, none of which can exist within an ideologically neutral zone. That beauty is seldom, if ever, disinterested need not lead us to regard it as some kind of ideological swear word, as many critics of beauty have done. Amelia Jones' tone is not untypical: 'There is always leakage polluting the supposedly disinterested authority of the discourse of beauty . . . That pollution is the stench of ideology'[35]. If beauty is never disinterested, then the key point is not for teachers to ignore its power or regard it as necessarily suspect; they need to consider in specific examples, be it expressed through art or language, in a scientific experiment or a mathematical theorem, where its *interest* for their students is to be located—culturally, morally, intellectually, politically. In this way, if they can bring the aesthetic pleasure of a beautiful poem, a beautiful idea, a beautiful piece of music or a beautiful theorem into their classrooms, beauty, as well as being interest*ed*, might help make the curriculum interest*ing*.

Disinterestedness is not the only area of contention we have inherited from Kant's theory of beauty. In situating the aesthetic experience firmly in the mind, Kant effectively imposed a split between perceiver and object which from then on became generally accepted. Coupled with the idea of aesthetic experience as disinterested contemplation, this served to drain the concept of beauty of much of its dynamism. The discourse of aesthetics went on to privilege the spirit over the body, reflection over intensity of experience, detachment over passion. In the words of Nehamas, it became isolated from the everyday world, promising nothing that was not already present in whatever work of art was under study, seeking to divorce perception and appreciation from desire[36]. It no longer conversed in the language of ordinary people and did not seek to do so. By concentrating on the question 'How is the aesthetic experience stimulated by the art object?' it naturalised the idea that the arts have a specific vocabulary that needs to be learned if we are to evaluate them successfully. However, as Clifford Geertz has pointed out, the idea that in order to understand beauty we need to approach it through technical attention to specific aesthetic qualities is an entirely Western idea that dates from the time of the Enlightenment. In all other cultures, beauty is commonly understood by attending to the broader cultural concerns that it serves. He writes, 'The means of an art and the feeling for life that animates it are inseparable and one can no more understand aesthetic objects as concatenations of pure form, than one can understand speech as a parade of syntactic variations'[37]. Similarly, Nehamas has questioned the idea that aesthetic judgments are necessarily autonomous, detached from context and purpose and hence in need of an exclusive vocabulary. Words that we use in order to make such judgments, he argues—words such as 'elegant', 'delicate', 'profound', 'subtle'—do not imply values that specifically relate to the arts. They are words that we use in our everyday lives and that we make use of in our discussion of the arts as and when appropriate. Such critical discussions, he suggests, should begin from what we get personally from the work in question and should not amount to an attempt to judge its worth in any objective sense. This, after all, mirrors why we go to see a performance of Hamlet, look at a painting or read a novel—to get something out of it, not to analyse its component parts, put everything back together again and then deliver a verdict[38]. And when we see something that strikes us as beautiful, we long to share this experience with others who matter to us—our friends, our family and, as teachers, our students—to encourage them to feel what we have felt. But this can only ever be in the form of an invitation, not an instruction, as no one will ever appreciate beauty by simply being told to. By implication, for beauty to weave its spell in the classroom, the teacher must first and foremost find beauty in what she is working with; seek out ways for her students to share in the passion and enthusiasm she feels for it; and encourage them to discover a shared language, not one imposed from without, as a means to articulate their experience. This does not mean that there is no place for technical language to help with this articulation; of course there is. What it does mean is that we do not start with it but from an attempt to stimulate the 'feeling for life' that the object of beauty needs to animate in our students before there can be any experience for them to learn from in the first place.

USEFUL ASPECTS OF KANT'S THEORY

Kant makes it clear that I can only come to value something as beautiful if I come to feel it as such; in other words, any education in beauty has to work through the emotions. But at the same time he describes how aesthetic experience engages the capacities of the imagination and of understanding, both of which are cognitive processes. He thus implies a close inter-relationship between emotion and cognition, between feeling and knowing, what amounts to a theory of the emotions as cognitive in nature. We can usefully, if briefly, consider the implications of this for the teaching of a giant such as Shakespeare. Whether we take our lead from Kant (that Shakespeare should be taught because of the strength and number of claims as to his importance) or from Bourdieu (that he ought to be taught as a principle of social justice, so all, not just the cultural elite, have the chance to benefit from the cultural capital that a knowledge of Shakespeare brings with it), he will not be understood, and hence be valued, by young people unless they learn to *feel* the beauty of his writing. This is equally true, of course, of those who teach Shakespeare—an obvious enough point, perhaps, yet recent work by the Royal Shakespeare Company's education department has shown that many secondary English teachers in the UK do not like Shakespeare themselves and/or lack confidence in their ability to teach him; and research has revealed widespread disaffection among secondary students with the way he is traditionally taught in the classroom[39]. As Shakespeare is the one author enshrined in the English National Curriculum that every child must study, this is something I return to at greater length in a later chapter. It is enough to say here that Kant's ideas imply a pedagogy that directly addresses the emotions and that is playful in its approach.

Kant's position on play, seeing it as the fulcrum of aesthetic experience, had a major effect on its subsequent conceptualisation in Western thought. As Rob Pope has argued, it was only after Kant that play came to be seen as 'a form of liberation and creative fulfilment'[40]. That Kant saw play as essentially a process of the intellect, involved in both the creation and appreciation of beauty, has implications as to how teachers should view all of the art forms, including those that are often taught as highly academic exercises, such as poetry. Let us take metaphor as an example. When in *Othello* Brabantio protests,

> *. . . my particular grief*
> *Is of so flood-gate and o'erbearing nature*
> *That it engluts and swallows other sorrows' (1.3.55–57)*

we do not literally believe that his grief takes material form and breaks through a set of flood gates. We recognise that Shakespeare is drawing an imaginative parallel between the power of grief and that of a flood. In making such a playful connection, however, he is not being trivial, nor is he being arbitrary or linguistically self-indulgent. In John Armstrong's words, 'It is not a chancy or arbitrary linkage; it is rich in implication and suggestion. It does not yield explicit understanding but speaks to understanding'[41]. Shakespeare's playful use of language engages our minds in a particularly sophisticated form of play whose beauty depends upon its 'richness of implication and suggestion'. So Kant's theory implies three things about the arts: that they are playful, and therefore pleasurable; that this play is a play of the intellect as much as it is a play of material form; and that beauty is the highest form of creative play.

Finally, as Austin Harrington has argued, Kant's insistence that we claim validity in our aesthetic judgments takes them beyond mere expressions of opinion—they are, in fact, invitations to others to enter into a critical discussion with us[42]. Although issues of class, gender, age, sexual orientation and ethnicity will influence my judgments, they are not the grounds upon which I base them; my liking for the David portrait of Mme

Recamier might well be *influenced* by my being a heterosexual male and a Francophile, but my critical discussion is not *grounded* in that fact. Similarly, the fact that my working-class background denied me access to certain kinds of art—opera, for instance—does not make the works of Verdi any the less beautiful for that, no more so than my lack of education in the philosophy of Hegel or the mathematical principles of Bertrand Russell invalidates their work in any way. Conversely, if someone educated in the appreciation of classical music fails to recognise the subtle beauty of Eric Clapton's guitar playing, then it does not mean that beauty is only in the eye (or in this case the ear) of the beholder, just that this particular person's cultural education has worked against them hearing and responding to this particular expression of it. And although it might be plain silly to compare Clapton unfavourably with Verdi, it would be perfectly acceptable to compare Clapton's guitar playing with my own and find the former's rendition of the theme tune to *Edge of Darkness* far more beautiful than anything I can play. In a similar way, I can coherently argue that one production of *Hamlet* is better than another and make valid judgments when comparing—as Christopher Ricks has done—the lyrics of Bob Dylan with poets such as John Donne and John Keats, comparisons he makes not to bury Dylan but to praise him[43]. The implication, then, is that we *can* evaluate beauty and argue that certain works of art, or cultural productions, are worthy of our attention (and hence worth learning about) due to their intrinsic merits and not simply because they afford us cultural or social capital; and, indeed, that some works are worthier of our attention than others. As David Shumway puts it, 'These qualities (of art works) are relative; they depend upon the context of reception to be realised. But they are also intrinsic in the sense that they exist in the texts and not merely in the minds of critics'[44]. In other words, beauty is more than a matter of opinion.

THE BEAUTIFUL AND THE SUBLIME

Before we leave Kant, there is a further aspect of his theory that requires our attention, namely, his subdivision of beauty into two contrasting experiences, those of the *beautiful* and the *sublime*. In this, once again he was building upon the theories of previous writers on the aesthetic, noticeably Edmund Burke, whose *Philosophical Inquiry into Our Ideas of the Sublime and the Beautiful* had been published in 1756. At its most general, the sublime stands for those things, both in art and in nature, that overwhelm us and fill us with awe—a storm at sea, for example, the vastness of the ocean; whereas the beautiful relates to those things whose pleasures are lighter and more domestic in nature—the physical charms of a person we love, or the delicate song of a bird or the gentle melody of a lyrical ballad. Elaine Scarry summarises the division as follows:

In Kant's newly subdivided aesthetic realm, the sublime is male and the beautiful is female. The sublime resides in mountains, Milton's Hell and tall oaks in a sacred grove; the beautiful resides in flowers and Elysian meadows. The sublime is night, the beautiful day. The sublime moves, beauty charms. The sublime is dusk, disdain for the world, eternity; the beautiful is lively gaiety and cheer. The sublime is great; the beautiful small. The sublime is principled, noble, righteous: the beautiful is compassionate and good hearted.[45]

The sublime, then, is an aesthetics of transcendent and spiritual power, the beautiful an aesthetics of worldly charm; and as the female member of the binary, the beautiful, as Scarry points out, suffers in comparison: 'Each attribute or illustration of the beautiful became one more member of an oppositional pair, and because it was almost always the diminutive member, it was also the dismissible member'[46]. Such binary oppositions are, indeed, open to challenge. Even when it had only recently been formulated, William Blake invited us to forego it and see the beautiful and the sublime as integrally connected—the small with the mighty, the natural with the infinite, the fragile with the powerful:

> *To see a World in a grain of sand*
> *And a Heaven in a wild flower,*
> *Hold Infinity in the palm of your hand*
> *And Eternity in an hour.*[47]

Ruskin, too, did not accept this distinction so readily. The sublime, he wrote, 'is not distinct from what is beautiful, nor from other sources of pleasure in art, but is only a particular mode and manifestation of them'[48]. Despite this, however, and despite the determination of Postmodernists to do away with any lingering stench of a binary opposition, they are tendencies still present in schools, with similar effects to those noted by Scarry. The arts are beautiful, for example—charming, a distraction, but not as important as the sciences, sublime in their attention to the powerful forces of nature. Within the arts themselves, many secondary English teachers are uncomfortable with the cosier aspects of the beautiful, favouring literature that is more in tune with the aesthetics of the sublime, powerful and moving, reflecting the uncomfortable realities of the modern world and the sensibilities of their students. Robert Swindell's novels, for example, such as *Stone Cold* and *Junk*, are popular studies in the lower secondary years, powerful depictions of teenage life that explicitly deal with uncomfortable social issues such as homelessness, rape and drug addiction. To understand why so much of contemporary aesthetic taste chimes with the idea of the sublime rather than the beautiful, however, we need to go beyond simply seeing it as a response to the realities of the modern age. Such horrors have always been with us; we need to engage with the legacy of a further and more recent cultural tradition, that of Modernism.

THE 'TERRIBLE BEAUTY' OF MODERNISM

All changed, changed utterly:
A terrible beauty is born[49]

Towards the end of the nineteenth century, advances in technology led to a sudden and marked increase in the pace of change. The years between 1879 and 1903 witnessed inventions such as the electric light bulb, the first synthetic fibre, the Ford motor car, the cinematograph, the gramophone record, radio telegraphy and the first aeroplane. At the same time, there were developments in scientific thought that were to revolutionise how we understand and think about the world. Darwin's theory of evolution and Marx's theory of capital had already shaken the religious and political foundations of Western civilization and were now followed by Freud's mapping of the unconscious and Einstein's theory of relativity. All of this had a profound cultural effect. It was a widespread belief, and not only among artists, that, in Robert Hughes' phrase, the world was witnessing 'the end of one kind of history and . . . the start of another': 'From now on the rules would quaver, the fixed canons would fail, under pressure of new experience and the demands for new forms to contain it'[50]. For some this induced a feeling of heroic optimism in the cultural possibilities of the future, mingled with a sense of awe and/or terror at the sure knowledge that the power that had previously been thought of as belonging to God was now being usurped by technological advancement and new forms of knowledge. The future no longer lay in old belief systems but in science, in machines, in social and political revolution, in a celebration of the forces unleashed by modernity that fed a desire to sweep away the past and invent a new and better future. The cultural movement that this heady mix inspired we now call Modernism.

Modernism's rejection of the cultural, moral and political values of the past had a major impact on the concept of beauty within the arts. One of the prophets of Modernism, the French poet Rimbaud, had challenged artists to be 'absolument moderne', and integral to this call to modernity was an out and out rejection of beauty: *'Un soir j'ai assis la Beauté sur mes genoux—et je l'ai trouvée amère—et je l'ai injuriée'*[51]. Whereas Baudelaire and others in the Aesthetic Movement had actively divorced beauty from goodness, Modernism sought to reject beauty outright. Rimbaud's call was echoed in the many manifestoes of Modernism, a good number of which emerged from the group of Italian artists collectively known as the Futurists. 'There is no longer any beauty except in battle', wrote their leader, Marinetti: 'We want to glorify war, the world's only hygiene'. The Futurists declared ugliness, not beauty, as their artistic goal. 'We will no longer have verbal symphonies, lulling harmonies, soothing cadences . . . We will courageously be that which is "ugly"'[52]. At the heart of this self-conscious rejection of beauty was the continuing desire to shock contemporary bourgeois sensibilities and to replace the idea of a comforting, consolatory aesthetic with one more attuned to the immense power of the machine, to the power that humans now had at their disposal to transform the social and cultural world, an aesthetic that could embrace the thrill of terror at the heart of this promise of modernity. Modernism was in fact rejecting an aesthetic of the 'beautiful' in favour of one of the 'sublime'.

The work of the Futurists has been dismissed by many apologists for Modernism as 'precisely violent but empty and unaffiliated': an illustration of how 'innovative vitality' can be replaced by 'empty dynamism'[53]. Picasso's *Les Demoiselles d'Avignon*, painted in 1907, is, on the other hand, recognised as one of the early masterpieces of Modernism and serves to illustrate the achievements of its revolutionary aesthetic, in particular the violence it inflicted on the idea of the beautiful and its embodiment in the female form. For centuries in Western art, the female nude had been painted as both desirable and reassuring in her sexuality. Take, for example, Ingres' celebrated painting *La Grande Odalisque*, in which a naked young woman, stretched out on a bed with her back towards us, offers herself to our gaze within the erotic surroundings of a harem. In the centre of the picture, her right hand delicately holds a fan, whose shape has distinctly phallic connotations. Like her, the four naked figures in Picasso's *Demoiselles* make a living by dispensing sexual favours, but this time there is no exotic setting to disguise the fact; these are prostitutes, not royal concubines. Ingres' painting has been noted for the distortion in the length of the neck and the torso, intended to enhance the erotic desirability of the woman. The distortions in the Picasso painting serve quite a different purpose. The sensuous curves of the Ingres figure are replaced by bodies that are flat and angular; instead of the comeliness of the face we have an ugliness modelled on the sharp features of tribal African masks. Like masks, these faces, although they gaze at us, do not reveal their secrets; they are distorted and disturbing, their meanings difficult to decipher. The bodies themselves adopt aggressively sexual postures, and there is a slice of melon in the central foreground that resembles a blade, a weapon of castration. It is positioned behind a bunch of grapes and other fruit that together form a grotesque cartoon of dismembered male genitalia. Such imagery is a long way from the erotically charged fan in the foreground of Ingres' painting and the sexual favours promised by the lingering touch of the concubine's hand. If female sexuality in *La Grande Odalisque* is depicted as seductive, sensual and pleasurable, in *Les Demoiselles* it is frightening, bestial and ugly. 'The further removed from the animal is their appearance', wrote Georges Bataille of women, 'the more beautiful they are reckoned'[54]. The whores in Picasso's painting exemplify this principle by inverting it.

Figure 2.4   Les Demoiselles d'Avignon (1907), Pablo Picasso. © 2009 Estate of Pablo Picasso / Artists Rights Society (ARS), New York.

The *Demoiselles* also illustrates Modernism's break with the foundational conventions of Western art in the way that its form is abstracted from the reality it is representing. This is most evident in the background. In the Ingres painting, there is a background of what are quite clearly drapes, luxuriously colourful and carefully textured, whereas Picasso rejects both perspective and referentiality. The jagged patterns of blue and white that form the backdrop do not necessarily represent anything; they are form, they are paint organised in particular ways to provide patterns and colours to complement the figures in the foreground, without pretending to be anything else. The *Demoiselles* thus declares itself, on all fronts, as difficult—cold, remote, discomforting. It does not speak to the heart or to the senses in the same way that a picture such as *La Grande Odalisque* is intended to. Instead, it illustrates what Crispin Sartwell has defined as the core of Picasso's art:

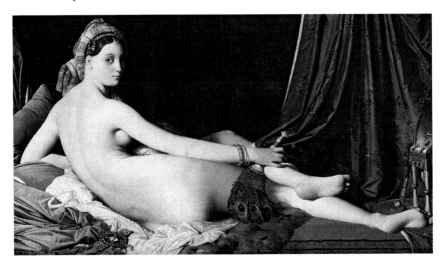

Figure 2.5   La Grande Odalisque (1814), Jean Auguste Dominique Ingres. Courtesy of the Musée du Louvre, Paris.

> Picasso's beauty is a disturbed beauty or a distressed beauty and a complicated or disgusting beauty. But whatever kind of beauty it is, it is the beauty of power . . . Picasso's aesthetic lionized the power of his will in the form that he imposes on us: as we look at his work, he is our master.[55]

Difficulty and incipient ugliness came to characterise all forms of Modernist art—the novels of Faulkner and Joyce, the paintings of Braque and Pollock, the poetry of T. S. Eliot. Eliot indeed saw difficulty as an essential quality of poetry in the modern world: 'The poet must become more and more comprehensive, more allusive, more indirect, in order to force, to dislocate if necessary, language into his meaning'[56]. Rejecting the 'easy' verse of poets such as Tennyson and Browning, his own poetry included another landmark of Modernism, *The Waste Land*. Published just four years after the end of the First World War, there is no optimism in the vision of modernity he portrays. The war had illustrated all too well the dark, murderous power of the new machines as well as the bankruptcy of the old European political systems. In Eliot's poem the modern, post-war, industrial city of London is ugly—a city of brown fog, dull canals, gashouses, creeping rats with slimy bellies, a place where *'the river sweats / Oil and tar'*[57]. It is a loveless world of spiritual emptiness, sordid sexuality, faceless crowds and lonely death. What beauty there is in the poem, as with Picasso's painting, is to be found in the material of the art form itself, in the cinematic force and surprising rhythms of its language and imagery; there is no beauty in what these images represent, only in what is forged through the will of the artist.

Modernism's conscious efforts to create art out of ugliness had a political motivation in the work of groups such as the Dadaists and the German Expressionists, who forged an alliance with ugliness in order to attack bourgeois hypocrisy and moral degeneracy. In the years after the Great War, the streets of Berlin were full of ex-soldiers, many of whom had been disfigured. *Card Playing War Cripples* is one of several paintings in which

Figure 2.6   Card-Playing War Cripples (1920), Otto Dix. Alte National Galerie, Berlin. bpk/ Nationalgalerie, Eigentum der Freunde der Nationalgalerie/ Jörg P. Anders.

Otto Dix and others used them as subject matter for social commentary. If Plato saw beauty as reflecting the inner goodness of the individual, Dix uses ugliness to portray the hidden corruption of those running the Weimar Republic—the policeman, the army officer and the capitalist, crouched around their café table as they gamble. Here beauty is more than an irrelevance; it is an ideological enemy, a soporific to hide political truths only an artful use of ugliness can convey. The work of artists such as Dix conforms to the comments of the American artist Barnett Newman, who was later famously to say, 'It is the impulse of modern art to destroy beauty'[58].

FROM MODERNISM TO KITSCH

If, as Sartwell suggests, the Modernist aesthetic was centred on power, it was the power that Kant had associated with the thrill of transcendent freedom at the heart of the experience of the sublime; the sense that, despite her immense force, nature, in the final analysis, has no dominance over us. If Kant had meant this in a moral sense—that we are creatures with an autonomous sense of morality that transcends our nature as sensible beings—Modernism celebrated it as an expression of human will, detached and above the common comforts of ordinary living. It is precisely this aspect of Modernism that Wendy Steiner has savagely criticised in her book *The Trouble with Beauty*, in which she focuses on how its dismissal of the beautiful in preference for the sublime rejected the female form and with it the virtues we associate with the feminine that go beyond physical shapeliness—charm, sympathy, domesticity, pleasure and love. She sees this legacy as having reverberated throughout every aspect of modern life to the detriment rather than the benefit of women; so the vision of Modernism which saw beauty as a lie and a myth within the world of art has echoes in our contemporary culture in which beauty is conceptualised as an ideological construct that dominates and victimises women. The result for Steiner is that, for women, this sets freedom and pleasure at odds with one another. 'Eschewing beauty', she writes, 'comes at a high price for it closes off passion, procreation and self understanding'[59].

To illustrate the virtues of beauty, Steiner invokes the myth of *Cupid and Psyche*. Here, the mortal Psyche (the soul) is married to the immortal Cupid (love), but he visits her only in darkness. When she finally lights a candle in order to gaze upon his sleeping figure, she is overwhelmed by his beauty. In his anger at her disobedience, Cupid now deserts her, but Psyche's love for him is so strong that she performs a series of superhuman feats in order to be re-united with him. She thus gains immortality and therefore equality with Cupid, and together they give birth to a daughter, Pleasure. This concept of beauty, of course, recalls that proposed by Plato, where 'the soul, moved by beauty, becomes worthy of love and its delights'. Steiner continues, 'Sympathy is the product of the interaction we call beauty, an interaction in which both parties become aligned in value and, in the process, become in some sense equal'[60]. 'Insight, understanding and empathy' are the three key virtues that can result from an experience of beauty thus defined[61]. This she contrasts to the Modernist sublime, where the emotions of awe, admiration and fear are ends in themselves, producing a 'thrilling detachment' that is sometimes called freedom but is in fact a freedom devoid of solicitations for involvement, reciprocity or empathy[62]. Hence the close proximity between the sublime and the horrific; for those artists who attempt to transcend human limitations run the risk of destroying 'the common values and pleasures of human existence'[63].

Steiner's critique of Modernism brings us, in some ways, back to where we began. In attacking the sublime she is proposing a theory of beauty that resonates with Plato, one that includes the qualities of love and interconnectedness and that recognises ethical as well as aesthetic values as inherent to it. These she invokes through the softer charms of the beautiful—of domesticity, ornament, good heartedness and compassion—whilst implying that the sublime is a false polarity, inhuman and culturally dangerous. She sees recent work in abstract art as challenging the cold misogyny of Modernism. In Rachel Whiteread's *House* and *Untitled (One Hundred Spaces)*, for example, she detects a cultural shift towards a rediscovery of the values of charm, wit and ornament in work that is 'deeply pleasurable, providing an almost childlike aesthetic bliss'[64]. Such a shift does, indeed, seem to be in evidence, certainly in the world of cultural commentary. Since the 1990s, as we have seen, there has been a surge of interest in the concept of beauty and a steady re-evaluation of its positive qualities[65]. But if the age of Modernism has passed, its sensibilities have not. The structures of feeling we have inherited from it have not been so readily displaced. Besides, as T. J. Clark informs us, 'the "modernity" that Modernism prophesied has finally arrived . . . what we are living through is modernity's triumph'[66]:

> Modernity means contingency. It points to a social order which has turned from the worship of ancestors and past authorities to the pursuit of a projected future—of goods, pleasures, freedoms, forms of control over nature, or infinities of information. This process goes along with a great emptying and sanitization of the imagination.[67]

This bleak vision is one in which the predictions of Modernism have come about without the triumph of a just, new order. Fascism and Socialism, the twentieth-century grand narratives of political reform for re-making history, both turned out to be murderous. Since 1989 capitalism alone has reigned supreme, and even the unprecedented banking crisis of late 2008 has not provided us with a real alternative. Mass consumerism still brokers the promises of happiness we are being sold, flooding our homes with seductive images of package holidays, supermarket binges and the latest fad in portable technology. Thus the projected, happy future is one of instantaneously satiated pleasure, commodified, sanitised and empty, rooted only in the economic values of perpetual novelty and innovation. At the same time, the images of Modernism that were previously so shocking have entered the iconography of popular culture devoid of their contextual reference points and intellectual content—Munch's *The Scream*, for example, pastiched in the mask from Wes Craven's horror film of the same name. Revolt has well and truly been turned into style; or, as Fred Inglis puts it, '[e]ven the avant-garde, once the shocking gypsy-cousin of the bourgeoisie, has been paid off as designer of the next fashion but one'[68]. Sartwell comments that the Modernist urge was to transform the darkness of human desire into art: 'Their art makes a beauty that draws on a lust for power, and our experience of the beauty they created reveals our dark desire to be overwhelmed'[69]. In the world of contemporary modernity, however, such desires are readily channelled into the entertainment plied by horror films and computer games, products that, if not sanitised of shock and gore, have been purged of any radical intellectual challenge or attempt to help us imagine the world afresh. They bring to mind Frederic Jameson's argument of how the visible can be '*essentially* pornographic, which is to say it has its end in rapt, mindless fascination'[70].

Beauty, meanwhile, held in contempt by Modernism, is in danger of being drained of its substance and emptied into the shallow consolations and saccharine sentimentality of kitsch. 'Chopin's Sonata in B flat minor sung by Perry Como in an arrangement by Liberace and accompanied by the Marine Band'[71]—Umberto Eco's witty conceit neatly captures the essence of kitsch, the kind of artistic or cultural product that self-consciously seeks to create beauty entirely through the arousal of superficial response. It targets the emotional reactions of the consumer, demanding *only* to be looked at or *only* to be listened to; critical inquiry or reflective contemplation are not its concerns. In the words of Hermann Broch, 'The essence of *Kitsch* consists in exchanging the ethical category with the aesthetic category; this obliges the artist to pursue not a "good" work of art, but a beautiful work of art; what matters to him is beautiful effect'[72]. The mere *effect* of kitsch can thus be contrasted with the *experience* of beauty, inasmuch as its very shallowness, ease of reception and absolute lack of cognitive challenge guarantee that we learn nothing but mindless conformity from kitsch:

> Kitsch removes the truth from art and substitutes consolation; it tells us, sweetly, that everything will be all right . . . kitsch consumerism is the narcotic which suppresses the mighty question of how to live well; instead, it turns the home of our culture into an unacknowledged prison for the gratification of trivial desires.[73]

Contemporary educational discourse may be resistant to beauty, but it is by no means immune to kitsch. TV ads to recruit for the profession with

carefully selected images of smiling teenagers, radiant-faced, their honest
laughter shared by their young, smartly dressed teacher, who is doubtless
on the fast track to middle management; local news items that celebrate
the nativity play in a neighbourhood primary school, in which reporters
solicit cutely naive comments from suitably innocent young mouths—such
are the shallow, consolatory appeals of kitsch: everything is fine and there
is nothing in our schools that cannot be sorted through smartness, fun
and clean-cut professionalism. More insipid are the exhortatory stories of
those dedicated educationalists who, in the desire to spread the good news
of their own genuinely held beliefs, reduce to images of pure kitsch 'the
beautiful world of making and thinking, creating and criticizing' that is the
educational endeavour[74].

An extract from the writing of Guy Claxton will serve to exemplify
this trend. Claxton is a figure who currently commands much respect and
admiration among educationalists in the UK and was recently featured as
one of the '[t]hinkers who have shaped Modern Education' in the *Times
Educational Supplement*[75]. *Building Learning Power* (BLP), perhaps his
most influential book, opens with a three-page introduction to Darren
and Katie, both described as 'powerful learners in the making'[76]. Darren
is eleven years of age and about to start at St Edmund's Comprehensive
school. He is in bed, thinking ahead to his first day at his new school, and
from his musings we learn that he is a keen and avid learner—'much better
now than he was at five'—thanks largely to his Years 5 and 6 teachers at
Beckley Road primary school, who followed the approach to learning the
book goes on to explain in detail. Darren has benefited from a range of
strategies: 'fun' classroom activities, such as making posters with suggestions for what to do when stuck with your reading or maths or if you have
fallen out with your friend; keeping a regular learning journal; memorising
routines such as 'Predict—observe—explain'. He can hear the voice of his
Year 6 teacher in his head, coaxing him to write about the hopes, fears
and expectations he has about his new school so he picks up his learning journal and writes for a few minutes before going to sleep. Meanwhile
Katie, his seventeen-year-old half sister, is busy washing her kit and thinking ahead to an essay she needs to write for the leisure management course
she is studying at the local college. She, we are told, has 'started to develop
her "learning muscles" (being a fitness fanatic she likes the metaphor)'. We
then learn about Darren and Katie's family holiday in Greece through the
thoughts of Darren's father, Charlie. Darren evidently had the time of his
life, and we are left in little doubt that this was because of the confidence
he now has as a learner—learning to snorkle out of his depth; chatting to
two German girls he had befriended, despite being unable to speak their
language; creating 'playful projects' with them at the hotel; observing carefully before joining in with the evening Greek dancing classes. Katie, too,
had soon lost her teenage sulkiness and become infected by Darren's enthusiasm for learning, unselfconsciously and persistently practising her diving

with a 'gaggle of boys half her age'. The final paragraph of this introduction is worth quoting in full:

> And now it's a bright September morning. Darren in his new school uniform and Katie in her designer sweat-suit are grabbing a bowl of cereal and getting their things together. Katie is off to the library to see what she can find on the relationship between self-esteem, body-image and attitudes to exercise—bit of a mouthful, but she's quite gripped by the idea. And Darren has to hurry to meet Leon for their walk to St Edmund's. 'OK, mate?' says Charlie to Darren as he flies out of the door. 'Bit wobbly, Dad' he calls back, 'but I'll be fine.' And Charlie thinks to himself 'Yes, you will.'

All of this is pure kitsch. Domestic happiness is evoked through images of a sun-drenched holiday, smartly dressed but appropriately fashion-conscious children, and a suitably laid-back father figure. This vision of reality, straight from a corn-flakes advert, spills over into images intended to connect learning and school with the good life. In the world of BLP, young, healthy, fit bodies explicitly mirror young, healthy, active minds. Everything—from reading and swimming to how to make friends, have a good time and change your attitude to life—can be learned through a set of techniques, fun exercises and memorised routines. The technology of this formula for 'powerful learning' is marketed in a narrative that suggests by implication its potential to magic away not only the problems of education but also those of family breakdown, obesity, teenage sex and social prejudices and divisions of all kinds. Our Darren is not the scallywag his name conjures up for many English primary teachers but a model of learning who flourishes despite having endured the trauma of his parents' divorce. His educational trajectory connects the state sector (Beckley Road) with the religious sector (St Edmund's), and he bridges the divides of nationalism and misogyny as well as religion, choosing two German girls as his holiday companions. A wholesome holiday this, too, with not a whiff of sex in the air, certainly not for seventeen-year-old Katie; the boys she spent her time with were not only a lot younger than her but safely pre-pubescent (half of seventeen being eight and a half). Later in the book we meet Darren's inspirational teacher from Beckley Road Primary, Ms Rita Salbiah (evidently though not explicitly black), who also had a wholesome, healthy summer break, this time in an 'alternative holiday community' where she windsurfed, wrote poetry, performed a risqué Aretha Franklin routine and 'let herself be massaged by the guy with cerebral palsy'[77]. In the world of BLP, social prejudices are breezily wished away and everything is, indeed, all right—squeaky clean, in fact—and irony is an undiscovered concept. For lurking beneath it all is the uncomfortable Modernist vision of power and the will as ultimate virtues. Darren is a 'powerful learner in the making', and at one point his father muses, 'If Darren wanted to master something there was no stopping him now'. We can imagine him striding confidently to school, he and Leon side by side, smart new uniforms, hair neatly combed, humming in synchrony *Tomorrow Belongs to Me* . . .[78]

To begin with Plato and end with the introduction to *Building Learning Power* may be bathetic in the extreme, but such is the chasm between beauty and kitsch that it needs to be recognised and held on to. The history of beauty as a value related in this chapter has been intended to account for the various and conflicting nuances of meaning we find in its modern uses. These nuances can now inform a consideration of beauty's relationship to learning and its place in a humane and ethical educational project. But although our approach so far has been critical and historical, beauty as a value, like education, is future oriented and optimistic. As Denis Donoghue has written, 'It seems clear that the tense of beauty is the future and that its apprehension is propelled by a politics of hope and of anticipation, a surge of feeling beyond the merely given present moment'[79]. As such, it can readily be corrupted into the glossy sentimentality and easy imaginings of kitsch. If the experience of beauty is hopeful, in an educational context, it must never be imagined as easy. It inspires passion, not sentimentality, is resistant to formulae and pre-ordained goals and is best considered through the reality of a lived past than in the possibilities of an imagined future. And the past I begin with is my own.

3 Beauty as Educational Experience

EPIPHANY

And twenty minutes more or less
It seemed, so great my happiness,
That I was bléssed and could bless.[1]

At the age of fifteen I bought an old battered copy of one of Bob Dylan's early albums from a boy in my class. It featured songs such as *Don't Think Twice, It's Alright* and *A Hard Rain's Gonna Fall*, all played and sung by him alone to the accompaniment of his guitar and harmonica. I had for some years been able to blow a simple tune out of a harmonica and had been taught how to play the viola at school. Here, however, was something much cooler than a viola. The cover featured a large photograph of the young Dylan walking arm in arm with a very pretty girl down a street somewhere in New York. The first time I listened to the album I sat alone in my bedroom, staring at the cover, mesmerised by both the music and the lyrics. The next day was a Saturday. I spent what little money I had on a cheap acoustic guitar and the rest of the weekend using my rudimentary knowledge of how to play the viola in order to figure out how to play the guitar. By the end of the weekend I had listened to the album several times, scribbled down the lyrics to one of the songs and worked out a simple sequence of chords that allowed me to sing it in my own version of his very particular, plaintive style. I had discovered the voice I wanted to have and the person I wanted to be and had embarked on a love affair that was to last for several years.

What exactly had I fallen in love with? First and foremost it was the poetry, the words he used and the way he used them. He sang songs about a world I could recognise, of injustice but also hope that things could be made to change for the better, with emotions I could identify with in lines of beauty that I would write down again and again as if, by doing this, they might somehow become mine. And they could become mine in a very real sense because I could learn to play them and sing them quite quickly. The folk-blues tradition from which he emerged is very tolerant of imperfection and does not require a great deal of skill in order to obtain tolerable competence in it. There was also the glamour, of course—the promise of a way of life. His smile on the album cover had a hint of thoughtful and witty rebelliousness, whereas his clothes—flat cap, suede jacket, jeans—conveyed an air of freedom, of casual disregard for wealth making. And he had a beautiful girl on his arm, and they were both laughing, delighting in each other's company. I had soon bought cap, jacket, jeans and harmonica holder, as well as the guitar. The girl, unfortunately, did not come with the package, but I could dream and for me it was a dream of perfect happiness. To imitate was to hope, to desire a future in which I could flourish, be seen, listened to and loved. It was a very youthful, very common, very human dream.

Of course things did not work out that way, and the world was spared my talent. I wrote songs and sang them, even professionally for a while, played in a number of bands, never made a record, and eventually other dreams in life took over. Many years later my sister sent me an old photograph, and there I was, seventeen years old, guitar and cap, posing in my imagination for the cover of the album I was never to record. I felt no sense of loss or regret on looking at the forgotten image, still less any contempt for the young man I once was. In the story of my life so far, it made sense. I still love music, and his lyrics sparked in me a love of poetry. I earn my living through words and through performing, if we consider teaching and delivering lectures as performing; and whenever I play those early albums of Bob Dylan, as I occasionally do, I am still inspired by their sentiments and struck by the power of their stark and simple beauty.

* * * * * * * *

Such is the experience in my youth that comes closest to what is often called a 'moment of epiphany', defined by Armstrong as one of revelation 'in which we suddenly—and for a short time—gain a great insight into ourselves and the world'[2]. More precisely, perhaps, what I have described is an intense encounter with beauty that had a profound and dynamic effect on my formative years[3]. Such experiences are not uncommon and can be found in the biographies of writers, in particular. I once heard the author Philip Pullman speak of a time when he heard a group of older boys at school reciting T. S. Eliot's *Journey of the Magi*. He described how the quite unexpected tingling in his spine made him realise in an instant that this kind of poetic language was going to be of great importance to him in his future life[4]. The philosopher and historian R. G. Collingwood writes in his autobiography of how, at the age of eight, he chanced upon a volume of Kant in his father's library and, although he could not understand the ideas, he knew that they were somehow his business, a matter personal to some future self of his own[5]. We might speculate that if, for Pullman, the rhythms and sounds of Eliot's poetry were what had such an impact upon him, for Collingwood it was the mysterious elusiveness of the ideas that Kant's language was conveying, the beauty hidden within it. But for both boys, as for me, this sudden encounter with beauty was more than an experience isolated in time; it brought with it a realisation that there was important work ahead of them. It also had a highly significant afterlife, with recurring moments of beauty and pleasure that, in my case, constituted the soundtrack of my adolescence.

The inspiration for the children's novels of Arthur Ransome came not in the form of an epiphany but more in this form of significant recurrence, the accumulation of happy childhood experiences spent holidaying near Coniston in the English Lake District:

> We played in or on the lake or on the hills above it, finding friends in the farmers and shepherds and charcoal-burners whose smoke rose from the coppice woods along the shore. We adored the place. Coming to it we used to run down to the lake, dip our hands in and wish, as if we had just seen the new moon . . . *Swallows and Amazons* grew out of these old memories. I could not help writing it. It almost wrote itself.[6]

Like Ransome, the French novelist Alain Fournier drew inspiration from his intense love of the rural setting where he grew up, in this case the Sologne region of central France. As a teenager in Paris, however, he had his own epiphany in the form of a brief but overwhelming meeting with a beautiful young woman whom he fell immediately in love with. Both experiences fused to inform the one, great novel he wrote before his early death. *Le Grand Meaulnes* has as its subject 'the fading of that visionary gleam with which, in retrospect, even the simplest sights and sounds of his outwardly ordinary childhood seemed to him to have been invested'[7]. If Ransome's work re-created again and again a paradise where adventures could be continually and seemingly perpetually enjoyed without ever the need for the protagonists to grow up, Alain Fournier used his memories to recapture a world of nascent adult desires, irresistibly exciting yet painfully nostalgic, where the promises of the future inexorably fail to live up to the vanished happiness of the past.

Both kinds of experience—the beauty that recurs in our day-to-day lives and the beauty that hits us suddenly and overwhelmingly—share, I argue, a similar aesthetic topography and differ only in degree. Nor are they the privilege of artists, philosophers and novelists such as I have quoted here—it is simply they who write or speak about them most often and who are heeded most readily when they do. When we are young, beauty will impact on us in different forms according to the environments we are brought up in and the opportunities they afford us. As someone born on a council estate in Liverpool, I did not enjoy the same pastoral closeness to nature that Alain Fournier or Arthur Ransome did, but I had books, the cinema, parks, old churches, my Roman Catholic religion, canal walks through aging industrial landscapes and the immense, now desolate beauty of Liverpool's crumbling Dock Road to shape my aesthetic consciousness—not to mention the Beatles and players like Roger Hunt and Ian St John who then graced the field at Liverpool Football Club. We can always find beauty close to us in people and in nature; in art, dance, music, song and literature; in sport; and in ideas, whether mathematical, scientific, philosophical, political or spiritual. The great English painter William Turner was the son of a barber and did not grow up in a privileged background with access to works of art and holidays in the countryside but in an alley close to London's Covent Garden. However, as John Ruskin speculated, he knew where to see beauty around him: 'Dusty sunbeams up or down the street on summer mornings; deep furrowed cabbage leaves at the greengrocer's; magnificence of oranges in wheelbarrows round the corner; and Thames' shore within three minutes race'[8]. As Armstrong comments, 'Experience of special, privileged objects is not, then, the needful thing; what counts is that the experiences are delighted in, dwelt upon, mobilized and made use of'[9].

The significance of the account with which I opened this chapter lies therefore in its ordinariness as well as its intensity. Against the background of more common aesthetic experiences, my youthful dream reflected that of many of my contemporaries and, as for the vast majority of them, it did not materialise. Yet it motivated me to learn as nothing else in my adolescence did. As an overwhelming experience of beauty it provided me with an ideal which I internalised and strove to emulate for many years. It will serve as an example to investigate the nature of such experiences and what characterises them as educational.

EXPERIENCE, KNOWLEDGE AND BEAUTY

In his philosophical inquiry *Experience and Its Modes*, Michael Oakeshott offers several significant propositions about the nature of experience and its relationship to knowledge. First of all he defines it as inclusive of both the act of experiencing and what is experienced, which, if taken separately, become meaningless abstractions. Thus, according to Oakeshott, we cannot separate the experiencing of beauty from the object that embodies beauty for us; both together constitute the experience, which only makes sense in its particularity. Secondly, he argues that we cannot define experience in terms of sensation exclusive of thought as we need to exercise judgment at the immediate level of sensation in order to make sense of it. In his words, 'Sensation implies consciousness, consciousness implies judgment and judgment is thought'[10]. Thus any experience of beauty we might have is not simply a sensorial response to a beautiful stimulus; at its very roots, quite prior to any Kantian concept of a judgement of taste, it involves our primary thought processes in an initial and immediate evaluatory response to it. The same holds true for feeling. A given feeling—of pleasure or of fear, for instance—is always connected to prior knowledge and is therefore inseparable from thought. Thus Oakeshott states that there is 'no experience which is not thinking, nothing experienced which is not thought, and consequently no experience which is not a world of ideas'[11]. So despite the emotional intensity of my initial encounter with the music of Bob Dylan, in the light of Oakeshott's theorising, the experience was cognitive as well as emotional, a world of thought and feeling fused together.

Oakeshott proceeds to explain the significance of this theory of experience to how we should understand knowledge. Experience is as real as it gets for us: 'The thinker who demands a reality beyond experience is certain of disappointment'[12]. The implication here is that experience provides the frame within which we should look at how we learn, for the way that we gain knowledge is dependent upon the way that we make sense of it—of how people treat me; of what people tell me; of things that happen to me; of the consequences of actions I take; of ideas I come across; of what happens to me at school and so on. For this reason, knowledge should not be thought of as mere accretion, as something we simply add extra facts or bits to as we learn new things. As it centres around a world of ideas, the struggle to learn from experience is a striving for coherence as a basis for understanding: '[W]e can be said only to know a system of ideas which is, or appears to be, coherent. . . . Whatever we know, we know as a whole'[13]. If new knowledge was merely an increment, an addition, collected as a series of ideas, then it could only ever touch what he calls the circumference, or the raw end of our cognition. He goes on:

> But since it is a system, each advance affects retrospectively the entire whole, and is the creation of a new world. Knowledge . . . is not the extension of a mere series, or the enlargement of a mere collection of ideas; it is the achievement of the coherence of a given world or system of ideas by the pursuit of the implications of that world.[14]

Oakeshott is not suggesting that we do not ever learn facts, skills or ideas piecemeal or in sequence, or that we cannot learn in an accumulative fashion; rather, he is saying that things we learn in this way do not count as knowledge unless they have changed in some underlying, coherent way how we see or act upon the world. In this sense, knowledge is more accurately to be understood as transformative rather than incremental; and in this light, we can see how intense encounters with beauty are at base knowledge-creating experiences of the most transformative kind, providing as they do a renewed sense of coherence between subject and world. As Elaine Scarry writes, 'The beautiful thing seems—is—incomparable, unprecedented; and that sense of being without precedent conveys a sense of the "newness" or "newbornness" of the entire world'[15].

Experiences such as this, from which we learn so profoundly, that 'achieve permanence, weight and significance from out of the transience of experiencing', have been defined by Gadamer through the German term

Erlebnis: 'An experience (*Erlebnis*) is no longer something that flows past quickly in the stream of conscious life; it is meant as a unity and thus attains a new mode of being one'[16]. The concept of *Erlebnis* echoes Oakeshott's emphasis on coherence, standing out from other forms of experience as unique in itself but relating deeply to the 'meaningful whole of life'[17]. Scarry expresses this in terms of its physical effects: 'Beauty quickens. It adrenalizes. It makes the heart beat faster. It makes life more vivid, animated, living, worth living'[18]. Such an experience, writes Gadamer, lasts in the memory of the person who has it, as 'unforgettable and irreplaceable', something that no amount of description or definition can ever exhaust[19].

Erlebnis, then, is the most powerful expression of *an* experience as distinctive from the continuous flow of *general* experience. This was something John Dewey attended to in his book *Art as Experience*, where he theorised in detail what having *an* experience consists of. In language reminiscent of Oakeshott, he links it to what we would nowadays call a constructivist theory of knowledge: '[T]aking in any vital experience is something more than placing something on the top of consciousness over what was previously known. It involves reconstruction'[20]. Like Gadamer, he saw an experience of this kind as integrated with but demarcated from the stream of ordinary experience and defined its nature in terms of unity and coherence, as something that ends in a sense of consummation and not mere cessation. Importantly, too, he did not see such experiences as confined to the arts but dependent upon qualities such as absorption and purpose that could just as well emanate from a scientific inquiry as much as from one's experience of painting or viewing a landscape. His sober, pragmatic approach to analysing the nature of such experiences provides us with a lens through which we can theorise the more common, recurring experiences of beauty, less intense than those peak experiences we have such as the more sudden and intense epiphany or *Erlebnis*. Ransome's holidays, for example; or the numerous times I listened to a Dylan album after the original revelation of his music; or the sense of fulfilment I felt whenever I had managed to play a new song. Dewey is particularly attentive to the *narrative* aspects of such experiences, and we therefore return to him later in the book when we examine how teachers can learn from beauty by using aesthetic ideas to shape their pedagogy[21].

We might venture at this point that Oakeshott's definition of knowledge centres around ideas rather than skills, privileging conceptual understanding over 'know how', something that would put his epistemology at odds with much of the practice of modern schooling. But Oakeshott does attend to the world of thought-in-action, as Schon might have described 'know how', when he examines the nature of *practical experience*, which he describes as the world of concrete reality itself[22]. He does not, however, conflate know how with the acquisition of skills or techniques; this would be mere accretion, touching only the raw end of learning. Knowledge gained through practice, he argues, is reached through action and the exercise of the will and is driven by 'a felt discrepancy between what is and what we desire shall be'[23]. If desire is the engine that powers our will to learn, it is our values that shape our desires, and hence, in practical experience, the coherence we seek whenever we create new knowledge is located in a world of values. Values provide the motivation for action inasmuch as the knowledge that we seek is knowledge that we value. The very business of practice is 'to realize in the world of practical fact what exists and is already real in the world of value'[24]. Without this underpinning sense of value, practical experience risks the danger of incoherence—in Oakeshott's terms, of becoming 'a world of mere activity' rather than one of purposeful action[25].

Let us look at what this means in terms of the relationship between my own experience of learning the guitar and the coherent world of ideas that drove this process. Like any craft, learning to play the guitar in the folk-blues tradition consists of a series of skills, in this case various styles of fingering and plucking, different rhythms and methods of strumming, the ability to move the hand from one chord formation to another with speed and minimum effort and so on. Some of these skills need to be mastered before others can be attained. For example, a particularly satisfying skill is that of 'hammering on', where the player plucks a discordant note, immediately rectifying the sound by hammering on his finger to hit the correct fret. This creates a more fluid sound, seemingly eliding one chord into another, but cannot be used effectively until the player can change chords quickly and effortlessly. In this sense the 'know how' or skills are indeed incremental in terms of how and in what order we best acquire them. But this is only part of the picture and would have been incoherent if not for a broader conceptual framework that determined my progress—my knowledge of music, or more precisely the kind of music I wished to create, what it sounded like in my mind's ear in comparison to the actual sounds I was producing at any given time. I was working, therefore, as Collingwood tells us all artists work, with the artistic product existing in my head, discovering it by working until I was satisfied[26]. This was a world of value, the value being beauty, the beauty of the music I wished to make and the words I wanted to sing. Without that sense of value, I would have been engaged in 'mere activity', lacking in any sense of direction or purpose or any idea of what should count as quality. There would have been no coherence or sense to my learning to play and hence very little desire to do so. I would not have bothered with it, just as I have never bothered to learn to play the oboe, never had the wish to strip and re-assemble a motor cycle's engine and never harboured the inclination to become a boat builder. The knowledge I gained from beauty framed the skills I learned as I learned them and indeed provided the impetus for learning them in the first place. And this, in turn, was deeply related to what I liked, who I felt I was and who I wanted to be.

Richard Sennett tells us that the modern world has two key methods for urging us to work hard and work well: the one is a moral imperative—to do it for the good of the community—the other is through invoking the spirit of competition. 'Both recipes have proved troubled', he tells us: 'Neither has—in naked form—served the craftsman's aspiration for quality'[27]. The reason for this, I would venture, lies in the nature of craft as a practice and of practical experience as knowledge. In my case, I was driven neither by a sense of communal, moral purpose nor by any sense of competition. I was not trying to be better than my friends, nor was I working on dreams of becoming rich—famous, yes, but trying to achieve fame through an ideal of beauty that was internal to the practice I was engaged in. None of the external considerations would necessarily have impeded my learning, but they could never have had the motivating energy of beauty as they were not integral to it. Beauty was the value that made it all matter and that anchored me to the process.

It would be wrong, however, to regard this experience of beauty solely in individual and psychological terms. Passion and desire were at the heart of its future-oriented momentum, and these had an outwardly social as much as an inwardly personal dimension. The envisioned future, in which I would write songs, perform them and become visible and loved, was not something that I thought could be achieved overnight and without work. It involved embarking upon a project that was practical as well as creative and social as well as personal because, once I had bought and begun to play the guitar, I became part of a fluid but well-defined community of other, like-minded young people who did the same. It led me to meet new friends from whom I learned new songs and new techniques of playing, friends who could also learn from me. So I became a teacher as well as a pupil, gaining in self-esteem in the process. It also led me in unexpected directions. There was the obvious musical route back to an older generation of black blues singers such as Leadbelly and Robert Johnston, as well as forward to then emergent musicians like Neil Young, Joni Mitchell and Ritchie Havens. Although these artists were fairly standard tastes among the aesthetic community I had opted into, all of them affected how I wrote songs and played the guitar and consequently expanded my education within this closely defined musical field. But when I learned that Dylan was influenced by the poetry of Arthur Rimbaud, his difficult, visionary and irreverent poems became a new avenue of fascination, which in turn led me to read the more lyrical poems of Verlaine and the Modernist verse of Apollinaire. As a result of this new and growing interest in French literature I opted to study French rather than history at university, and it was there, in the avant-garde theatre of Beckett, Tardieu and Ionesco, that I discovered a new passion which eventually brought me to the job I hold now. So despite the twists and turns along the way, my current vocation can be seen, partly at least, as the outcome of a largely self-directed learning journey, an outcome I could never have envisaged when first I embarked upon it, scribbling down the lyrics of *Blowing in the Wind* in a cramped bedroom at the age of fifteen.

BEAUTY AND 'UNSELFING'

And tortures him now more, the more he sees
Of pleasures not for him ordained.[28]

Although beauty itself might be a universal human value, how and where
we find it will differ between individuals, cultures and historical eras. My
son does not rate Bob Dylan very highly at all. He is more interested in hip-
hop and his decks than in the acoustic guitar that I somewhat misguidedly
bought for him a few years ago, which now gathers dust in the corner of
the spare room. New technologies open up new fashions but also new possibilities for creating beauty, and, if anything, beauty has a bigger hold over
his life than it had over mine. For me it was the guitar and performing in
bands; for him it is contemporary dance, but he has shown more tenacity
than I did by making a career of it. Young people's need for the aesthetic is
ever present, even if its expression is ever changing. If they do not find it in
the classroom, they will certainly find it elsewhere; and it can be challenging for teachers to help young people connect aesthetically with the content
of a proscribed curriculum.

A graphic example of a student's failure to engage with beauty—and
one that is likely to resonate with many secondary school teachers—is
provided by Kathleen Gallagher in her book *The Theatre of Urban*. She
writes of a boy called Rally who, in her words, 'rules the classroom with
his wit and dominant persona'[29]. He does not use his charisma to help
the teacher, who, recognising a class leader when she sees one, gives him
opportunities to perform responsibly that he consistently undermines
or rejects. Gallagher illustrates this in her description of a drama lesson
focused on Shakespeare's *Macbeth*. When Rally volunteers to take on
the lead role in dialogue with Lady Macbeth, he deliberately subverts the
text, sexualising every exchange with his female partner, constantly playing up to his friends. Amid the laughter this generates one of them calls
out, 'He's like a kid in a candy store'. Gallagher's observation is typically
astute: 'He is indeed getting all the attention he craves but like a sugar
high it is never enough'[30].

Shakespeare is an iconic example, his works generally accepted internationally by academics, theatre practitioners and the general public as among
the very best in the entire history of human cultural achievement. More-
over, *Macbeth* is regarded as one of his most powerful plays. In a search
for beauty within proscribed curricula, we need surely look no further.
Despite this, what Gallagher describes is the antithesis of any engagement
with beauty and any learning through it. Iris Murdoch helps us identify
what is missing for Rally. It is not that he is failing to pay due reverence
to the object of art under study; it is much more to do with a process she
calls 'unselfing' which, in his case, is entirely absent. 'Unselfing', claims
Murdoch, happens when we forget about ourselves, our anxieties and our

day-to-day preoccupations and is at the heart of the experience of beauty. She describes this as a form of 'unpossessive contemplation' of something excellent in art or in nature and as an experience which 'alters consciousness in the direction of unselfishness, objectivity and realism'[31]. Here is how she exemplifies it:

> I am looking out of my window in an anxious and resentful state of mind, oblivious of my surroundings, brooding perhaps on some damage done to my prestige. Then suddenly I observe a hovering kestrel. In a moment everything is altered. The brooding self with its hurt vanity is disappeared. There is nothing now but kestrel. And when I return to thinking of the other matter it seems less important.[32]

There is a moral thrust to Murdoch's argument—that beauty can make you a better person—for which she has been criticised by writers such as John Carey. He accuses her of being a 'well-fed academic, fond of poetry', failing to see that her vision of the kestrel would be seen as one of menace rather than beauty by 'a Chinese peasant watching over a batch of chicks that will soon be ready for market'[33]. There is a tacit insinuation here that beauty in nature and in art is something that ordinary people do not have time for; that only the well fed and educated can be expected to value it (I assume he counts himself amongst their number). We might, too, question Carey's assumed authority to speak on behalf of a Chinese peasant. Anyway, his criticism misses the point. Murdoch is describing this as *her* vision of beauty; she is not claiming that everyone in the world will see the kestrel as she does; rather, she is using it as an example of the positive effects an experience of beauty can have on us. Her central point is that to experience and hence learn from beauty we must, to some extent, lose ourselves; and Gallagher's is a good example of the validity of this proposition exemplified in its negative form.

Rally steadfastly resists any engagement with Shakespeare's dramatic verse by resolutely performing a version of *himself* rather than of Macbeth, at no point releasing himself from the tyranny of his own, closely guarded identity, thus avoiding any exposure to the possibilities of something different. He conducts a one-person show with no space for the teacher, his co-student/performer nor indeed for Macbeth. This is not to say that he is a bad person or that he is somehow morally or affectively deficient; it is simply to state a quite obvious fact.

The reasons for this might be various. Adolescence is a time of acute self-consciousness, when young people need to declare their own autonomy at the same time as they define who or what groups they belong to. We might speculate that Rally maintains his social capital among his friends by continually performing a witty, rebellious and subversive persona. We might, on the other hand, follow current accountability practices and blame the teacher for not deploying an appropriate pedagogy, or for not keeping strong enough discipline. Or we might broaden our speculations to consider the political construction of curricula, what counts, to use Michael Apple's term, as 'official knowledge'[34] and see in Shakespeare an icon of a culture that Rally and many like him feel not only detached from but also hostile towards—hostile in a way similar to Milton's great rebel, who saw in Eve a beauty that could never be part of his world and hence felt compelled to destroy it. If this is the case, then Rally will regard Shakespeare in a way that is similar to how Carey's Chinese peasant would respond to Murdoch's kestrel—seeing it as a source of threat rather than of beauty. All of these could play their part in Rally's rejection, but at the heart of the problem, I would argue, are issues of identity that cannot be entirely reduced to those that Apple would associate with sanctioned abuses of cultural authority[35].

As we have seen, beauty *as experience* inspires love and admiration as opposed to a sense of rejection. At this intense level, Nehamas tells us, we are engaged in a complex process of desire; a desire to possess but also *be* possessed by the object of beauty, where the Platonic connection between beauty and love is at its most evident. It is a moment when I am prepared to let something or someone other than myself shape my desires. If I love you, suggests Nehamas,

> I don't approach you with a settled sense of myself, taking my plans and my wishes for granted . . . Instead, I expect them—I want them— to change when I expose them to you. I hope that you will make me wish for what I have never wished for before and give me what I now can't even imagine.[36]

As with love, so with beauty, and this is a far cry from Kantian disinterestedness. Murdoch implies that, in an encounter with beauty, rather than being protective of my identity, I acknowledge that it will in some significant way be changed. Not only do I acknowledge it, I desire it. This kind of language does not fit readily with the politics of recognition that currently dominate the discourse of identity, but to resist beauty for ideological reasons is to deny ourselves the possibility of finding new pleasures which are integral to a process of learning[37]. We cannot experience and hence learn from beauty unless we are able or prepared to loosen the ties that restrict our identities. Instead of celebrating their fixity, we need to embrace their fluidity.

John Berger provides us with an example of an intense encounter with beauty that helps theorise its connection with identity a little further. In his short essay *Field*, the field of the title is one alongside which he sometimes has to stop on his drive home. Describing it precisely and in great detail he concludes, 'Suddenly an experience of disinterested observation opens at its centre and gives birth to a happiness that is entirely your own. The field that you are standing before appears to have the same proportions as your own life'[38]. The 'disinterested observation' may carry echoes of Kant but it is not at the heart of the experience here, which only becomes *an* experience when it opens up and is transformed into passion, with the resulting happiness and elation being akin to love. It is a clear example of unselfing as defined by Murdoch, but it is the spatial analogy that is of particular interest to us here as it supplies us with a metaphor through which we can find a definition of the experience of beauty that takes due account of identity. Beauty, we might postulate, is located in the expressive poise between the individual experiencing and the object under consideration, when both are in balance or harmony[39]. This is not a simple, two-dimensional idea. To refer back to my personal example, the poise was between my identity at the age of fifteen and the songs and persona of Bob Dylan. My naïve idealism, my rudimentary knowledge of music, my youthful sexuality were as equal a part of that experience as were the music and poetry of the songs themselves and the image and age of the performer. This balance was the basis upon which the contact between subject and object could be made, and without it any process of unselfing could never have happened. We lose ourselves to find in ourselves a renewed sense of coherence to our lives.

Only one of the examples that I provided at the opening of this chapter happened in a school setting—that of Philip Pullman—and I doubt if the teacher was aware of the depth of the impact he had had. Teachers may not be able to *plan* for epiphanies, and there is no denying beauty's elusive, surprising and intensely individual qualities, but in the way they teach they can make them more or less likely to happen. As argued earlier, there exist those recurring, more frequent aesthetic experiences that share the qualities of overwhelming experiences of beauty, albeit in less intense a form. We can be moved, stirred, captivated, suddenly excited by something mysterious but fascinating, taken on a journey of discovery that we wish to continue, to places we long to revisit and further explore. If we are to bring the potential to learn through beauty into the classroom, then we should find the underlying principles to inform our pedagogy within the experience itself. So what might these be?

Firstly, such a pedagogy must not rely on the object of beauty itself to do its work—whether it be found in a scene from Shakespeare, in a geometrical theorem, in a painting by Mondrian or in an episode from the life of the Buddha. The teacher must pay equal attention to the expressive capacities of the students in her class, which she therefore needs to be interested in and aware of. This goes beyond their levels of literacy and includes their likes and dislikes, the aesthetic opportunities afforded by their gender, class and cultural backgrounds, their aesthetic interests and tastes both in and outside of school and so on. Secondly, she must have an ability to make the object of study match these expressive capacities as far as she can; in other words, she needs to find ways to make the object of beauty connect with the lives of her students. This is implicit in the often-quoted idea that good subject teachers imbue a love of their subject in their students—which leads to our third point: that the teacher must herself be responsive to the beauty in whatever it is she is teaching. Fourthly, the pedagogy itself must attend to those features that we have seen as integral to the experience of beauty—the possibilities of surprise, for example, and the need to help students forget themselves through strategies that can loosen the tyranny of their everyday identities. Fifthly, teachers must be prepared to live with something close to what Keats described as 'negative capability'—'capable of being in uncertainties, mysteries, doubts, without any irritable reaching after fact or reason'[40]—this despite the fact that it flies in the face of current, dominant accountability practices. To these principles we might add one more: the need for the teacher to allow for different forms of replication, different ways for students to respond to and communicate their experiences of beauty. An episode from the life of the Buddha could be expressed as a piece of art; a geometrical proof as a colourful wall display; a painting by Mondrian might inspire a story, as could be the case with Sean Tan's wonderful book *The Red Tree*[41].

This last point is important for, as Elaine Scarry insists, beauty will always have what she calls 'a deeply beneficent momentum toward replication'[42]. Beneficent as it is inspired by generosity, an urge to invite others to share the experience with us. Sometimes this might consist of making a direct copy, as I attempted in my singing and song writing; sometimes an urge to share the experience of the original, as when I introduced the songs and the recordings of Bob Dylan to my friends. For John Berger the urge towards replication was expressed in a piece of writing but perhaps the most common way most of us replicate an experience of beauty is through talking about it with people whose good opinion we value. What matters is that appreciation and creation, what Dewey distinguishes as the aesthetic and the artistic experiences of beauty, are integrated rather than treated as separate; for appreciation leads to a desire to communicate and replicate, which are themselves creative acts.

JOHN RUSKIN AND THE LIMITATIONS OF TECHNIQUE

If the experience of beauty is equally dependent upon the expressive capacity of the individual in harmony with the beautiful object, then it is not necessarily dependent upon a high level of specific skills that approach perfection. A dance by eight-year-olds can be beautiful, provided it is not attempting to imitate the perfection of classical ballet; seven-year-olds can sing beautifully, but no sane teacher would rehearse with them the Hallelujah chorus. John Ruskin had very interesting things to say about this relationship between beauty, creativity and the appearance of perfection. When still a young man he visited Venice and was struck by the complex expressivity of the Gothic Doge's Palace, in which he noted how the individual masons, all of them unknown to us, had left the mark of their own creative identities in the different carvings that surmounted each pillar, in the complex brick patterns and even in the varying levels at which they had positioned each window. This for Ruskin was a beautiful building—'the central building of the world', he called it—as it reflected the subtle, shifting patterns of natural beauty[43]. It was not perfect vis-à-vis ideas of classical regularity, balance and symmetry, but it was humane, as during its construction the masons had not been treated as the slaves of a pre-ordained plan in which each of them had had to produce work that was anonymous in its perfect synchronicity. This was a quality he did see, however—and deplored—in the renaissance museum that stands opposite the Doge's palace in St Mark's Square. The perfection of its matching, slender columns and the exact symmetries evident in its design and execution, where not a brick is positioned out of place, were, for him, signs of an inhumane civilisation that placed the virtues of order and conformity above those of individual creative expression and the common humanity of its workforce.

Ruskin saw in Venice a direct analogy with Victorian Britain and the ruthless, mechanised processes rife in factories and workshops which contrasted unfavourably with the vigorous, creative freedom enjoyed by the Gothic masons. 'Men were not intended to work with the accuracy of tools, to be precise and perfect in all their actions', he writes: 'Let (them) but begin to imagine, to think, to try to do anything worth doing and the engine-turned precision is lost at once'[44]. Imperfection, states Ruskin, is an essential part of life and integral to nature: 'And in all things that live there are certain irregularities and deficiencies which are not only signs of life but sources of beauty'[45]. He argued that no good work could be perfect and that to demand perfection was to misunderstand the nature both of art and of beauty.

Richard Sennett has argued that Ruskin's views were a Romantic reaction not only to rampant industrialisation but also to the new cult surrounding virtuoso performers, such as Paganini and Liszt, who made a virtue out of reaching heroic heights of technical skill that could only diminish how amateur members of the audience felt in comparison. In describing the effect such virtuosity had on the amateur performers who flocked to see them, Sennett makes interesting use of the language of the sublime:

> The rise of the virtuoso on stage coincided with silence and immobility in the concert hall, the audience paying fealty to the artist through its passivity. The virtuoso shocks and awes. In exchange, the virtuoso unleashed in listeners passions they could not produce using their own skills.[46]

Ruskin, he believes, moved this concept of the virtuoso from the concert hall to the engineering works with the purpose of criticising what he saw as oppressive practices. To hold out against the advance of machines instead of embracing their emancipatory potential, creating a myth of the craftsman as 'defiant but doomed' was, Sennett argues, a delusion on his behalf.

Sennett's ideas echo the judgments of Modernism which made Ruskin's ideas seem unfashionable and naïve. Preoccupied as Modernism was with the hopes, dreams and nightmares of modernity, Ruskin's arguments were thought of as hopelessly medieval and romantic. But now, as the art critic Matthew Collings has pointed out, the Modernist dream has vanished, and once again Ruskin's arguments speak to our contemporary concerns[47]. For the pressures of the industrial revolution, read those of globalisation; for the conformities of mechanisation, read those of corporate managerialism. If Ruskin was preoccupied with nature, with the need for us to find ways of living lives and shaping our desires that would be closer to its rhythms, then this is forcefully relevant to our most pressing challenges as we are faced with the need to change the way we live in order to rectify the damage we are doing to our planet, in natural and economic terms.

As Ruskin argued, beauty is not coterminous with technical excellence, which is in itself unnatural; and if we make the mistake of restricting it to ideas of technique and virtuosity then we render it ever more remote from common practices and fail to recognise both its value and its nature as experience. In the words of Collingwood, 'The means-and-end or technique terminology . . . is inapplicable . . . Expression is an activity of which there can be no technique'[48]. The most technically skilful guitar playing will not necessarily be the most beautiful; beauty always has something mysterious at its core and consists of something that is both more and less than technique. Ruskin attacks the error that confounds perfection of technique with beauty which, in effect, imposes a split between the experiencing and the object, positioning beauty as a preserve of the latter and not in the expressive poise between it and the subject of the experience. This tendency fits readily with the underpinning ideology of technicism, which dominates contemporary educational thinking and works against individual creative expression both of student and teacher in ways that Ruskin would have recognised as echoing the conditions of the factory workers of his day.

Derived from management theory, technicism supposes that technique and skills are applicable when freed from purpose and intention. This serves not only to demoralise them but also to drive a wedge between the knower and the known, between the learner and what is being learned. The so-called skills of flexibility, literacy, numeracy, critical thinking and so on are necessarily defined as goods external to what is being taught. They are emphasised as those needed to meet the realities of a competitive, globalised world and thus serve a moral and social vision dominated by the requirements of economics, something that Ruskin recognised and deplored within his own era. Even creativity, so obviously a conceptual ally of beauty, has been appropriated by the language of instrumentalism[49]. Unlike beauty, which involves a deep emotional connection between learners and what they are learning, skills-based curricula are founded upon an absolute split between the one and the other. So a technicist approach to the teaching of Shakespeare, for example, would reduce it to a series of points to be learned, listed by the teacher in the form of objectives, whose achievement must be visible in order to be noted and assessed. The danger here is that the incoherence of 'mere activity' will replace the coherence of practical experience and hence there will be little possibility of achieving real knowledge. And it is a danger all too prevalent as the accountability structures of contemporary education encourage these very characteristics of curriculum planning and pedagogy to flourish at the expense of beauty.

THE FRAGILITY OF BEAUTY

Beauty is connected with fragility, with the fact that it is passing.[50]

Throughout this chapter, I have emphasised the energising potential of beauty, its hopefulness and future orientation. But there is also a fragile quality to beauty, and we often find in it a sadness stirred by the ever-present possibility of its loss. Sartwell explains this by seeing beauty as dependent upon the time-bound nature of our existence and its inherent mortality. In his words, '[B]eauty is made possible by temporality as loss is made inevitable by it'[51].

For a British teacher of my generation, Murdoch's kestrel inevitably brings to mind the story of Billy Casper, the young boy at the centre of Barry Hines' novel *A Kestrel for a Knave* and of his close friend Ken Loach's film version, *Kes*[52]. Billy is the younger son in a one-parent family living in a mining town in Yorkshire. He is unhappy both at school and at home; in the one he is seen as a failure, in the other he is uncared for by his mother and bullied by his elder brother. But when he finds a young, injured kestrel it becomes the centre of his life; he cares for it and learns how to train it from books on falconry that he finds in the local library. One of his teachers is concerned enough about Billy's welfare to take an interest in him and is enlightened enough to go and watch him demonstrate his skills with Kes one evening after school. He is both amazed and enormously impressed by what he sees.

At this point in the story, Billy's relationship with Kes would appear to exemplify Elaine Scarry's contention that beauty is life saving. She quotes the words of Odysseus when he is shipwrecked and comes face to face with the stunning beauty of Nausicaa: 'I look at you and a sense of wonder takes me'[53]. Like Odysseus, Billy's life before that moment was 'a long campaign . . . doomed to hardship'[54]. Kes is Billy's Nausicaa as, through the beauty of this small bird, his life becomes 'more vivid, animated, living, worth living'[55]. But Scarry's eulogy comes with an important qualification. 'Like a small bird', she writes, 'beauty . . . has an aura of fragility'. It is among 'the truly precious things that bad fortune can destroy'[56]. One evening Billy returns home to find Kes dead, his neck broken by his older brother in revenge for Billy's failure to place a bet on a winning horse for him. There is no lasting place in his life, it appears, either inside or outside of school, for the beauty Billy had found.

The fragility of beauty as a value within mainstream schooling has more recently been explored in another fictional tale set in Yorkshire, Alan Bennett's *The History Boys*. Set in 1982, it tells the story of a group of eight sixth formers from a grammar school whose examination results at A Level show exceptional promise and present the school with the possibility of a record number of places in Oxbridge for history. In his excitement, the head hires a young teacher, Irwin, to train them in the techniques of how to pass the entrance examination and interview. Irwin shows the boys how to make an argument that they do not necessarily believe but that will make them stand out interestingly from other candidates. Truth, in this sense of the word, does not matter; historical knowledge is simply a means to an end. The entrance examination is a game, and what matters is that the boys learn how to win it. In contrast to Irwin is Hector, an older teacher of English, whose lessons follow no curriculum guidelines and have no instrumental purpose. He denounces examinations as 'the enemy of education'[57] and proclaims in mock pride that his own lessons are 'a waste of time' providing the boys with '[u]seless knowledge'. His classes are improvised and responsive to their suggestions. Music and singing are common, and poetry peppers the dialogue of the classroom, with the boys quoting verse as freely as their teacher. Irwin coaxes them to use this ability to impress in their essays, but the boys are initially resistant: 'Mr Hector's stuff is not meant for the exam, sir. It's to make us more rounded human beings'[58]. In the end, however, they follow his advice, learning to be clever rather than sincere in their arguments, using the poems they have learned '*by heart*' ('and that is where they belong', adds Hector) as 'handy little quotes that can be trotted out to make a point'[59]; and as a result each of them obtains their place in Oxbridge. The celebrations on their return to school are, however, quickly silenced by the sudden death of Hector in heavily ironic circumstances. Giving Irwin a lift home on his motor scooter, there is a crash; Irwin has leaned in the wrong direction as they turned a corner. He survives with a broken leg.

The play is comic, complex and not at all didactic, but one way it can be interpreted is as a dance between two opposing approaches to education; and although set in 1982, its concerns are vividly contemporaneous. Hector exemplifies a liberal tradition of education for education's sake, an ideal which shuns examinations and sees knowledge as its own reward. As the headmaster puts it, 'It isn't that he doesn't produce results. He does. But they are unpredictable and unquantifiable and in the current educational climate that is no use'[60]. So Hector—as the irony of his name suggests— belongs to a defeated, heroic, perhaps mythical past. At the end of the play he is, quite literally, history himself, his death caused by the oppositional leaning of his ideological adversary (the heavy symbolism is saved by its comic irony). The future, then, belongs to Irwin, who tellingly does not stay long in the teaching profession, quickly moving on into journalism and ending up as a politician. With his pragmatic rather than moral approach to historical truth one can well see his charm, cleverness and gift for spin in the service of a modern political party. More broadly, he represents the professional of the postmodern era, advancing his career through displays of efficiency rather than commitment and judged by the ends he achieves rather than by the means he uses to achieve them.[61]

Yet it is the doomed character of Hector who dominates the play and provides it with its heart. Like Cyrano de Bergerac in Rostand's great comedy, he is gifted in language though not in looks, vainly in love with physical beauty, expressing lines of beautiful dialogue that contrast with the pathos of his unrequited love for the boys he teaches. At the midpoint of the play there is a strikingly moving scene immediately after the point where the head has requested his resignation. Hector is sitting alone in the classroom, when a student called Posner enters, evidently for a tutorial. He has chosen a poem by Hardy to learn for this session, *Drummer Hodge*, which has as its subject the death of a young English drummer boy on a battlefield in Africa late in the nineteenth century. Posner recites the poem, and Hector explains why he finds it particularly moving:

> The important thing is that he (the drummer boy) has a name . . . Before this, soldiers, private soldiers anyway, were all unknown soldiers, and so far from being revered, there was a firm in the nineteenth century which swept up their bones from the battlefields of Europe in order to grind them into fertiliser. So, thrown into a common grave though he may be, he is still Hodge the drummer. Lost boy though he is on the other side of the world, he still has a name.[62]

The reference to the battlefield serves on one level as a metaphor for the kind of education that Hector resists, one that regards young people not so much from his liberal perspective, as individuals whose characters are to be nurtured, but in utilitarian and technicist terms, as fertiliser, as a percentage contribution to the nation's overall welfare, as a statistic of attainment that can nourish the school's reputation in the local community. At the end of the scene (which is also the end of the lesson) Hector comments,

> The best moments in reading are when you come across something—a thought, a feeling, a way of looking at things—which you had thought special and particular to you. Now here it is, set down by someone else, a person you have never met, someone who is even long dead. And it is as if a hand had come out and taken yours.[63]

This is a very different idea of education from the one that dominates in our schools today. Instead of the technical aims, stated objectives and emphasis on generic skills, education is here envisioned as something of a conversation between the learner of the present and the achievements of the past. Like all good conversations, its content cannot be entirely structured in advance, nor can it be expected to have easily defined objectives that will shape a pre-determined conclusion; we do not engage in conversations for these purposes. A conversation can be expected to have focus, shift to different but related areas, provide space for all parties involved to engage in and shape and—if it is worth having—should provide satisfaction of a very human kind; a sense of companionship, of time well spent, of something lingering within us that we are happy to go away and think about. Such a metaphor for education does, indeed, make room for beauty[64].

The subsequent stage direction is very important. *He puts out his hand and it seems for a moment as if Posner will take it, or even that Hector may put it on Posner's knee. But the moment passes.* The moment passes but it is a beautiful moment, especially when viewed retrospectively at the play's conclusion. By this time we have learned that Posner is the only one of Hector's pupils who 'truly took everything to heart', who 'remembers everything he was ever taught'[65]—and in the film version we learn that he goes on to become a teacher himself. This act of teacher and student reaching towards one another is given added resonance by the words of Hector that conclude the play:

> Pass the parcel.
> That's sometimes all you can do.
> Take it, feel it and pass it on.
> Not for me, not for you, but for someone, somewhere, one day.
> Pass it on, boys.
> That's the game I wanted you to learn.
> Pass it on.[66]

Hector's game is very different from Irwin's; for Irwin education was a means to an end, for Hector an end in itself and it ends *in* and *as* the common good. It is a fragile, perhaps doomed model because it resists quantification and is ready to see a worthwhile statistic in just one pupil being truly affected by the content of a lesson, taking its beauty to their heart.

Although the word beauty is never used in the play, there is plenty of it about, woven into the dramaturgy created from the snatches of poetry the boys constantly recite, the popular music they play and sing, their youthful, articulate exuberance and liveliness, the warmth of their relationships, in the tenderness of Posner's unrequited love for one of his classmates and in the pathos of Hector's death. Plato, Wilde and Proust are mentioned in one breath by the head master, contemptuous of their homosexuality but also, by implication, the way each placed such a high value on beauty. And Hector orchestrates this beauty by the way he teaches and in the ideal of teaching he aspires to. Bennett has described the play as 'sentimental and unrealistic'—which in one sense it is[67]. As a counterpoint to the urgings and imperatives of the head, which chime so readily with contemporary educational discourse, we are, throughout the play, reminded of Hector's love of the subjunctive; in an early scene, for example, when the boys are speaking in French, he insists that they speak *only* in the subjunctive. The subjunctive is the mood of possibility, contingency and hypothesis, the mood of uncertainty. Such a mood does not chime easily with the pressures on today's schools and, if the choice were presented as an either/or, then the need for schools to achieve visible and socially valued test results would always triumph over a more idealistic but openly uncertain vision, as indeed it does in *The History Boys*. The beauty of the play is that it manages to celebrate the boys' achievements but also what is lost in the process—the vision of a classroom where a teacher, doomed and defiant, like Ruskin's craftsman, has beauty at the centre of his vision. Given the popular appeal of both the play and the film, Hector's exuberant defiance and ultimate demise spoke profoundly to the many who watched and were moved by it.

EPILOGUE

Despite my experiences as a musician, in all my years as a teacher and head teacher, I never felt comfortable teaching music. If ever called upon to cover a music lesson for an absent colleague, I was more aware of my limitations than anything else. I could hardly sight-read music, could not play the piano and felt competent only to lead classroom singing and some very basic pitched percussion work. In my final year as head of a middle school, however, I faced a crisis as one dynamic music teacher left to be replaced by another, far less competent, who could only teach part-time. I was aware of a small group of girls in Years 7 and 8 who could sing exceptionally well and also of a boy in Year 6, skilful on the keyboards, who, like me, played by ear and read music only with difficulty. One lunchtime, I brought them together and proposed that we form a small band in which I would play the guitar. Our bargain was that I would teach them to sing in harmony and that, for every song I chose, they could choose one of their own for us to learn.

The results exceeded my expectations. The girls were so good that we were soon working on songs with complex, three-part harmonies, whereas the boy could pick up a tune and rhythm so quickly that I only ever had to play a song through once for him to be able to figure out his accompaniment. This was an experience I was very much at home with, like being back in a band, rehearsing new material. We played a number of gigs—at our school concerts, at the school fete, at the county show. We performed during the interval of the PTA annual dinner dance and were even invited to play at some neighbouring schools.

At the end of the year, we spent a day in a local recording studio and cut a hundred copies of our favourite six songs on to cassette tapes. These were all sold within two days, at a price fixed to cover costs. Walking around the school on the last day of the summer term, the tape could be heard playing in most of the classrooms. The favourite track seemed to be our version of *Eternal Flame* by the Bangles, and groups of younger girls could be seen to be singing along to it, emulating the girls' movement routine. My own particular favourite, however, was and remains an arrangement of Donovan's *The Mandolin Man and His Secret*. The surging harmonies of the first line that the girls sing so beautifully still take my breath away.

As with *Kes* and *The History Boys*, a death marked the end of this happy period. Nothing so tragic, however; it was the school that died, the victim of a local authority reorganisation and their plans to merge it with a nearby first school. I was not enthusiastic about the prospect of re-applying for my job and then, if successful, being faced with the task of sacking half of the current members of staff. So, at the end of the year, I left to take up a position in teacher education. 'Mr Winston is leaving the band to take up a new career in the West Midlands', reported the local newspaper; it was the closest I ever got to musical fame.

I kept in touch with former members of the band for about a year or so. Four of the girls went to the local high school where their reputation preceded them. Immediately on arrival, they were invited by a group of boys in Year 11 to sing as part of their music GCSE projects. I met one of them a few years later, quite by chance. Her parents had since been divorced and she was now living with her father in another town, studying sciences in the sixth form. 'We still play our tape', she told me. She and the other band members will now be about thirty years old, and I do not know what any of them are doing in life, or how music features in it. But, for me, that little cassette tape is one of the possessions I cherish from my years of teaching and is always what I think of when I hear or read Hector's lines at the end of *The History Boys*:

Pass the parcel.
That's sometimes all you can do.
Take it, feel it and pass it on.

4 Beauty, Education and the Good Society

BEAUTY AND THE CARING VIRTUES

> *Let us cultivate (beauty) to the utmost in men, women and children—in our gardens and in our houses. But let us love that other beauty, too, which lies in no secret of proportion but in the secret of deep human sympathy.*[1]

It is forty years since Iris Murdoch mounted a strong and influential argument for placing beauty at the heart of any project whose central question is, 'How can we make ourselves better?' The Kantian emphasis on duty, 'the proud, naked will directed towards right action', is, she argued, an unrealistic and inadequate response to the question's moral thrust as it ignores some of our deepest human needs[2]. Ordinary people know instinctively that states of mind such as pureness of heart and meekness of spirit create what she termed the 'genetic background of action'[3]. They know, too, that they need help if they are to achieve a better quality of consciousness, one that might provide 'an energy for good action which would not otherwise be available'[4]. This energy was once generally thought to be provided by religion, in the form of prayer, for example, but Murdoch recognised that, in a secular age, anything which succeeds in altering consciousness in the direction of unselfishness should be connected with virtue. She proposed that the most obvious thing in our surroundings to help us with this 'unselfing' is beauty, reminding us that, as Plato pointed out, beauty is the one spiritual quality that we love by instinct. Her conclusion—that an education in the enjoyment of beauty is 'a training in the love of virtue'[5]—boldly restated the Neoplatonic tradition in terms suitable for a secular age.

Although Murdoch's argument flies in the face of later feminist commentaries on beauty, it presages the subsequent feminist re-evaluation of moral theory by philosophers such as Annette Baier, Nancy Chodorow and Martha Nussbaum[6]. A key landmark in this re-interpretation was Carol Gilligan's influential study of the moral thinking of girls and young women, *In a Different Voice*, published in 1981, in which she contrasted how men and women respond differently to the same moral dilemmas[7]. Her one-time co-researcher, Lawrence Kohlberg, had proposed a theory of universal moral development based upon reason and the over-arching principle of justice. In this he had been highly influenced by John Rawls' *A Theory of Justice*, itself written from within the Kantian moral tradition that Murdoch had criticised[8]. Gilligan read in the data she had gathered that men and women tended to think differently about the moral issues posed to them; whereas women were more concerned with the particularities and relational aspects of the ethical dilemmas—in particular the emotional consequences of a particular course of action—men were more pre-occupied with rules of conduct, questions of fairness and absolute moral principles. She concluded by proposing an 'ethic of care' as a counter balance to Kohlberg's morality of justice; if a justice perspective emphasises reason, autonomy and civil society, then a care perspective stresses the emotional needs of individuals for networks of attachment and interdependency in both civic and domestic settings. As Annette Baier has recognised, Gilligan's argument suggests that we blur the boundaries between public and private virtue and advocates 'a union of male and female moral wisdom' in order to counter the ways in which gendered thinking might distort or limit moral action[9].

Wendy Steiner helps us make the connection between feminist moral theory and the potential for beauty to develop those virtues that have traditionally been most evident in environments and tasks associated with female sensibilities. Such practices at their best are characterised by the virtues we associate with care and attachment—love, generosity, trust, gentleness, sympathy, cheerfulness, patience and so on. As we have seen, Steiner emphasises the significance of what she calls the 'softer' values found in an aesthetic of charm, sentiment and sympathy, describing them as 'the common values and pleasures of human existence'—values which have been devalued by Kantian theory[10]. The aesthetics of homely activities such as decorating a child's bedroom (or an early years classroom, perhaps), preparing and cooking food, gardening, making and presenting gifts are demonstrative of a specific set of domestic virtues and also, as Steiner points out, can be identifiable with those softer values of 'the beautiful' as opposed to the more detached and awesome qualities of 'the sublime'. Although we have seen this conceptual binary as one open to challenge, it nonetheless mirrors the different gender tendencies of the care and justice perspectives outlined by Gilligan. Both the aesthetics of the sublime and the perspective of justice are associated with qualities of autonomy and detachment and the emotions of admiration, respect and fear for powers and principles greater than ourselves. In contrast, the aesthetics of the beautiful and the perspective of care centre upon emotional attachment, mutual dependency and the virtues of human sympathy. Just as Gilligan and Baier stress the significance of the caring virtues, so Steiner urges that we privilege these more feminine aspects of beauty as they help us become connected with life and with the 'other', rather than detached from them, and enable us to recognise and value those things which are our dearest concerns: 'If we can discover the bonds between value and mutuality forged in aesthetic response . . . that pleasure will be seen as life-enhancing rather than exclusive or oppressive'[11].

The garden is a key metaphor for these ethical and aesthetic values—a place of domestic culture, tranquil and secure, in which we labour creatively in order to cultivate and enjoy natural beauty and see it flourish as a result of the due attention and care we pay to it. Small wonder, then, that the Romantics closely identified the cultivation of the garden with the education of the child and that these values should find expression in those classic children's stories in which the needs of young children for both care and beauty become the central subject matter. Frances Hodgson Burnett's *The Secret Garden* is a well-loved example, in which the character of the young, orphaned heroine, Mary Lennox, flourishes and blossoms as she learns to tend and cultivate the garden of the title. In doing so, she establishes the first caring relationships of her life with the local boy, Dickon, and her sickly, hysterical cousin, Colin, on whom she has a healing and redemptive effect. Typically, these social and moral benefits extend beyond the world of the children and transform the life of the adults whom they come into contact with. In the final chapter, Colin's widowed father, who has been grieving for his wife since she died giving birth to his son, is travelling alone through the mountains of the Austrian Tyrol (the aesthetics of the sublime are unmistakable). His mood, as ever, is dark and tormented, unaware as he is of the children's transformation of the secret garden, so loved by his wife, and of Colin's restoration to health. He rests by a small stream and is touched for the first time for years by the natural beauty of the world and feels its life enhancing qualities:

> He sat and gazed at the sunlit water and his eyes began to see things growing at its edge. There was one lovely mass of blue forget-me-nots growing so close to the stream that its leaves were wet and at these he found himself looking as he remembered he had looked at such things years ago . . . 'What is it?' he said, almost in a whisper, and he passed his hand over his forehead. 'I almost feel as if—I were alive!'[12]

Soon afterwards he returns to England and of course discovers that, through the 'Mystery and Magic' of the Garden—that is to say, through its beauty and its charm—his child has been restored to health, and happiness has returned to his home.

In Michelle Magorian's *Goodnight Mr Tom*, the young evacuee, Willie Beech, is forced into the care of the curmudgeonly recluse, Tom Oakley[13]. On discovering the extent of the emotional abuse and physical neglect Willie has suffered, Tom's care for the young boy develops into the genuinely felt love of a parent, and both man and boy begin to flourish within this newly discovered mutual dependency. As with the earlier novel, the garden becomes a central metaphor of Willie's need for nurture in order to grow into health and maturity, a symbol of the domestic ideal as the site where nature, culture and beauty meet; or, as Fred Inglis puts it, a 'Garden of Eden . . . where culture is detached from labour and returned to creativeness'[14].

This Romantic alliance of childhood with the qualities of nature at her best is at the heart of another favourite children's story, *The Selfish Giant* by Oscar Wilde[15]. Once again, the garden is the central symbol from which, this time, the children are banished, an action which brings a permanent state of winter into it. Only when they manage to climb through the giant's fence and begin to play there once more does spring return. On seeing the flowers blooming again and on hearing the song of a linnet, the giant's 'unselfing' explicitly occurs, this fusion of children, nature and domesticity marking the moment when he is rescued from his selfishness and can begin to share once again in a life that contributes to the common good. *The Selfish Giant* has been variously interpreted as an allegory for the British presence in Ireland and as a sublimated expression of Wilde's homosexual love for younger men[16]. Such is not how the tale is apprehended by children or teachers in primary schools, where it is more often than not treated as a moral tale about selfishness. Its true educative power, however, lies not in any lesson that it illustrates but in the qualities of beauty that are intrinsic to it and the softer values of sympathy and attachment that it conveys, illustrative of Wilde's own principle that 'a beautiful thing helps us by being what it is'[17]. The popular writer Gervaise Phinn tells of how, during his time as a school inspector, he witnessed a female teacher break down into sobs at the climax of the tale, and of how a six-year-old boy gently took the story book from her hands and finished reading it aloud to the class. 'I always have to do that when she reads that story', he told Mr Phinn afterwards[18]. Wilde himself would have understood:

> His son, Vyvyan, records that when his father read this story aloud he used to cry: 'Cyril once asked him why he had tears in his eyes when he told us the story of *The Selfish Giant* and he replied that really beautiful things always made him cry'.[19]

Wilde would doubtless, too, have made the connection with Plotinus; that it is the moral force integral to the tale's beauty that touched their common humanity. Unfortunately, however, the value of the tale is seldom if ever articulated in such terms, as the language to do so is simply not extant in educational discourse. Without this articulation, the sensitive teacher may well *privately* apprehend the power of beauty in her practice but lack the discursive resources to talk about it *publicly* and hence develop and promote it.

BEAUTY AND THE GOOD SOCIETY IN THE EARLY YEARS: A CASE STUDY

That beauty can indeed be its own point when the virtues it embodies and promotes are worthwhile in themselves is unfortunately given no credence by policy makers or commentators who concern themselves with the educational value of the arts. Gordon Lidstone, writing for the UK's left-leaning *Institute of Public Policy Research*, recognises that it can be difficult to evaluate the social benefits of the arts but makes his argument in the reductive, technocratic language so characteristic of our times. Those working in the arts need to provide evidence of the 'social impact of long-term investment', we are told.[20] Whereas he recognises the difficulty in 'determining value through objective measures of outcomes', he nonetheless stresses that there is a need for the arts to do precisely that.[21] He concludes, 'When examining social impact it will be less a case for setting benchmarks for achievement than being comprehensive in understanding how the mechanisms of impact may work and finding appropriate modes of measurement'[22]. Impact, benchmarks, mechanisms, measurement. The language, typical as it is of the economic, positivist and managerial jargon that reflects the dominant assumptions of our age, is more than a technical means of communication; it constructs the moral boundaries within which not only the arts but also education in general are today being discussed, conceptualised and evaluated. And the moral language that characterises our era, as MacIntyre informs us, produces in turn human characters who typify it in the way that they 'morally legitimate a mode of social existence'[23]. In other words, there are those who come to embody this morality and enact its principles.

A few years ago, I undertook the evaluation of a community arts project for pre-school children and their parents in the suburb of a city in the West Midlands, UK. The project, entitled *The Emerald Cave*, was a joint venture between Sure Start and a Theatre in Education (TiE) company that regularly tours its work in local primary and secondary schools[24]. It was an interactive, participatory theatre programme for pre-school children and parents to experience together. A professional visual artist was heavily involved in the design of the programme which had many sensorial qualities, using light, cloth and playful objects as well as actors to embellish the participants' experience. As part of the evaluation, I interviewed the local strategic project co-ordinator for Sure Start. He had seen a preview of the show, and his response was polite but sceptical. Although expressing support for the initiative, his language was always guarded, and he displayed little enthusiasm. He indicated that there was a strong 'doubting Thomas' within him—a phrase he used four times in a twenty-minute interview—and he suggested that there would be many 'doubting Thomases' that the company would need to win over, who would probably see the programme as 'a bit arty farty'. He qualified his support for the project by describing it as a 'stepping stone towards meeting our objectives' rather than in any sense actually meeting those objectives; and he stated clearly that he was most interested in the arts being used to address particular targets, specifically referring to the encouragement of breast feeding.

This response from a key manager exemplifies the pervasive mistrust of the 'uselessness' of beauty, underpinned by an ideology that values only visible objectives and practical outcomes deemed to be socially desirable. More than this, he personified not only the philistine vision at the heart of this ideology but also the moral distortions that it inevitably produces—a certain ideal of the rational man of Modernist moral philosophy against whom Iris Murdoch's own vision is targeted: '[His] ideal rationality would leave us without art, without dream or imagination, without likes or dislikes, unconnected with instinctual needs'[25]. Mercifully, she writes, this man does not exist. Unfortunately, ideological forces seem to have since conspired with government agencies to create him.

Working within such a climate, TiE companies have no choice but to express their aims in the outcomes-based language of social utility. My evaluation, of course, also had to address these objectives, yet, in doing so, I did not accept for one minute that the real qualities of *The Emerald Cave* could be properly expressed from within the reductive language of measurable objectives. For me it was the *beauty* of the experience that mattered most, and the word 'beautiful' was one I heard used unselfconsciously by parents and Sure Start workers as an immediate response in the aftermath of the event.

At the heart of the interactive nature of *The Emerald Cave* children and parents were invited to relate to three fantasy creatures, called simply Troll, Imp and Bird. The simple plot involved them all being taken to the seaside and going on a magical voyage during which they discover the land of Troll and help him find a new home as his old one has been destroyed by the storm that blew the children ashore. This home is the emerald cave which they help to decorate before singing Troll to sleep and slipping off quietly back to the world of their everyday lives. The programme ran for a month in three rooms within a disused secondary school which the participant visual artist had transformed into the fantasy world. The first room became a beach and seascape, with sand, shells, blue and white cloth, theatrical lighting and a soundtrack of waves breaking on the shore. The second room was darker, a magic forest, with netting, treescapes, chocolate wood shavings on the floor and a cave with a variety of percussion instruments inside it. Suitable play materials were scattered around the space, model birds and butterflies suspended from the branches and netting. Children and parents could also interact with Bird here and see the egg in its nest transform into several chicks. In the final, darkened room was the emerald cave itself, a large, wicker creation with coloured lights flashing above it.

As is generally the case in early-years settings, the adult presence in *The Emerald Cave* was overwhelmingly female. The visual artist who designed the set and the actors who devised and performed the programme were also female. It is small wonder, perhaps, that the virtues of the programme embraced the softer, feminine values of charm and sympathy advocated by Steiner, and it is through these that I attempt to analyse the moral power of *The Emerald Cave*, as Iris Murdoch implied we should, from within the parameters of beauty itself.

Figure 4.1 From *The Emerald Cave*, a production from The Play House.

The ornamental was a key aspect of the programme's design. In the sea world, for example, there were strands of long grass that many children enjoyed stroking and shells of different colours and sizes that they played with by putting them to their ears or sorting them into piles. From the ceiling there hung model jellyfish that they stared at and pointed to; green strands of plastic seaweed that they tugged at; shiny wind chimes that played softly when brushed; a large swathe of blue material that children would jump up at and try to reach as it moved in the breeze created by the wave. Collecting ornaments was a key activity of Troll. Children saw that he liked articles that were soft and furry or hard and shiny. They were encouraged to collect and offer such items to him as presents throughout the programme and, at its climax, they helped him decorate his new home with his favourite things.

As Steiner points out, the ornamental is culturally mistrusted as having no practical purpose beyond the economics of the shopping mall and the bling factory, being decorative rather than functional; and what 'charm' it is seen to exercise contains cultural echoes of the magical, and hence of irrationality and trickery: 'To be merely ornamental is purportedly to be useless or without practical effect and yet the ornamental is also taken as a black magic of utility and power associated with deception'[26]. This mistrust is exacerbated as the ornamental is also closely associated with domesticity and family feeling, with private bourgeois comfort rather than grander social sentiment. These qualities of the domestic and the decorative were, indeed, integral to the charms of *The Emerald Cave* and should be viewed as a positive force for good, providing, in Murdoch's phrase, a genetic background for action. The ornamental did exercise a power over these young children, charming them, drawing in their attention, encouraging them to play with the shells, to stare at Troll's trinkets. These objects were comforting to him as any prized possessions would be. He would gaze at them, handle them fondly, and they were eventually used to decorate his new home. Educationalists will surely not view these qualities of comfort, warmth, cheerfulness and a shared sense of attachment in anything other than a positive light. Whilst recognising that their presence may indeed be muted in the lives of some young children, their very absence we regard as a form of deprivation. Any early-years setting would interpret the presence of such qualities, accessible through the ornamental qualities of beauty, as beneficial if not necessary to enable children to flourish. And if this is an insight we have inherited from the Romantic tradition, so be it; we need neither be embarrassed nor held in contempt for this if it provides us with a morally superior vision than exists in the arid, utilitarian agendas currently promoted by any number of government agents.

Central to the plot of *The Emerald Cave*, then, was a form of altruism. In discovering and playing with beautiful ornaments, the children were encouraged to share them in order to help a homeless creature. Even that most suspicious of aesthetic commentators, Terry Eagleton, writes that aesthetic experience can be seen to provide a discourse of utopian critique as much as it can be used to 'oil the wheels of hegemony': 'Before we can begin to reason there is already that faculty within us which makes us feel the sufferings of others as keenly as a wound, spurs us to luxuriate in another's joy with no sense of self-advantage'[27]. This harnessing of what Aristotle called the *orectic* potential of the children—their innate tendency to reach out to others and, in this case, luxuriate in Troll's joy—was integral to the programme's moral energy and worked through the experience of beauty it provided[28].

The point made by Eagleton is dealt with more fully by Elaine Scarry in her striking argument that an education in beauty can also be seen as an education in social justice. Many of her aphorisms chime with *The Emerald Cave*, and, once again, the symbolism of a bird was a powerful one. In the second of the rooms, the forest world, children, like Billy Casper, came across a small bird. This was a beautifully crafted hand puppet (I choose the adjective carefully to describe the puppet's ornamental qualities, its charm and reassuring domesticity). It made its appearance through a hole in a nest, with the puppeteer hidden from sight. Children enjoyed answering the bird's call ('Tickle, tickle!'), and later, when it had gone, some of them discovered a large egg in its nest, which parents and workers encouraged them to handle gently and with care. Later still, four chicks appeared in the nest—in reality a glove puppet, with each finger operating a chick. Some children would stick their own fingers in the chicks' wide-open mouths, some would stroke the tiny bodies, others would simply stare for several seconds. This small side show, with its own agenda of domesticity, sympathy and family life, paralleled the unfolding story of Troll and displayed an 'aura of fragility' that lay not so much within the materiality of the puppets, but more in what they represented of the real world—the fragility of birth, of babies, of life itself. 'Beautiful things always carry greetings from other worlds within them'[29]; and these greetings, Scarry goes on to argue, through the porous nature of the imagination, lead the perceiver back into her own world with a more capacious regard for it.

Beauty, according to Scarry, is a compact or contract between perceiver and perceived[30]. In this she is in agreement with Steiner who describes it in similarly relational terms, not as a static, objectified property but as a 'particular interaction between . . . a "self" and an "other"'[31]. In analysing the etymology of the word 'fair', which in English means both beautiful *and* just, she traces it to its Germanic root, the verb *fegen*, meaning to 'decorate' or to 'adorn', but also to 'pact', to 'make a covenant or an agreement'[32]. At the base of this pact is a radical decentring on the part of the perceiver, which is how Scarry defines Iris Murdoch's concept of 'unselfing'. The power of beauty to help children decentre was physically observable in their interactions with Troll and Bird, and this unselfing can be understood as the dynamic that makes the pact between perceiver and perceived actively possible. Its power emanates from the fact that it is sensuous and pleasure bearing rather than principled and dutiful. In Adorno's words,

Figure 4.2 From *The Emerald Cave*, a production from The Play House.

As radiant things give up their magic claims, renounce the power with which the subject invested them and hoped with their help himself to wield, they become transformed into images of gentleness, promises of a happiness cured of a domination over nature.[33]

Very possibly, they were sowing the seeds of compassion and equality in the process.

BEAUTY AND THE UTOPIAN IMAGINATION

> Implicit in every good story we tell our children (setting aside the storytellers who are rancid with cynicism) is the moral: 'Look, this is how the world ought to be. Try to make it like that when you're grown up. We haven't managed it, we older ones; perhaps you will.' Whatever has happened to the idea of beauty and happiness in adult art, our children must keep faith with their radical innocence. That is our own, and the novelist's, act of faith for the future. It expresses our faith that our children will *have* a future.[34]

As Inglis is suggesting here, beauty in stories such as *The Secret Garden* and *The Selfish Giant* and in educational programmes like *The Emerald Cave* expresses its moral power through the social utopias brought alive in their narratives and the promise of happiness they thus make tangible. Oscar Wilde, himself a socialist, saw the utopian imagination as intrinsic to his progressive ideals. 'A map of the world that does not include Utopia is not worth even glancing at', he wrote, 'for it leaves out the one country at which Humanity is always landing . . . Progress is the realisation of Utopias'[35]. Not all social philosophers have shared Wilde's enthusiasm, of course, and whether utopianism can ever lead to a good society or will inevitably produce dystopic, totalitarian nightmares has been a rich source of social and political debate since the Enlightenment. Walter Lippmann was in no doubt where he stood on the issue:

> The Good Society has no architectural design. There are no blueprints. There is no mould in which human life is to be shaped . . . The supreme architect, who begins as a visionary, becomes a fanatic and ends as a despot. For no-one can be the supreme architect of society without employing a supreme despot to execute the design.[36]

Of course, the likes of Thomas More and William Morris were hardly cast in the mould of fanatical despots, utopian visionaries though they were; but the twentieth-century experience of Fascism and Communism, both of which were utopian narratives that proved to be murderous, does add historical weight to Lippmann's scepticism. In our current postmodern world of fractured narratives and local knowledge, such grand visions have in any case lost their currency, and many, not simply those with a conservative bent, would claim this as a good thing. However, as Oliver Bennett has pointed out, Postmodernism has brought with it a growth in negative thinking, what he has identified as four general 'narratives of decline' that relate respectively to morality, intellectual life, the environment and political culture. The danger, he suggests, is that they lead to fatalistic, impotent attitudes and produce 'an endless cycle of automatic negative thoughts, resulting in an incapacity to see the self, the world, or the future in anything other than negative terms'[37]. In the face of this, and from an educational perspective, David Halpin has argued for the continuing significance of utopian thinking as necessary to combat the pervasive cynicism and sense of helplessness that such negativity can generate, so destructive of any educational enterprise that, of necessity, must hope for a better world. Quoting Zygmunt Bauman, he writes, 'By scanning the field of the possible . . . utopias pave the way for a critical attitude and a critical activity'.[38]

The German philosopher and playwright Friedrich Schiller would have agreed with Bauman. Writing at the end of the eighteenth century in the wake of the vanishing utopian promise of the French Revolution, he, too, was concerned with how education might keep alive the possibilities for a better, freer, more egalitarian world. What many contemporary progressive educationalists may find startling is that, in his *Letters on the Aesthetic Education of Man*, Schiller proposed that an education in the appreciation of beauty should be at the heart of such an enterprise. These letters were written over a number of years as a response to his disenchantment with the revolution, a disenchantment shared by many radical thinkers and artists of his day, as its ideals degenerated into disorder, violence and terror. However, as Wilkinson and Willoughby have pointed out, they did not mark 'a recoil into the timeless world of beauty, an apolitical retreat into the ivory tower of aestheticism'[39]. Rather were they his way of continuing to pursue his ideal by attempting to define an approach to education that might bridge the evident rift between the good that humans seemed capable of imagining and rationally hoping for and the failures that marked their attempts to achieve it; their potential to conceive of a better society, but their tendency to lose sight of it too readily under the political pressure of actual experience. For Schiller the answer lay in beauty, and to understand this we need to appreciate that, like Murdoch and Steiner, he did not conceive of beauty as a pleasant feature of objects, but as, in John Armstrong's words, a moral and social necessity, 'an ideal by which it is always possible for us to be guided in reflection upon ourselves and our lives'[40].

The letters themselves are complex and difficult, but at base his argument relies upon some simple but powerful proposals. Schiller suggests that humanity has two basic, conflicting drives, those of sense and of reason. What is necessary for the happy life of the individual and of society is that both remain in harmony, neither gaining superiority over the other.

(Although he did not relate these drives to gender, the parallels with the arguments of later, feminist thinkers are striking.) In order to manage this harmony, Schiller took on Kant's idea of 'playful disinterest' and proposed that there is a third human drive—that of play—which has the potential to keep both reason and sense in their rightful place. For the object of play, he suggested, is to unite in perfect balance our desire for sensation with our desire for order; and the highest expression of play, he believed, was to be found in the form of beauty itself, through the achievement of what he called 'aesthetic necessity'. Aesthetic necessity is a quality evident in all good works of art; in a beautiful poem, for example, when every word seems to be in just the right place; in a beautiful melody, when the passage from one note to the next seems logical, effortless, as though there were no other satisfactory alternative; in a beautiful painting, where the shapes, colours, textures and details balance to provide a totally satisfying visual experience. Importantly for Schiller, aesthetic necessity did not *symbolise* the harmony and order that should characterise the good and happy society; rather, it is what allows us, as sensuous beings, to apprehend what it actually feels like. It is through our feelings, then, that we can begin to appreciate what the good society would be like should we ever manage to achieve it. As John Armstrong explains, '[I]n apprehending aesthetic necessity, in giving ourselves up to it, in letting ourselves be moved by it, we are actually encountering, in the reality of lived experience, what it might be like to live the happy life'[41]. Or in the words of Schiller himself: 'Beauty alone makes the whole world happy, and each and every being forgets its limitations while under its spell'[42].

THE GOOD SOCIETY AND THE BEAUTIFUL GAME

In the era when Schiller was writing, he could conflate the meaning of beauty and art quite readily, something that, since Modernism, we are no longer able to do. But, conversely, his description of beauty as a high form of play encourages us to consider the implications of his theory in those more openly playful curriculum subjects, which include not only the arts but also sports and team games. In this, we find in Schiller an anticipation of one of the arguments of Elaine Scarry, who saw the ideals of beauty and justice embodied and enacted within the ethics and aesthetics of team games and of the political thought of John Berger as expressed in his novel *A Painter of Our Time*[43]. First published in 1958, Berger's novel is written in the voice of Janos Lavin, a refugee from Hungary who works as an artist in London. The central part of the novel deals with his struggle to paint a huge canvas of the 1948 Olympic Games, to capture what he remembers as one of the purest experiences of his life: 'thousands of people with tears in their eyes, which were tears of pure disinterested admiration' as Zatopek won the 10,000 metres[44]. The fusion of Platonic passion with Kantian disinterestedness is characteristic of Berger's particular understanding of the experience of beauty[45], and Lavin's struggle to capture this utopian moment through the materiality of paint leads him to reflect upon the connections between the beauty of art and the beauty of sport, in particular, of football[46]. In tones reminiscent of Schiller, he defines the beauty in both as dependent upon 'controlled freedom of intuition'—the need to consciously lose one's self-consciousness, to 'return to a reliance on intuition within certain consciously created limits'. The beauty of soccer, he reflects, is that this is a collective rather than an individual effort and hence becomes a model for the kind of free, productive, creative relations at the heart of his political ideals. 'I have seen games of football', Lavin concludes, 'in which I have glimpsed all I believe the productive relations among men might be'[47].

If Schiller and Scarry provide us with an impetus to reconsider the relationship of beauty and play within the curriculum and locate how they relate to an education in and for the good society, then Berger points us explicitly towards the game of football, tellingly eulogised as 'the beautiful game' in the country where its practice excels, Brazil. In the UK, the fact that many young, working-class boys aspire to be professional footballers is often viewed in an entirely negative light, as an unrealistic aspiration, a sad, masculinist delusion, a distraction from academic energies, an impediment to their finding a more rational career choice. What if, however, we were to begin by considering the strong appeal of the game itself and see this, as Berger did, in terms other than the external goods, such as wealth and fame, that being a successful footballer can bring with it? What are the *internal* goods inherent to the game of football as a social practice? Many of these are, of course, associated with the acquisition and demonstration of skills—controlling the ball, delivering an accurate pass, scoring a goal— and the satisfaction associated with the mastery of desired skills. There are, too, the pleasurable aesthetic qualities of grace, flow and balletic gesture that we associate with these skills in action. However, the unselfing which Berger's reflections evoke is dependent on 'consciously created limits'— in other words, the rules of the game—and to carry the moral force that Berger implies they do, these rules are best understood as encapsulating a set of *virtues* which frame the skills and artistry of the game, providing it with its moral energy and its fundamental appeal.

As MacIntyre tells us, a virtue is an acquired human quality without which we will be unable to achieve those goods that are internal to a specific practice[48]. They are not just admirable traits, but cardinal features of a practice, presupposing a set of ideals, a sense of what it is good to strive for. Peter Arnold writes, 'Such virtues are moral because they constitute the very qualities by which a person's conduct is morally appraised both within and across the different contexts of his or her life'[49]. In the case of football, these virtues will include determination and patience (without which I will not improve my skills); self-control (without which I will be violent and over aggressive); generosity (without which I will be a poor team player);

honesty and a sense of fair play (without which I will cheat and be suscep-
tible to the will to win at all costs). Crucially, however, these virtues rely
for their moral power upon their intrinsic connection with the state of aesthetic necessity that players of soccer aspire towards, that 'reality of lived
experience' upon which their love for the game is founded. In this sense,
every game holds a promise of and is a quest for moments of beauty. Some
of these are dependent on the skills and artistry of the game—a beautiful
pass, for example, or a beautiful goal—others on its social virtues, such as
a beautiful display of sporting behaviour.

Of course, it is hard not to sneer and point to the absence of these virtues
in the professional game today, readily characterised by cheating, greed,
selfishness, arrogance, disrespect, chauvinism and the corrupting influence of capital[50]. The fact remains, however, that the vices listed here are
appreciated as recognisable signs of corruption, as contrary to the virtues
of the game in its ideal form. Despite the blatant examples of its lack, the
ideal retains its power because, when played in a way that approaches it,
players—and, indeed, spectators—can experience the utopian sensation
stressed by Schiller that, for them, this is how life feels at its best. When
pundits use the phrase 'the beautiful game', as they often do, it is this vision
they are referring to, one embodied in 'the best traditions, customs and
conventions' of the game *as a practice*[51]. Macintyre is explicit that skills
themselves do not constitute a practice, hence do not develop the virtues,
and uses football as one of his examples: 'Tic-tac-toe is not an example of
a practice . . . nor is throwing a football with skill, but the game of football
is'[52]. So although skills acquisition is integral to the practice of football in
schools, it is a flawed educational vision that defines its core curriculum in
terms of these skills, dissociating them from the virtues of the game, the
moral vision at its heart, which is, I am arguing, best apprehended through
the concept of beauty. We might go so far as to say that any teaching of the
game that did not take due account of this moral vision would have a corrupting effect on all concerned—teacher, players and the game itself—an
argument supported by recent empirical research into both girls' and boys'
participation in sports, which has demonstrated a significant link between
the kinds of moral behaviour young people demonstrate on the sports pitch
and the educational values of their teachers and coaches[53].

PLAY, CRAFT AND BEAUTY IN THE PERFORMING ARTS

Not everyone, of course, will appreciate or want to experience the beauty
of soccer or any other sport, and there are no specific experiences of beauty
we can point to as human universals. But play and beauty themselves *are*
universal concepts that find specific forms of expression through innumer-
able cultural and social practices. In the curriculum we can find an interesting comparison with soccer in the performing arts—dance, drama and

music—each if which is openly playful and has a strong, social or group dimension to it. The manner of this playfulness, of course, differs as each art form has its own discipline of practice, but 'playing' is a verb applicable to the creative process (dancers play with movement motifs, musicians with melodic and harmonic possibilities), to the development of skills (practised through playing), and, in music and drama at least, 'playing' is an expression coterminous with performing itself.

In his book *The Craftsman*, Richard Sennett defines play as a craft that connects children to work, as it is in play that they learn to dialogue with materials, testing out what he calls their 'truth' just as the craftsman must dialogue with the 'material truth' of clay or glass or whatever he is working with[54]. So a child pulls at the eyes of her teddy bear not because she is destructive but because she is testing out its nature as matter, its resistance to her own material strength. In learning to play a musical instrument, this truth is located in a world of fact; for example, can I place my finger on the string or on the valve so that the note sounds right? Can I release it so as to play rapidly and cleanly? Sennett emphasises the virtues of sustained repetition, another feature of play, that are inherent in the practice and rehearsals necessary to attain such truth; playing something through again and again until it sounds right. This is what he sees as the key point to Schiller's definition of play as connecting the sense drive with the form drive; that 'play negotiates between pleasure and rigor'[55]. Furthermore, he suggests, strikingly, that practice motivates desire in children rather than vice versa, as practice teaches them how to concentrate which in turn leads them to appreciate and enjoy the subtler beauties of the art or craft they are learning and the pleasures of producing work of quality. Thus, he implies, we learn the virtues of patience, of diligence, of taking pride in our work. In this way, as Julian Bell points out, Sennett's book is a philosophical essay with moral implications, in which he seeks 'to ground the idea of the good in physical circumstance; to derive his *oughts* from a clutch of ascertainable *ises*'[56].

Sennett is much influenced by Enlightenment figures and has little truck with the writings of Romantics and post-Romantics such as John Ruskin, which he sees as sentimental and tainted by nostalgia for an unrecoverable past. Nevertheless he shares with Ruskin a concern that the creative, productive capabilities of ordinary people are being neglected, and craftsmanship for him is an educational model that can foster their development. 'The innate abilities on which craftsmanship is based are not exceptional', he writes; rather, 'they are shared in common by the large majority of human beings in roughly equal measure'[57]. This is a useful and necessary counter to the elitist idea that subjects like the performing arts in schools are either recreational, and thus of no real educational value, or the province of those with talent alone. It suggests that, as crafts that can be learned, their development is dependent as much upon opportunity as talent and that they develop a set of skills and virtues directly connected to the world of work. But it is an argument that omits any reference to beauty, and, indeed, grounded as it is in the values of cultural materialism, it could be seen as implicitly dismissive of anything so reminiscent of Ruskin's rhetoric. Without negating Sennett's argument, I wish to add beauty to the mix within both the artistic and the social domains of the performing arts as curriculum subjects, in particular to see how it connects them with an idea of the good.

As with soccer, we can grasp much of the educational power of the performing arts through the virtues that frame their skills and the aesthetic necessities that shape their practices. In their more complex and subject specific forms of play, such as devising theatre or dance in small groups, or rehearsing an orchestral composition, success can be seen to depend upon the practice of a range of virtues similar to those we listed for soccer, but different in terms of the specific skills they call for. So determination and patience are equally important in devising a drama, dance or a piece of music, but they are demonstrated in activities such as group discussion and decision making, the reading and learning of lines (or dance motifs/ phrases, or parts of a musical score), trying out and, if necessary, discarding ideas, making commitments and sticking to deadlines. Performing arts students, too, must be generous as team players and exercise self-control of a physical and mental kind if they are to be successful. Ultimately, however, as with football, these virtues only matter for the players in terms of the pleasures promised in performance, and for those students who pursue the performing arts because they love them, this pleasure is intrinsically associated with the concept of beauty. Sennett reminds us that playing is a craft that binds rigor to pleasure and thus develops good working practices; but Nehamas also reminds us, in Platonic tones, that finding beauty in what we do can, despite Sennett's subordination of desire to practice, inspire us with the love that drives us onward, that makes the rigors of practice worth the effort[58]. This was certainly the case with my own musical apprenticeship, described in the last chapter. The practice involved in being taught the viola lay the foundations for my ability to play the guitar, but it was the force of beauty and its close associations with love, desire, aspiration and pleasure that motivated me to take up the guitar in the first place. In my case, the satisfaction of good work, of a job well done, was something I derived from doing a history essay, whereas the satisfactions of composition and performance were much deeper than that. Craft and artistry, quality and beauty, love and satisfaction were all in the mix when everything went well; and it was love that kept me going through the times of frustration and disappointment, when the songs were not coming or the performances were not good enough.

Let us consider, then, beauty in the artistic dimension of learning for those students who love the performing arts. For them, I would suggest, when preparing for performance, the concept of the beautiful is paramount as a motivational force, even though the form this will take will necessarily be a source of argument and debate among the individuals concerned.

To draw once again from Schiller, they will need to develop a shared sense of aesthetic necessity in order to guide their reflections, decisions and evaluations during the creative process. For students who love performing, there is nothing quite so thrilling as the moment when their work is shared, watched and/or listened to. As with any live performance, this thrill is inseparable from a sense of risk that everything can go wrong. Risk is the rigor upon which their pleasure depends but their level of pleasure will equate with their experience of beauty; and this we can define as *an experience of aesthetic necessity created and shared with their audience.*

Julian Bell points out that Sennett, in concentrating upon finding the good in the manual and mental activity of craftsmanship, misses out the key element of the receptive, of standing back, looking at and *seeing* that one's work is good[59]. In the performing arts, this takes on an added level of significance, inasmuch as the performers make the aesthetic object out of their own bodies; instead of scrutinising it themselves, they offer themselves to others for scrutiny. In this sense, the 'good' is indistinguishable from the body that produces it at the instant it is apprehended by others. For young people, this provides them with a chance to be looked at, admired, adulated and praised, a small opportunity to leave their trace on the world[60]. It is a chance for them not only to create something beautiful and good but also, for that moment at least, to be *seen themselves* as beautiful and good. For those young people who are physically attractive, popular and with high self-esteem, this may not be personally and socially so significant; but for many young people, this moment of unselfing can feed back into, strengthen and transform their own sense of self-worth.

As with football, the professional need for teachers of the performing arts to attend to educational values that are both artistic *and* social reminds us that, in the final analysis, schools are not craft workshops or coaching establishments and that their educational project, although concerned with the identification and development of individual talent, is not reducible to this. Within this specific context, it is the difference between concentrating on the individual artistic talents of a few—the virtuoso model—and fostering the innate abilities, social *and* artistic, of the many—the ensemble model. Excellent teachers can aspire to the values of the ensemble in the way that they organise their lessons and through the ethos they encourage in their classrooms. Such is not to deny the struggles they are faced with, ranging from overwork, bureaucratic record keeping, examination pressures and disaffected student behaviour, but it is a model that can help them recognise moments of real value when they happen. I am defining these as moments of beauty in order to suggest that the social as well as the artistic ideals of the performing arts can be apprehended through aesthetic necessity. I can recall, for example, during a visit to Romania, watching a presentation given by eight-year-old primary children in which an extremely talented little girl spent as much time happily and unselfconsciously supporting those around her as she did concentrating upon her own performance—helping one child off with his jumper, guiding another to a specific space. This was a *beautiful* moment as it encapsulated not only the value of what this teacher had herself achieved but also the ethos of shared endeavour and mutual support and consideration at the heart of the ideals of the ensemble. Such are the potential achievements of beauty within the performing arts—joyful, profound, morally significant and reaching far beyond the educational limitations of skills-based curricula.

SEEING BEAUTY IN THE DISABLED BODY:
BILL SHANNON, THE CRUTCHMASTER

Oh body swayed to music, O brightening glance,
How can we know the dancer from the dance?[61]

A very unusual utopia is imagined by John Varley in his story *The Persistence of Vision*. Here the inhabitants of a society called Keller live permanently in darkness and silence for they are blind and deaf. Their lives, however, are peaceful, ethical and sensuously fulfilling and they communicate with one another at a level deeper than any speech could manage through a language system called 'Touch', which involves the physical contact of naked bodies. The culture they have created renders the non-disabled narrator of the story the outsider, envious of what they are capable of. He comes to appreciate their blindness and deafness as a culture rather than a disability, even as gifts that he might welcome if as a result he were to attain their levels of happiness and fulfilment. The story is referred to by Lennard J. Davis in his book *Enforcing Normalcy* as illustrative of a central point in disability politics, namely, 'that our construction of the normal world is based on a radical repression of disability, and that given certain power structures, a society of people with disabilities can and does easily survive and render "normal" people outsiders'[62]. But the story also makes another point: that the aesthetic possibilities of such a society are radically different from that of a non-disabled society. Not only this, but also that the beauty of such an aesthetic, when appreciated by the non-disabled outsider, can be a potent source of 'unselfing', achieving not only a political rupture but also a revolution in moral and spiritual understanding of the kind postulated by Iris Murdoch.

Davis uses this story as a counterpoint to what he describes as the implied 'Utopia of the Norm', an ideal pursued during the nineteenth century whose assumptions still permeate the social fabric of our lives. As societies became more urbanised and industrialised, he argues, the science of statistics became increasingly significant as a classificatory and organisational system and gave rise to the concept of the average (or normal) human being. Davis traces the growing influence of the concept of the norm in modern social and economic theory—in the concept of the average worker, for example—but principally in the ideology of eugenics that this idea of the norm gave rise to. For eugenicists, blindness, deafness and other forms of physical disability were no longer seen as either inevitable or acceptable and became pathologised as undesirable, outside the norm, to be eradicated like criminality and disease. He makes the uncomfortable point that eugenics was far from the sole pre-occupation of a group of right-wing extremists and argues that it was equally influential in progressive socialist thinking, 'seeing in the perfectibility of the human body a Utopian hope for social improvement'[63]. Although eugenics has since the Second World War been understood as morally reprehensible, the concept of the norm, of which it was an extreme expression, still permeates common social assumptions concerning disability, marking it as deviant, a mark of deficiency, a cause of embarrassment for the non-disabled majority, entirely as a medical rather than also as a cultural condition.

Interestingly, Davis claims that the concept of the ideal body propagated by eugenics was politically very different from that shared by pre-industrial western societies, derived as it was from classical Athens. Here, the perfect body was essentially a property of the gods, with the varieties of its human form being exaggerated in the grotesque representations of mediaeval carnival. These he sees as a celebration of the multiple, necessarily imperfect material forms of the human body, in which all forms of physical disability were viewed as part of the human continuum, not as deviations from it. Like Ruskin, therefore, his argument is directed towards the more pernicious effects of normative, technicist ideologies, in seeing industrial ideas of perfectibility as a dehumanising force, driven by an ideal of sameness and conformity rather than by the creative expressiveness of individual human bodies.

This normative concept of beauty was defined by the French statistician, Quetelet, as follows: '[A]n individual who epitomized in himself, at a given time, all the qualities of the average man, would represent at once all the greatness, beauty and goodness of that being'[64]. Beauty as an ideal thus became beauty as an expression of the average—or rather, beauty as an ideal or composite of the average. The sheer nonsense of this has since been demonstrated by two Russian artists, Komar and Melamid, who, in an ironic search for the true normative ideal, researched into what the public in different countries considered to be beautiful art and produced a series of composite paintings in response to their findings. As Kimmelman comments, 'The results were kitsch and predictably awful, proving, in case we didn't know it, that beauty, by definition is irreducible to a common denominator'[65]. Kimmelman quotes Francis Bacon to drive home his point: 'There is no excellent beauty that hath not some strangeness in its proportion'[66]. This is a highly significant use of the word 'strangeness', not as indicative of a property of 'the other' but rather as an intrinsic quality of *everything* that we find beautiful—be it the elongated back of the female concubine in Ingres' *Grande Odalisque*, the haunting, graphic imagery of

The Waste Land or the abundant, gothic expressivity of the Doge's Palace in Venice. To these we might add the armless (disabled?) statue of the Venus de Milo and its striking, modern echo recently exhibited in London's Trafalgar Square, Mark Quinn's sculpture of Alison Lapper, a celebration of female beauty not only as disabled but also as pregnant.

As Davis points out, history does not lack its fair share of successful and recognised disabled artists; Milton, Joyce and Beethoven are notable examples. In all cases, however, their achievements are seen as triumphs over disability as they worked from within a conventional rather than a disabled aesthetic. Their disabilities are an irrelevance to their art, invisible factors in its reception, never, as in the culture of the inhabitants of John Varley's utopia, celebrated as potentially beautiful in themselves. In the work of contemporary disabled artists, this, too, is often rare. I have remarked upon the sculpture of Alison Lapper as something that I, as a non-disabled observer, see as beautiful, but a similar work by photographer Mary Duffy, who is also without arms, did not have beauty as its intended outcome. In a series of three photographs entitled *Cutting the Ties That Bind*, she, too, explicitly compares her own body to that of the Venus de Milo, but her stated artistic intentions are entirely political, offering herself as a challenge to the accepted view that disability must *per se* be tragic or pathetic: 'I wanted to hold up a mirror to all those people who had stripped me bare previously . . . the general public with naked stares, and more especially the medical profession'[67]. Davis' commentary re-enforces the confrontational nature of this challenge, using the language of horror rather than pleasure: '[I]t is now the "object of horror" who holds the mirror up to the "normal" observer'[68]. For the non-disabled observer, then, the aesthetic purpose of this work is one of rupture and discomfort, not pleasure, in which the political/ethical challenge takes precedent over any possibilities of rendering it beautiful[69].

The work of the disabled dancer, Bill Shannon, also known as the Crutchmaster, has offered a similarly disruptive challenge. Shannon has a rare form of arthritis which prevents him from putting weight on his legs for any length of time[70]. Consequently he moves, whether walking or performing, with the aid of crutches and a skateboard, which he has developed to a very high level of skill. As a performance artist, he often works in outdoor settings, performing a set of complex movements that challenge the perceptions of non-disabled passers-by who, unaware that this is a performance, have the opportunity to intervene if they wish. Petra Kuppers describes one of his pieces as follows:

> Shannon creates a highly sophisticated and complex action out of walking down a flight of stairs with his crutches, developing this everyday action into a ballet of swoops and falls, graceful and comic, clumsy and artistic at the same time . . . Some of the people intervening are so unskilled in their movement and weight transference that the 'helpers'

hinder Shannon, or even lose their balance themselves. Movement competence becomes destabilized from 'known' differences between disabled and non-disabled.[71]

The experience of the non-disabled (and unwitting) member of the public, then, is one of surprise, perhaps shock and embarrassment as they learn that they have made assumptions about disability, unconsciously assuming the role of the powerful, of the helper and finding the position reversed. This experience is not intended to be pleasurable and the language of beauty would therefore seem to be out of place in explaining it.

This is not, however, how I first saw or learned about—and from— the work of Bill Shannon, during a television programme which showed excerpts of him dancing in his own unique style[72]. Growing up in Chicago, this style is strongly influenced by the street culture of hip-hop, but the form of dance he has developed is entirely new. Unlike Petra Kuppers, whose appreciation of Shannon's aesthetic is framed within a political commentary, the non-disabled Dani Kasrel's words respond only to the prowess of his movement:

> He has taken what others would consider a disability and turned it into an opportunity to devise a unique and wholly entertaining dance technique. Shannon flips and casts his body about with the agility of a gymnast. He effortlessly glides his feet, both on and off the ground, and even twists full-circle while riding a skateboard.[73]

Is it simply the case that, as non-disabled observers of his art, both Kasrel and myself shut out the political challenge in order to enjoy the aesthetic qualities of his movement? I do not think so; in fact, I wish to use my own response to seeing Shannon perform to argue that, as a non-disabled observer, it was precisely through seeing beauty in his work that I learned something profound from it.

Beauty's aura of fragility, its nature as a compact, those aspects of it that we saw as integral to the experience of *The Emerald Cave*, are equally integral to the experience of watching Shannon dance. The frailty of his legs becomes the very focus of our attention, the essence of our compact; as non-disabled observers, we are being asked to stare, not to divert our gaze, and one of our deepest prejudices—that disability must of necessity be deficient—is being challenged not by rational appeals or political shock tactics but by the experience of something beautiful: 'Shannon shatters conceptions about the nature of what it means to be disabled. Rather than feel sorry for him, you are exhilarated by his awe-inspiring movements'[74]. When Shannon dances, he brings into sharp focus three points argued by Scarry: that beauty makes us conscious of error, that beauty is unprecedented and that beauty exerts what she calls a 'pressure towards the distributional'[75].

When I first saw Shannon dancing, I was transfixed, unable to look away. I was immediately conscious that I was witnessing something not only that I had never seen before but also that I had never *imagined* seeing before. Scarry stresses how this unprecedented quality of beauty makes us wish to change our perceptual field in order to continue gazing at it, and in this she implies a revision of one's mental as well as physical location. For, on seeing Shannon performing, one is immediately forced to reconsider one's perspective on the potential abilities rather than the *dis*abilities of disabled bodies and their relation to the aesthetics of the non-disabled body. In my case, I was confronted immediately with the error of my previous misconceptions about dance and disability. Shannon offers us a new aesthetic and, in doing so, he invites us to change our perception of disability in general. There is no sense of pity or compensation, merely celebration. And he achieves this through the grace, energy and control of his dancing; in short, by displaying those physical virtues that render it beautiful to look at. In making our gaze pleasurable, at the same time, he ensures that we remain acutely conscious of his difference from, rather than any imitation of, the non-disabled dancer. And although he may be unique within this social category we label as 'disabled', Scarry argues that it is one of the gifts of beauty and its aura of fragility to make us gaze with renewed attention and care at those persons or objects within a category we have now recognised as beautiful. The first time we feel an appreciation of a painting, a poem, a play or a 'disabled' person *for their beauty*, we extend this acquaintance to others in that category with an innate appreciation of their potential and worth. In this sense his dancing exerts a 'pressure towards the distributional', and herein lies its affective potential as an education for the purposes of social justice and the attainment of a better society: 'Like the political complaint about inattention to problems of social justice to which it is related, it (beauty) explicitly confirms the value of human attention'[76]. In establishing rather than rupturing a bond of attachment with the observer, Shannon's aesthetic raises the observer's awareness to a higher quality of consciousness by inspiring awe and wonder, aspects of beauty traditionally associated with the sublime. A key point made by Murdoch is that this raising of consciousness brings us closer to a truthful, more objective vision of things as they really are, a vision often masked by our prejudices and common, everyday anxieties. She calls this the 'realism of compassion', a phrase that may not chime well with the politics of disability but that nonetheless defines the aesthetics of such art in moral and political terms, releasing the observer as it does from their 'blinding self-centred aims and images'[77].

RECLAIMING BEAUTY AS A POTENTIAL FORCE FOR GOOD

In this chapter I have re-affirmed the moral case for an education in beauty that broadly conforms to the Platonic tradition. This is not an uncontroversial claim:

Again and again, history has smashed to pieces Plato's assurance that to love the beautiful is to desire the good. Beautiful villains, graceful outlaws, tasteful criminals, and elegant torturers are everywhere about us. Salome, Scarpia and Satan do not exist only in fiction.[78]

Nehamas' position is not an unusual one. The evidence, he argues, is stacked against the argument that an education in beauty is also an education in goodness. At best, he suggests, we might propose that the moral dangers of beauty are small; after all, 'how harmful could George Eliot be?' he quips[79].

The mistake that Nehamas is making here, I think—and this is one I have been arguing against throughout this book—is to isolate beauty, as Kant did, from the web of values it must necessarily interconnect with in its expression. It is as though it should be stripped bare and expected to do the work of education on its own, as beauty alone, removed from influences, contexts and histories rather than be allowed to work with and within them. In each of the examples examined in this chapter, there is a necessary implication that for beauty to have any kind of virtuous impact within an educational setting, it must be consciously framed within a set of values and practices that will work in harmony with it, or that will release its positive potential. In *The Emerald Cave*, for example, the educational values of the company and of the artists involved in its delivery matched the caring values fostered by the narrative of the story, which themselves were enhanced through the interactive and enacted nature of the programme. These values reflected very much those of Reggio Emilia and many early years educational settings, where beauty is perhaps manifested most readily in schools. In the case of sports and the performing arts, the values of the teachers were seen as central, for, if they fail to recognise or harness the communal virtues that their subjects *as practices* can embody then they may aspire to technical excellence but never release the utopian energies inherent to beauty[80]. The final example reminds us how beauty, as well as being domestic and familiar, can find moral energy in its power to surprise and can be surprising in its very manifestation. As Geertz reminds us, our interpretation of beauty is bound up with our interpretation of culture, and the same can be said, of course, of our interpretation of disability. Hence Shannon's dancing is a form of cultural and aesthetic exchange, a dialogue across differences that includes the physical and the aesthetic, the cultural and the political[81]. In reshaping his body to surprise and delight us, Shannon can also reshape our perceptions and hence our spirits, reclaiming beauty as a social force for good, not with transcendental pretensions but with transformational possibilities, one whose moral potential is worthy of our full attention as educators, as Iris Murdoch suggested it should be.

5 Beauty and Creativity
Examples from an Arts Curriculum

One day we shall win back Art, that is to say the pleasure of life; win back Art again to our daily labour.[1]

When John Ruskin compared the Gothic with the Renaissance architecture of Venice and drew for his contemporaries the moral conclusions that he did, he was arguing for a particular view of human creativity which linked it to the rhythms, patterns and infinite varieties of nature. In doing so, he was very clear about the relationship between creative work, personal fulfilment and social morality. Individual expressiveness was a necessary condition, he argued, for the production of good work—good not only in a practical but also in a moral sense. In *The Stones of Venice*, he urged his readers to see in the contrasting and surprising details of the Doge's palace—details that nonetheless created an organic whole of supreme beauty—'signs of the life and liberty of every workman who struck the stone . . . a freedom of thought and rank in scale of being, such as no laws, no charters, no charities can secure; but which it must be the first aim of all Europe at this day to regain for her children'[2]. In his sights, Ruskin had the factory system of industrialised Britain with its oppressively mechanistic and dehumanised practices which, in turn, corrupted the everyday aesthetics of the age, producing a taste for a kind of mechanised perfection, the triumph of technique over beauty, and what he saw as a 'diseased love' of novelty and change[3].

Ruskin, then, envisioned the relationship between beauty and creativity as an ethical one; how something was made and the social values it embodied was as important as the appearance of the final product and indeed could not be detached from it. He did not see the beauty of the Gothic palace as created by the architect, with the workers commissioned only to realise a pre-ordained plan, but as a result of the inter-relationship between the plan and its fulfilment. What he celebrated above all were the individual creations of ordinary labourers that the overall structure of the building nurtured and allowed for. This for him was indicative of a healthy culture, one which, in Matthew Collings' words, incorporated a 'shared vision of nature uniting the powerful and the poor'[4]. This vision was one in which all creative labour had a social and moral, as well as an economic, purpose, that of helping individuals experience an intensity of life that satisfied their spiritual needs by bringing them close to the rhythms and patterns of nature. Art he saw as the supreme cultural expression of such work.

Ruskin's ideas were highly influential in his time. They were taken to heart by the pre-Raphaelites, who, in their meticulous attention to colour and detail, celebrated the beauty of nature in its infinite variety; and in their content depicted moral lessons to illustrate the need for humans to work in harmony with it. William Morris, too, was a great admirer of Ruskin. His wallpaper designs domesticated the beauty of nature by bringing it into the homes of ordinary people, whilst the environments he created for the workers he employed were intended to foster their happiness by maintaining a connection between nature and creative labour. His workshops were places of space and light, in which machines served rather than stifled individual expression. A chair made by one of his workers would be fashioned from a local rather than an imported wood, its seat constructed from rushes rather than material, springs or upholstery. The fact that I am sitting on such a chair at this moment is indicative of the longstanding if now rather neglected influences of Ruskin's ideas. As Matthew Collings has also said, 'We are still living in the fallout of conditions Ruskin was attempting to describe when they were brand new'[5].

Ruskin's concerns remain our concerns. For him the Doge's palace was a metaphor for a vibrant civilisation; for us the lessons he drew are relevant to the education we conceive of for our children and the kind of future we hope they will create for themselves as a result of it. For Ruskin and Morris, the value of human creativity was inextricable from the value of beauty, with implications at once both practical and ethical as to how they conceptualised the organisation, purpose and value of work. As Morris wrote in his essay 'Useful Work Versus Useless Toil', '[T]he beauty that man creates when he is most a man, most aspiring and thoughtful—all things which serve the pleasure of people free, manly and uncorrupted. This is wealth'[6]. Ruskin had challenged the Victorian establishment to reconceive wealth not as the accumulation of capital and economic power but, in John Armstrong's terms, as 'the real appreciative possession of what is good': 'A nation becomes richer the more beautiful and fine things it creates and retains and—above all—the greater the education of its population in the enjoyment and appreciation of those things'[7]. By substituting the word 'school' for 'nation' and 'students' for 'population', we can use the moral ideas that Ruskin directed at Victorian industrialists to take a critical look at the current vogue for fostering creativity in schools. As well as suggesting a particular moral purpose for the teaching, creation and appreciation of the arts, such a re-consideration will prompt us to focus on the particular interplay between creativity and ethics and how the two can connect through beauty.

THE AMBIGUITIES OF CREATIVITY

That creativity is now firmly established as an educational value is beyond dispute. Since the Russians sent shockwaves through America in the 1950s with the launch of the Sputnik satellite, a perceived need for students to be creative and innovative as opposed to conventional and predictable has become an international concern for governments and a lucrative business for those psychologists and educators who can peddle tests, obtain research contracts, devise courses and offer training designed to stimulate the brain into ever-greater creative performance. Creativity has been embraced more or less uncritically by all who share a vested interest in education; politicians and the business community see it as vital for the development of new products and markets in an increasingly competitive and globalised economy; teachers harassed by oppressive accountability structures have welcomed it as licensing a break from rigid curriculum planning and a chance to reassert their individual values; artists and other 'creative professionals' in the UK have been able to find employment, working in partnership with schools, through the government sponsored agency, Creative Partnerships. Creative management, creative learning, creative pedagogies, creative curricula, creative minds, creative surroundings—practically everything in education can these days be qualified as creative and be guaranteed a nod of approval in response. Beauty may be absent from educational discourse but creativity is not only present but promiscuously so.

Various definitions have been provided for creativity, but the one current in UK schools was presented by the National Advisory Committee for Culture and Creativity in Education (NACCCE) in 1999: *imaginative activity fashioned so as to produce outcomes that are both original and of value*[8]. A shared definition, however, has not led to a shared understanding of its value or any agreement as to its nature. This has been illustrated in a recent publication called the 'rhetorics' of creativity, which attends to the discursive positions taken by its proponents in education and the claims they make for it[9]. For some, influenced by Howard Gardner, creativity is apprehended in psychological terms and its nature is best studied through attention to individual genius; for others, who admire the work of writers like Paul Willis, we should see it in socio-political terms and therefore attend to how young people interact with popular culture and creatively construct their identities. Other arguments revolve around whether we ought to see it as a free-floating, ubiquitous attribute of the personality or as only expressible through cultural practices; in other words, is everyone inherently creative in their everyday talk and actions or does creativity only gain legitimate expression through specific cultural practices that have to be learned? There are those—the most powerful—who emphasise the importance of creativity in economic and business terms, whereas others warn against this, worrying that a creative workforce is a euphemism for a workforce you can sack regularly in the belief that they will be adaptable enough to acquire new skills and find themselves another job. There are other contested positions within the field—whether creativity is innate or can be taught; whether it is a cognitive function or a cultural phenomenon; and whether it is inevitably a social good or potentially productive of anti social, subversive, even dangerous acts.

This last point, questioning as it does the moral value of creativity in education, is important but hardly ever made, and we shall return to it shortly. In schools, the general, received idea is that creativity is an educational good *per se*, and this not only blurs the underlying incoherence of its discourse but also masks the fact that it has a relatively short history as a human value, much shorter than beauty. In mediaeval times, the original words 'create' and 'creation' had an exclusively religious connotation in English, referring only to God's creation of the world, with humans as his 'creatures', who could not themselves create. This changed at the time of the Renaissance when the term 'creator' began to be used with reference to poets and thence to artists in general[10]. The adjective 'creative' did not come into use until the eighteenth century and still generally referred to artists as they were seen to create worlds which compared in richness, order and beauty with the world created by God himself. The noun 'creativity' was first entered in the Oxford English Dictionary as late as 1875, and John Hope Mason has argued that this date marks the moment when an understanding of human creativity as a value independent of spiritual and artistic frames of reference finally gained pre-eminence in Western thought, a change that had been gathering momentum since the explosion of technological inventions and commercial innovations that had produced the Industrial Revolution. So a concept of *creation* based upon a moral vision of the artist as a creator of beautiful things, incorporating the values of stability, order and harmony with nature became superseded by that of *creativity*, reflecting the values of technology and commerce, characterised by qualities of change and innovation, instability and disruption, competitiveness and conflict with nature. If by the late nineteenth century technological advances had made such creativity possible, he argues, economic conditions had led to it being seen as both necessary and desirable[11]. Once again, the parallels with the political rhetoric of our own era are evident[12].

The key figure in the Western tradition to embody the attribute of creativity thus understood, Hope Mason suggests, is Prometheus, who stole fire from the gods and thus enabled humankind to harness the powers of nature for our own ends. We might also consider here the figure of Arthur Rimbaud, one of the prophets of Modernism, who, in 1874 (the coincidence of dates is significant), gave up poetry before moving to North Africa to make a highly 'creative' living in the commerce of guns and slaves. This symbolic connection between the almost simultaneous emergence of creativity as a value and Modernism as a movement is further underlined by two readings of Mary Shelley's *Frankenstein*—subtitled *the Modern Prometheus*—the one by Hope Mason, the other by Wendy Steiner. For Steiner, the novel is an attack on the values of the sublime, which characterised the aesthetics of Modernism; for Hope Mason it is a warning against the energies of human creativity when unfettered from ethical values. (Torturers, for example, have throughout history proven themselves to be hideously creative.) Both see in the figure of Frankenstein a man driven by obsessive creative ambitions at the expense of other, less heroic human virtues, notably compassion. When he fails to create a wife for the Monster, Steiner sees this as symbolic of what she calls 'the irony of the sublime'—the elevation of freedom and creativity above love, family and pleasure, which she suggests have as much if not more purchase on how we should define ourselves as human[13]. Hope Mason sees Frankenstein's failure here as signifying the choice we have to make between conflicting values—an energetic, productive but all-consuming creativity or a gentler, unproductive but life enhancing compassion, a choice he suggests that is emphasised in the frame story of the book. When the novel opens, Robert Walton, a ship's captain, comes across Frankenstein in his pursuit of the Monster through the frozen wastes of the Arctic. As Frankenstein relates his tale, Walton sympathises with him, identifying the heroic qualities that drove Frankenstein to create the Monster with the urge that drives him on his voyage of discovery into the unknown regions of the North Pole. At the end of the novel, however, Walton shows himself to be unlike Frankenstein, responsive to other human feelings, finally turning back and abandoning his quest when faced with the fears and terrors of his crew. By contrast, Frankenstein shared no such failure: 'It was not his creative impulse or faculty which was frustrated. On the contrary, his creativity operated at full stretch. The problem was that it could do so only at the expense of other equally (or more) essential values'[14]. Like Steiner, who saw Modernism's rejection of beauty as a rejection of those values that connect us most closely to life, Hope Mason identifies the same terrible, amoral, thrilling but ultimately life-destroying potential in unfettered creativity. It is no coincidence, perhaps, that Stockhausen, one of the key figures of Modernism, declared the 9/11 attacks as 'the greatest work of art for the whole cosmos . . . Lucifer's masterpiece'. As Peter Conrad comments, '[W]ho else, except perhaps Prometheus, could be responsible for a maelstrom set off by tanks of aviation fuel?'[15] Of course Stockhausen was widely condemned for his comment, but Hope Mason finds in the figure of Prometheus, if not in Lucifer, a detail that leads him not to thrill at our creative powers of destruction but to glimpse hope for the survival of our children. We need to remember, he suggests, that Prometheus not only knew what fire could do but also, by carrying it away from Olympus in a fennel stalk, demonstrated something of equal significance. 'The knowledge Prometheus brought us', he concludes, 'was not only about creative capacity and power; it was also about how to contain it'[16].

These concerns over the potential dangers of 'unfettered' creativity, if still somewhat muted in educational discourse, are nonetheless being voiced. Peter O'Connor has pointed out that the key skills normally associated with its development—flexibility, the ability to innovate and come up with surprising, original ideas that are nonetheless achievable, the capacity to work autonomously in groups and as an individual and so on—are as useful in the training of a terrorist as they are for any other vocation[17]. A recent issue of the *Creativity Research Journal* has devoted a special issue to what it calls 'malevolent creativity'[18], and Anna Craft, an influential British writer on creativity in education, has criticised the drive in some schools to equate innovation with creativity and see it as a good in itself[19]. Her concern that we promote what she calls 'creativity with wisdom' is essentially a moral one, which returns us to Ruskin and Morris and their ideas about what characterised 'good' creative work and the particular role they saw here for beauty and artistic expression.

The rest of this chapter constitutes something of a dance between the fire of creativity and the fennel stalk of beauty, and, in its attempt to argue how Ruskin's vision for the arts can be achieved within school settings, it addresses a number of practical questions by attending to three specific examples. The first and second of these analyse two instances of children's work—one a poem, the other a painting—and examine the contexts and pedagogies that facilitated their creation. In doing so, I consider how the beauty of existing art works can help shape children's artistic creations in ways that guide them into expressing their own ideas or experiences of the beautiful; the kind of teaching that enables this to happen; and whether calling it 'creative' is in any useful way enlightening to educators. These analyses also consider the relationship between imitation and creation, creativity and self-expression, and the connection between rules, tradition and children's creation of art. The third example turns its attention to the recent work of the Royal Shakespeare Company's education department as I consider how creativity can be seen as a relevant concept for teachers who wish to make the work of a great artist such as Shakespeare *matter* to their students. I examine how creative pedagogic practices can sensitise young people to the beauty of Shakespeare's language and how, when sequenced with due attention to the aesthetics of narrative drama, they can charm students into a strong engagement with his plots. Each of these examples is intended to address in different ways a further, over-arching question implied by Ruskin, namely, how we might foster a vision for arts education in which beauty can bring an ethical dimension to children's creative work.

'ALL THE GOOD IN THE WORLD': BEAUTY, CREATIVITY AND SELF-EXPRESSION

The following poem was written by a Year 2 child as part of a cross-curricular science topic on pets:

Can I have a pet please?
Can we have a dog please?
A fish will do
We will clean its tank
We will feed it
We will love it every day.

We may smile at the sentiment behind this writing and approve of the caring attitude that it is promoting, but we would struggle to find any creative merit in it, artistic or otherwise, even for a six-year-old. The choice of the poetic form by the teacher would appear to be pragmatic and simplistic; poems help children write because they are short and do not require much in the way of punctuation, allowing for repetition and providing space on the page for a nice drawing. They are creative because they provide room for the expression of the child's emotions, which in this case are reduced to her liking for animals. The result, as all too common in primary classrooms, is superficial. There is, perhaps, a basic pattern to the verse, but no other poetic devices such as rhythm or imagery are detectable, and the content is trite even for a six-year-old.

The poem was published in a book for primary teachers[20] and is revelatory of some underpinning attitudes and assumptions about creativity that have long been common in education to the detriment of children learning and creating through the arts. These are embodied in the idea of creative self-expression, which has its roots in the philosophy of Rousseau, in which, as Fleming points out, the assumption is that it is 'the emotion of the creator which [is] the key determinant of quality rather than the work itself'[21]. Fleming calls this understanding misguided and unbalanced, as it leads towards relativism and uncertainty in judging the quality of work. Despite the recent attention to promoting an understanding of creativity among teachers, such attitudes can be hard to shift. I recently attended a day-long conference to celebrate the results of a year's partnership between artists, local authorities and primary schools, which had concentrated specifically on developing creativity through the arts. Time and again heads and teachers used the phrase 'with creativity, there are no right or wrong answers' to express what they and their children had learned from the project, consistently failing to add that there might be criteria for judging better from worse answers. However, teachers can hardly be blamed for harbouring such misconceptions when the artists who visit their schools make use of them themselves[22].

John Hope Mason suggests that we are wrong even to look for creativity in any of the artistic products that children produce. Although these might be imaginative and playful, he argues, they can never be significant enough to merit being described as 'creative'. He quotes Iona Opie to support this claim: '[C]hildren aren't really creative . . . [They] invent nothing. They adapt things. They are Tories of the whole and anarchists of the particular'[23]. Such arguments, however, are based on definitions rather than actual usage, and if, as Wittgenstein would have advised, we attend to how teachers actually make use of the term 'creative', we would find that the vast majority regard writing poetry as a creative exercise. But it does not ensue from this that the child who wrote this particular poem has created anything worthwhile or learned anything in the process; and we would be hard pressed to see it meeting the purposes of creative work that Ruskin and Morris argued for, which, to borrow the words of Richard Shusterman, should offer an 'enhanced, aesthetic experience that gives the live creature not only pleasure but a more vivid, heightened sense of living'[24].

The following poem was written by a nine-year-old boy during his first month in Year 5. It was part of a cross-curricular arts project based on Michael Morpurgo's picture book *Blodin the Beast*[25]. At the culmination of the tale, a young boy, Hosea, escapes across a river from the pursuing Blodin on a carpet that has been woven from 'all the good in the world'. The tale does not state what this 'good' consists of:

> *In my carpet I will weave*
> *A gleaming shark of metallic blue*
> *The sweet tickling taste of a rainbow*
> *The shining light of a panther's eye.*

> *In my carpet I will weave*
> *A smile from my best friend when I'm sad*
> *A moment with my teddy late at night*
> *The splash as I dive under the turquoise to the bottom of the river.*

> *I will ride on the vast waves*
> *With the enormous beast hot on my tail,*
> *Then reach my destination*
> *With Blodin swallowed by the crashing waters.*

The genesis of this poem is significant. The children were each contributing a section to the class' own, communal version of the 'carpet of good', a task they began by making designs based upon their ideas of what the good in the world might consist of. When most of the girls drew flowers and most of the boys footballs, the teacher did not accept these as legitimate examples of self-expression but instead decided that the children's imaginations needed a more structured and engaging stimulus. She turned for this to Kit Wright's poem for children 'The Magic Box'[26,] a wish list of fleeting or imagined items, impossible to keep, that the poet would nonetheless like to put into his box. Some of these are beautiful, such as *the swish of a silk sari on a summer night*; others amusing, such as *a snowman with a rumbling belly*. The poem culminates with a verse that celebrates the fusion of imagination, desire and natural beauty as the poet envisions using his box to surf the *high rolling breakers of the wild Atlantic*, to be washed ashore on a beach *the colour of the sun*. The children explored the poem's structure and imagery before considering what they would like to put in their own magic box, using the lines of the poem as models for how to express these wishes as vividly as possible. Only when their work was well under way did the teacher change 'in my box I will put' to 'in my carpet I will weave', a moment of surprise and revelation for the class as some children immediately grasped the relevance of the poem to their project and the possibilities it presented for the design of their 'carpet of good'. The boy whose poem is presented here went on to create his design from the three images expressed in his opening stanza.

This may well be an example of 'creative teaching', although it would be more illuminating, I think, to describe it as reflective, wise, humane and hence effective teaching. It also illustrates how the moral vision expressed at the beginning of this chapter can be clearly realised in practice. Although the children worked from an existing poem, they were not engaged in a merely technical exercise but were instead dialoguing with a form that helped them articulate their desires and wishes in new and playful ways. In the case of our example, these veer quite unsurprisingly from the domestic and reassuring to the wild and thrilling. They may be the boy's own imaginings, but they could not have been created, as Negus and Pickering put it, 'without reference to existing rules, devices, codes and procedures'[27]. In this sense, the structural model both freed and gave shape to his self-expression by presenting him with rules within which he could play with the sensuous possibilities of language and its potential to create beautiful images. That we should consider this as a fundamentally human, hence natural pleasure, albeit always shaped by culture, has been strongly argued by Carter in his research into the creativity that characterises the pattern formations of everyday speech[28]. It is also evident in children's common enjoyment of the non-literal, more playful qualities of language found in nursery rhymes, puns, jokes, chants and advertising jingles. That schools should fail to take advantage of this predilection was bemoaned forty years ago by Wilkinson and Willoughby in their extensive introduction to the work of Schiller. They complain of 'the frequent failure to make the teaching of language anything more than a mechanical and meaningless drill on the one hand, or an idiosyncratic and undisciplined expression of the inner life on the other'[29]. The UK's National Literacy Strategy has since tried to address this by providing a framework for the teaching of different genres of writing, but this has all too often reduced the teaching of poetry to yet another decontextualised, technical exercise where children learn the form of the haiku, for example, but are often given no better reason for wanting to write one beyond the fact that they are very short.

Both the ethical and aesthetic aspects of the boy's poem are highly contextualised, grounded in the art works that framed it. If the Kit Wright poem helped him make imaginative connections between his desires and the beauty of the natural world, the tale of *Blodin the Beast* provided an added moral dimension in which the beauty of the carpet had a particular symbolic value. Blodin, an oil-swilling, fire-breathing monster, ravages the world from which Hosea flees, and the illustrations reveal him to be as much machine as living creature. He represents the unfettered powers of capitalism and technology, enslaving entire populations to serve him and laying the planet to waste in the process. The moment of his defeat is replete with echoes of the Modernist sublime as the gigantic, machine-like monster is engulfed by the crashing waves of the river. But it is also a moment when beauty and nature combine to defeat his rampaging, unrestrained power, as Hosea rides to safety on the frail but beautiful carpet to a 'land of peace and plenty', something that the poem, too, evokes as the boy identifies himself with Hosea in the final stanza.

Ruskin judged the creativity of the Doge's palace by the way in which its beauty demonstrated a shared moral vision within which individual workers could nonetheless freely express themselves, and this is the model to help us judge the creative success of this work. Children are quite rightly resistant to sanctimonious preaching and overly moralistic pedagogies, of course; but here the moral vision shared by teacher and pupils for the duration of this project, something that Ruskin saw as a necessary underpinning for good, creative work, were integral to the story and did not need to be preached by the teacher or overtly stated as pre-determined objectives.

CAPTURING BEAUTY AND CREATING ART

> *By what means then shall those work who long for. . . . the development of the faculty that creates beauty?*[30]

Key to the creation of the poem analysed previously was the presence of a model for the boy to imitate, where the discipline of the form provided a structure to help him find the words to express his own emotions. Imitation of this kind was seen by Aristotle as central to the way we learn, and Elaine Scarry marks it out as an educational energy inherent to beauty. 'Beauty brings copies of itself into being', she writes: 'It makes us draw it, take photographs of it, or describe it to other people'[31]. She also makes a key link between the imitation or copying of beautiful objects and the human urge to be creative, claiming that 'by perpetuating beauty, institutions of education help incite the will toward continual creation'[32]. This close association between imitation and creation was a belief commonly held throughout the Renaissance, when the great art of antiquity was seen as a model for contemporary artists to emulate. This only began to be challenged in the eighteenth century when the concept of *originality* emerged as a value and took on its contemporary meaning, associated with the invention of something entirely new[33]. The Romantics embraced originality as a key quality of the free and creative artistic genius, and later it became a central value in the Modernist project, which, in rejecting the art of the past, attacked the very concept of tradition. As a result, originality is now fully enshrined as integral to contemporary definitions of creativity, thus obscuring the relationship between artistic creation, imitation and tradition[34]. Noel Carroll sums up the common sense attitude we have inherited:

> Insofar as the modern myth of creativity is tied up with ideas of originality, spontaneity, freedom, exorbitant claims to individuality, and the notion of artistic genius as thoroughly self-determining, it has little patience for the idea of an artistic tradition. Tradition stands in the way of creativity and artistic freedom by introducing something putatively not of the artist's own into the mix.[35]

This, Carroll argues, is the 'Ur-theory of artistic creativity in our culture, often masquerading under the name of self-expression'[36], and he then proceeds to reformulate the case in favour of tradition, claiming that it helps rather than hinders artistic creativity. Traditions, he states, act as conversations that present artists with a diverse range of live options. These do not act as a body of rules to be applied mechanistically, thus inhibiting freedom, but, instead, provide a rich combination of projects and voices, a 'collection of exemplars that include not only art works but also routines, techniques, conventions, effects'[37]. With this in mind, I propose to examine how children's experiences of natural beauty can be fostered and given expression through a proper engagement with the traditions, routines and conventions of art, viewing these not as a cage but as a flexible resource to spur children into acts of creation, which can themselves be beautiful.

If there is a phase of education where beauty is unselfconsciously valued it is perhaps the early years, particularly in those schools influenced by the now well-known philosophy of Reggio Emilia. Pioneered in the region of Italy from which it derives its name, the Reggio philosophy prioritises the development of children's creativity and places a particular value on the visual languages of art. In Reggio schools, trained artists are often employed as full-time *atelieristas*, or workshop leaders, to work with children alongside teachers. Numerous publications by American and English educators are testimony to the visual beauty of the schools and the striking quality of the artwork produced by the very young children who attend them. The enthusiasm and language of Susan Fraser and Carol Gestwicki are not untypical:

> In the Reggio Emilia preschools, beautiful objects, potted plants, and bowls of flowers are displayed on shelves and tables, and light is everywhere shining through coloured strips of plastic or reflected in the many mirrors in the room. The beauty so apparent in the classrooms is

designed to inspire children to become more visually aware and motivate them to create beautiful art work themselves.[38]

One of the core values of the Reggio approach is the promotion of 'a respect for the power and beauty of the natural world'[39]. This is complemented by close attention to the aesthetic organisation of the classroom environment, seen as essential, with all materials and work being displayed with care and attention; and by a clear understanding that art is a means of communication, a kind of 'graphic language', with a vocabulary that children can practise and learn. As one teacher explains,

> I used to see art as an important creative process for kids, but was 'hands-off' and 'anything goes' . . . I still highly value the exploratory, sensory aspects of art but now weave these aspects together with teaching about how to use a range of media . . . so that the children are able to communicate their theories, understandings and visions with clay, wire, paint, black pen etc.[40]

That this approach works is evident in the results[41]. It is also close to the ideas of Raymond Williams who, in his essay *The Creative Mind*, argued that art is best understood as a particularly powerful signifying system that humans have developed in order to describe and communicate experience. He pointed to scientific research that showed how the brain has to learn to see and interpret sensory information according to rules embedded in cultural codes: 'In each individual, the learning of these rules, through inheritance and culture, is a kind of creation, in that the distinctively human world, the ordinary reality that his culture defines, forms only as the rules are learned'[42]. The arts, he argued, are 'an intense form of general communication' but cannot even be seen, let alone understood, by someone other than the artist if they do not share 'the complex details and means of a learned communication system'[43]. All kinds of art are creative inasmuch as we share with one another a 'creative imagination', which Williams defined as 'the capacity to find and organize new descriptions of experience'[44]. Arguments that see inspiration as the source of an artist's creativity, or more recent ideas that situate it in novelty and originality, serve to obfuscate the simple fact that art is a language shared by communities and shaped by culture. For Williams, successful artistic creation was to be equated with the successful transmission of valued experience. In this sense, we can see that his understanding of art as a powerful communication system complements the argument that an artistic tradition should be seen as a help rather than an obstacle to creativity, 'an engine or catalyst that enables it to unfold'[45].

In Reggio Emilia, the creative success of the artwork is aligned to twin aspects of language and value; art is taught as a graphic language, and beauty is nurtured, both its experience and its expression, through the

Figure 5.1   Painting by ten year-old child.

learning environments created by the teachers. There are many practical reasons why these principles might be more difficult to apply to later phases of schooling in ways that suit the demands of the curriculum and the needs and interests of older children. But it is not impossible, as illustrated by the example of the following landscape painting[46].

This was judged by a panel of specialist art teachers to be good enough for a sixteen-year-old working towards a GCSE qualification. It was, in fact, painted by a ten-year-old girl during a week-long school trip spent drawing, sketching and painting in the Devon countryside. Before this, the girl had displayed no outstanding talent for art, yet the complexity of the colours and textures of the picture and the strength and coherence of the mood it evokes suggest that the painting she produced was more than a happy accident. By attending to the context of its creation and the pedagogy that shaped it we can see how the beauty of nature can act as a spur to artistic creativity and consider the contexts and pedagogies that can help children create their own, strikingly beautiful work.

At the start of the week, children were introduced to a range of landscape paintings which decorated for the next few days the hostel where they were staying—a converted barn next to an old farm house. These paintings were drawn from a range of traditions and illustrated a variety of interpretations and techniques. Reproductions of works by Turner and the Impressionists, for example, were complemented by watercolours painted by lesser-known, local artists and examples of paintings from other cultures, such as Wang Meng's fourteenth-century *Mountain in Autumn*. Different pairs of paintings were regularly brought together for children to discuss and compare how line, texture and colour helped determine their mood. On the day of this particular painting, towards the end of the week, children spent the morning outside, equipped with viewfinders and sketch pads. From different locations and in different directions they were questioned closely about what exactly they could see through the viewfinders before eventually choosing their own positions, where for over an hour they sat and sketched, wrapped up in warm clothing against the November chill. All children chose to work in different, quite isolated positions and were regularly visited by the teachers to be questioned and asked to comment on their work. In the afternoon, they returned to the hostel and began their paintings. At school in the previous week, the teachers had mixed a range of primary colours—powder paints in water thickened with PVA glue—and had brought them along to the centre in large pots. The pallets the children used to mix these colours were large enough only to hold small amounts of colour at one time, a process they were used to from their art lessons in school. As they painted their pictures, for which they were given plenty of time, the teachers continued to discuss, comment, praise and give advice to individuals.

On and around my desk as I write, I have a number of books on creativity. Taking advice from one of them[47] I have decided to surprise myself by making a random selection from among them and my hand has fallen upon *The Creativity Research Handbook*, volume 1, edited by Mark Runco. Within ten seconds I have found inside a list of the characteristics of 'creativity fostering teachers'[48]. None of these prove to be surprising and include having a co-operative, socially integrative style of teaching; encouraging flexible thinking in students; promoting self-evaluation in students; taking students' questions and suggestions seriously and so on (there are nine altogether). What is noticeable—and telling—is the omission of any reference to teachers' subject knowledge, of their need for an understanding of the creative qualities of good work in whatever field their students might be working in and the traditions which embody examples of such work. On another page[49] are listed ten cognitive aspects of creativity which include an active imagination, skills in convergent and divergent thinking, an ability to think up many ways to solve problems and so on. Again, lists such as this are now common currency in education, concentrating on potential rather than actual achievement, intentionally disconnecting children's learning from any specific disciplines of knowledge or valued areas of human endeavour. In this way, creativity becomes weightless, another tool of technicism, whose narrowly instrumental purposes and moral shortcomings we have already critiqued. We would not have to strain too hard to match most of these criteria to what these teachers and this particular child actually did without ever getting any closer to the heart of their achievement.

The creative process in this case was set up and sustained through conversation—conversations between the teachers and the children and between the teachers themselves; between various landscapes and the traditions of art that had been used to capture them; between different examples drawn from these traditions; between what children's eyes could see and the words they were encouraged to find in order to describe it; between themselves as perceivers, producers and evaluators[50]. There was also a productive tension between the children's individual, private experiences and the materials and styles they were presented with to express them. These materials and styles helped them create by acting as 'filtration devices', the importance of which has been argued by Noel Carroll: 'Too many options lead to paralysis rather than creativity: too many possibilities, without some way of narrowing down the field of alternative choices, will stop the artist in her tracks rather than promote the production of new work'[51]. The teachers' detailed preparation, planning and clear structuring of activities to scaffold children's learning were amplified by filtration devices that channelled individual creativity without stifling it, and also by their teaching of established processes inherent to the discipline itself—the use of sketchpads and viewfinders, for example. Of central importance, too, was their shared love of art and their love for teaching it, made evident to the children through the enthusiasm and energy they displayed. But something else must have been happening for this girl to paint the picture that she did.

There is always something mysterious, as well as familiar, about beauty. Strategies and techniques are necessary for its creation but can never determine or guarantee its expression. The week was planned so that an intense and memorable experience of the countryside would be the focus for all the children's activities. Taking place in November, the days grew dark early and the children spent a lot of their time outside in the darkness. On one evening they built and lit a bonfire, barbecued their food on it and sat around listening to stories before going to bed. On another evening they went on a walk through a nearby wood, lit only by the moonlight. These were children from a city school, and they interacted with the countryside in ways they were not used to and that were not normally permitted, all of them playful and exciting. When children spoke of the week afterwards, it was the nightly excursions that seemed to be most memorable to them. With this in mind, as I look again at this child's painting of a gloomy November day, it seems to be suffused by these night-time experiences. The blue hue of the hills in the middle distance suggests the quality and colour of moonlight; the flames of the bonfire are recalled by the red flecks of colour that permeate the muddy fields of the foreground, where the thick, black lines of paint also resemble the thin shadows of the long trunks of the trees in the pine wood. There is excitement and perhaps a thrill of fear in the bold lines of the foreground, which contrast with the tranquil if cold, pale washes that she has used to paint the hills directly below the skyline. All of these exist simultaneously under the grey skies of November where the clouds cast their shadows over the fields below. The beauty of her creation lies in the intensity of the experience it conveys, an emotional response to five days and nights spent in the wintry English countryside that this young girl has captured in a remarkable piece of work. But as an educator, I am also moved by the educational vision that enabled its creation, one that saw the value of beauty in the kind of childhood experiences that an intimate connection with nature can inspire.

RE-CREATING THE BEAUTY OF SHAKESPEARE'S LANGUAGE THROUGH A CREATIVE/AESTHETIC PEDAGOGY

> *You cannot point to the poem; it is 'there' only in re-creative response of individual minds to the black marks on the page. But—a necessary faith—it is something in which minds can meet.*[52]

In the two examples we have so far considered, children have made use of existing conventions to make their own artistic creations. In this sense, learning to appreciate has gone hand in hand with both learning to imitate and learning to create. Turning to the work of Shakespeare, the distinction between the appreciation and creation of beauty becomes more complex.

If asked to consider where we find beauty in Shakespeare, we might point to individual scenes, such as the climax of *The Winter's Tale*, when Leontes witnesses the 'statue' of Hermione come back to life, or to the aching beauty of the scene where Lear cradles the dead Cordelia in his arms. But for those who love Shakespeare, the beauty of his work is inseparable from his language. In the words of Richard Eyre, 'The life of the plays is in the language, not alongside it or underneath it. Feelings and thoughts are released at the moment of speech'[53].

To engage with Shakespeare's dramatic poetry is to experience the expressive power of language at its most intense and beautiful, and yet it is more often than not the very thing that can block a young person's access to the plays in the first place. It is for reasons such as this that Gingell and Brandon have attacked the current emphasis on creativity in the classroom, suggesting that its concentration on the hands-on, expressive creativity of students detracts from the benefits and pleasures of learning to appreciate the works of writers from the established canon[54]. This is, of course, one of the discursive positions highlighted by Banaji et al.[55], strongly contested by those who accuse it of cultural exclusiveness and elitism; but it also accepts the creation and appreciation of art as somehow oppositional, which, as we have seen, rests upon current assumptions that creativity is dependent upon acts of originality and inventiveness as opposed to imitation (or conservation) and discovery.

In the case of Shakespeare, we can begin to trouble such a claim by pointing to reader-response theory, as formulated by Iser[56] and Fish[57]. Iser pointed to the essentially indeterminate nature of any given text, which will of necessity have 'creative gaps' or blanks within it. These are what trigger the reader's imaginative involvement, stimulating her to construct her own meanings and thus engage more deeply with the text itself. Fish, too, emphasised the unavoidable need for readers actively to re-create the text in their imaginations, using the interpretive assumptions and procedures they bring to the reading process. These constructivist positions are particularly persuasive when we consider the nature of play texts, where so much is left unspecified; the tone in which any line should be spoken, for example, and the mood of the speaker; whether their words express true feelings or whether they mask them. These and other 'creative gaps' must be negotiated and filled in by the reader herself if there is to be any engagement with the text, let alone any appreciation of it. In such a process, the reader creates her own meanings by discovering them within the characters' words. Such creation of meaning can, of course, be guided by a teacher, but it cannot be forced or dictated. As Collingwood put it, 'To create something means to make it non-technically, but yet consciously and voluntarily'. This is achieved 'by people who know what they are doing, even though they do not know in advance what is going to become of it'[58].

Reader-response theory chimes with those writings on creativity by Carter and Craft, which emphasise its ubiquity within cognitive processes, and helps us understand discovery as a creative process in itself[59]. The issue of originality is thus conveniently bypassed, becoming absorbed in concepts such as *P-creativity*—a creative act of personal significance, new to the individual—as opposed to *H-creativity*, where originality is defined as being innovative in some historically significant way[60]. In this sense, we all make original discoveries—and are thus being creative—when we understand or appreciate something for the first time. But all of this pre-supposes that originality, as we currently conceive of it, is a necessary aspect of being creative.

It is precisely assumptions such as this that Rob Pope investigates—or more accurately 'deconstructs'—in his decidedly postmodern approach to the subject of creativity[61]. In the process of investigating the hidden val-ues and subordinated meanings in the words we associate with creativity, he makes some illuminating suggestions that can help us appreciate how an active appreciation of Shakespeare can be both ethical and creative. With regard to the word 'originality', for example, he reminds us that it only gained its contemporary meanings of 'novel' and 'innovative' in the eighteenth century[62]. Before then, it meant going back to a beginning, to the origin, a residual meaning still evident in phrases such as the 'original inhabitants' of a country, or, indeed, the 'original meaning' of a word. In this sense, then, we might suggest that we are being 'original' in our engagement with Shakespeare when we struggle to find 'original' mean-ings within the text itself—a conservationist attitude as it merges the value of the old and the new, recognising the necessity of both. Similarly, Pope suggests that we carefully consider the term *re-creation* and how this, too, might suggest a concept of creativity at once broader and more ethical in its intimations than is currently conceived. 'Recreation', of course, we asso-ciate with pleasurable activities that both relax and refresh us; the prefix 're-', implying 'again', includes rather than excludes the idea of imitation, or repetition; but as it also carries the meaning of 'afresh', it implies 'repetition with variation, not just—if ever—absolute replication'[63]. Here, then, is a concept of creativity as both sustaining and innovative, one which he sug-gests implies a more 'responsive' and 'responsible' vision than is normally offered in specialist literature:

> There the emphasis tends to be on the 'new' the 'novel' and the 'origi-nal' in their narrowly modern senses . . . *Re-creation* leaves more room for conserving and sustaining as well as recasting and refreshing, while resisting conservative, reactionary impulses of an unthinking and merely reflexive kind.[64]

We might argue, then, that activities which enable us to re-create an origi-nal Shakespearean text are creative in ways that refresh and sustain it, thus allowing it to be passed on in new and revitalised ways. This echoes Ruskin's position that we should learn to appreciate and sustain the beautiful and the good in our culture through acts of both creation and retention. It is also to propose creative engagement as the best form of appreciation, a very different idea from any elitist position that implies that Shakespeare's genius should be held aloft, to be admired and adulated from a respectful distance. It therefore shifts our attention to a consideration of the pedagogies that might enable students to refresh, revitalise and appreciate the beauty of Shakespeare's language by, in Pope's sense, *re-creating* it for themselves.

The education department of the Royal Shakespeare Company (RSC) has in recent years been working with teachers throughout the UK to improve the teaching of Shakespeare through a pedagogy that mirrors its own creative approaches and values. At the heart of these are ways of working with Shakespeare's language developed by Cicely Berry and praised by actors and directors as celebrated as Jeremy Irons and Trevor Nunn. Her methods are intensely physical and playful, exploring the beauty of the poetry through the voice—the muscularity of the language, the sensuality of its sounds, the rhythms and patterns of its dynamic. Here, according to Berry, we find not only Shakespeare's appeal but also his essential, dramatic meanings. So, for example, she will take a passage such as Ophelia's soliloquy in act 3, scene 1, and have the group of players read it aloud together, then re-read it pronouncing only the vowel sounds. This instantly draws attention to the quality of keening, of lamentation, in the extended vowels that dominate her final words:

> *Oh woe is me*
> *T'have seen what I have seen, see what I see.*

Sometimes she will take a scene where there is conflict between two characters and have it played physically as a game of tig, or with a football and two goals, or with one of them trying to physically attack the other, it being the duty of the rest of the players to prevent them from doing so[65]. Such work, she emphasises, is essentially an aid to discovery of what is already in the text, breaking pre-conceived patterns and releasing what she calls 'the physical vigour of the language'[66] or what, to paraphrase John Armstrong, we might call the hidden power of its beauty.

In adapting these approaches to make them suitable for English teachers working with secondary pupils, the RSC sees physical, creative play with the language as the key to unlocking its charms. So activities around a chosen dialogue or soliloquy could involve the students reading it in unison, in a circle, standing shoulder to shoulder; reading it individually, changing readers at every punctuation mark; reading in unison selected lines, emphasising the iambic rhythm of each (as in 'a *horse*, a *horse*, my *king*dom *for* a *horse*'). Pair work can include students sitting back to back, each taking the role of a different character, whispering the lines conspiratorially over their shoulders; then standing ten feet apart and repeating the exercise, this time shouting the lines at each other. Students might be asked to reduce every line to what they think is its key word and to speak it along with a strong, physical gesture. They might be asked to try out the scene with one character rooted to the spot, the other able to move wherever they like; or with each character given three choices of movement to perform at any point—to turn away, to move towards or to move away from one another. After each exercise, students will discuss with their partners and with the class the choices they have made and why they made them, and be asked to evaluate their appropriateness. In this way, the characters of the drama can start to live for them as, to paraphrase Coleridge, the words of the poet become their own words.

Of course the danger with such strategies, as with any set of techniques, is that they become little more than a series of things for students to do—Oakeshott's world of mere activity as opposed to purposeful action. Dewey's twin enemies of 'utter caprice or sheer routine' are still lying in wait for the teacher who fails to make the lesson coherent[67]. Consequently, which activities to make use of and how to structure them is key to the teacher's artistry; for, as we have learned from Dewey, the aesthetic shape of the lesson is what will provide it with a sense of unity, coherence and completion for the students. In his words, '[A]esthetic cannot be sharply marked off from intellectual experience since the latter must bear an aesthetic stamp to be itself complete'[68]. Such an experience, he suggests, is essentially narrative in its structure and he likens it to a journey whose success depends upon the pace of our progress: 'If we move too rapidly . . . the experience is flustered, thin, and confused. If we dawdle too long after having extracted a net value, experience perishes of inanition'[69]. In other words, it is pointless to attend to *creative* approaches to teaching Shakespeare if we ignore how we need to shape them *aesthetically* so that the words can release their energies and weave their charm.

With this in mind, and by way of a brief example, let us look at how we might approach the dialogue between Hamlet and Horatio in *Hamlet*, act 1, scene 2[70]. This is the scene in which Hamlet is informed by his friend that the ghost of his recently deceased father is stalking the battlements of Elsinore. It has been edited to make it manageable within a lesson of about fifty minutes duration and is intended to introduce the play to a class of eleven- to twelve-year-olds.

The lesson begins with the class sitting in a circle and the teacher taking on the role of Horatio. 'Do you believe in ghosts?' he asks: 'I didn't either . . . until this very night'. In a fearful tone he then describes the events of scene 1 to the children, the appearance of the ghost of the dead king to the soldiers on guard. He explains that he must now break the news to the king's son, Hamlet, whom he regards as a friend. How shall he do this? The students offer him advice to which he listens and also ask him questions to which he responds as best he can, informing them of the king's recent death and the queen's re-marriage to his brother in the process. In groups of four, the students are then asked to recreate the scene of the ghost's appearance as though it were an image in a graphic novel. Each group is given a different line from scene 1 that the image is intended to illustrate, such as 'What art thou that usurpest this time of night?' or 'Stay. Speak, speak. I charge thee, speak'. They can choose how they speak their line, whether by an individual or as a chorus.

Children are then handed an edited version of the scene between Horatio and Hamlet, with the characters of the guards omitted. The edits are intended to maintain the rhythm of the exchanges between the two.

HORATIO	My lord, I think I saw him yesternight.
HAMLET	Saw? who?
HORATIO	My lord, the king your father.
HAMLET	The king my father!
	For God's love, let me hear.
HORATIO	Two nights together
	In the dead vast and middle of the night,
	The apparition comes: I knew your father;
	These hands are not more like.
HAMLET	Did you not speak to it?
HORATIO	My lord, I did;
	But answer made it none: yet once methought
	It lifted up its head and did address
	Itself to motion, like as it would speak;
	But even then the morning cock crew loud,
	And at the sound it shrunk in haste away,
	And vanish'd from our sight.
HAMLET	Then saw you not his face?
HORATIO	O, yes, my lord; he wore his beaver up.
HAMLET	What, look'd he frowningly?
HORATIO	A countenance more in sorrow than in anger.
HAMLET	And fix'd his eyes upon you?
HORATIO	Most constantly.
HAMLET	I would I had been there.
	I will watch to-night;
	Perchance 'twill walk again.
	If it assume my noble father's person,
	I'll speak to it, though hell itself should gape
	And bid me hold my peace.

The class reads this together, shoulder to shoulder, after which the teacher invites the children to ask for a definition of any of the words they have not understood. The scene is read again, with readers changing at each punctuation mark. The children then work in pairs through a selection of the exercises presented previously. The whispering/shouting activity is particularly apt, as the former is so evidently more appropriate and can be given intentionality by asking the question, why might they be whispering? Who might they not want to hear their words? The different feelings that arise from Hamlet staying still as he speaks (shock? calm determination?) compared to those when he is constantly moving (agitation? excitement?) are also interesting to explore, as is the challenge of reducing the entire dialogue to key words, one taken from each of the characters' exchanges.

The lesson needs to end on a note of anticipation as well as reflection. Why might Hamlet want to speak to the ghost? What might the ghost want to tell him? What 'foul play' do the children suspect? Might the ghost want Hamlet to do something for him? What, perhaps? The children share their own ideas and are assured that they will be answered in the next lesson. The sense of consummation is, therefore, similar to that we feel when watching an episode of a favourite TV drama; it is not yet over and we want to tune in next week, but this episode has been coherent and satisfying in itself. In this way, the children are being introduced to a study of the play that will follow its dramatic progression. It will necessarily be selective, incorporating storytelling to connect specific scenes that the teacher will choose in order to provide a coherent and suitable focus for these young students, namely, should Hamlet avenge his father or not; and what do they think he should do at key moments of the play—when Ophelia is clearly distressed by his behaviour; when he notices someone hiding behind a curtain in his mother's bedroom; when he is standing behind Claudius, who kneels praying in the chapel? How does this compare with what he actually does do? Shakespeare's poetry will be at the heart of this aesthetic, intellectual and moral journey, as the class re-creates it in ways set to nourish their imaginative lives. And the key to making this work is a creative pedagogy sensitive to the aesthetic rhythms of the play itself.

* * * * * * * *

In his historical investigation into the emergence of creativity as a cultural value, John Hope Mason is not slow to point to the problems it has bequeathed. Human creativity has undoubtedly provided the developed world with the comforts, pleasures and conveniences of modern technology, but it has, in doing so, exploited and impoverished millions and now threatens the future sustainability of the planet itself. We thus need to find a new creative consciousness, he concludes, if we are to save ourselves from the future we have created. Artistic creation, he claims, no longer presents us with a viable, moral, alternative vision to that of amoral, rampant creativity—at least not in the concept of the artist we have inherited, as a free thinking, heroic creator, god-like in his aspirations[71]. It is a position echoed by Peter Conrad in his cultural history of artistic creativity. 'For good or ill', he concludes, in Nietzschean tones, 'man is now his own god: both a world-builder and a destroyer of worlds':

Perhaps we have no right to possess such powers, which may yet be our undoing. But it is too late to regret the audacity of the uncontrollable, invaluable beings who first questioned the limits placed on thoughts and dreams, supplemented nature with their own creations and came to be known—for want of a better word—as artists.[72]

Both writers, however, are viewing creativity and art through the lens of Modernism and uncritically so. This is perhaps unsurprising, as the heroic aesthetics of the sublime chime so readily with the values of unfettered creativity, as we have seen. In which case, a contemporary arts curriculum would have nothing to offer this search for a new, creative consciousness, different from the heroic hopes and dreams already registered by Modernism in the fields of politics, culture and technology[73]. But Hope Mason makes a further, interesting point, suggesting that we abandon the vision of the artist as hero or anti-hero in favour of gentler, more communal forms of artistic expression, exemplified for him by the creation and nurturing of a Japanese garden. In such a vision, he states, 'we would value the curator as much as (perhaps more than) the creator'[74]. This is to re-assert those values we have come to see as identifiable with the beautiful, values that can channel the creative energies of our children in ways that sensitise them to the rhythms and charms of nature, that encourage them to see the conservation and retention of beautiful things as communally beneficial as well as guides to their own individual creativity. Such was the vision of Ruskin and Morris, such is what I have been arguing for in this chapter. And such is what Elaine Scarry sees at the heart of the particular, creative dynamic of beauty—its forward momentum balanced by a continual urge to turn back, rediscover and learn from the beauty of the past:

> The very pliancy or elasticity of beauty—hurtling us forward and back, requiring us to break new ground, but obliging us to bridge back not only to the ground we have just left but to still earlier, even ancient ground—is a model for the pliancy and lability of consciousness in education.[76]

6   Beauty in Science and Maths Education

SCIENCE AND ARTS EDUCATION: TWO CULTURES?

Culture is activity of thought, and receptiveness to beauty and humane feeling.[1]

My science education was very poor. At primary school, we did no science, not even nature study, until my final year, where it consisted of copying paragraphs and line drawings from a textbook. At grammar school I met real science in a science laboratory and I hated it from the outset. The room had no aesthetic qualities whatsoever and reminded me of pictures I had seen of Victorian workshops. I remember it as dark and gloomy, with long benches covered in a sticky black polish that I could carve my name in with my fingernails, and what air there was seemed to be permanently polluted by the lingering smell of gas or the malodorous aftermath of some indeterminate chemical experiment. In my first year the teacher was old and white haired. He was a brilliant man, our form teacher told us, who had worked on radar in the Second World War, but his brilliance seemed to work against his capacity to communicate intelligibly. He spoke with a contemptuous tone as though everything he was saying was so obvious that only a fool could fail to comprehend, and I always felt extremely foolish in his lessons. He was also, we knew, an alcoholic and occasionally used to fall asleep in class whilst dictating notes. We were so frightened of him, however, that, whenever he did doze off, we remained still and silent on our stools until he awoke. My second-year experience was no better, as this new teacher had a non-interventionist approach to group work and also presumed our knowledge to be much greater than it was. Consequently, although I could draw neat diagrams and learn notes about experiments, I hardly ever understood what was happening in them and had very little desire to find out. I recall my deep lack of understanding whenever he balanced an equation on the blackboard—I and everyone else in the class apart from the three or four mathematical geniuses who always sat at the front. As a result, when offered the choice at the end of my second year between history and Spanish or physics and chemistry, there was no contest. I studied biology until

O Level, but my education in physics and chemistry came to an abrupt and unsatisfying conclusion at the age of thirteen.

This chapter, then, presents a particular challenge to me as it deals with subjects to which I failed to connect at school, both cognitively and affectively. It is guided by an attempt to see how the concept of beauty, as conceptualised by scientists and mathematicians, can help young people make such a connection. Two theoretical frameworks underpin this investigation, one psychological, the other cultural. These are intended to cast light on ways in which teachers can draw students into the pleasures and satisfactions afforded by science and mathematics as intellectual endeavours; and in passing they help cast a critical eye on current ideas that underpin collaboration between the arts and sciences in school curricula.

Science teachers (and maths teachers, too) face a particular educational challenge that is arguably less marked for their colleagues in the arts and humanities, and this centres upon the kind of concepts their subjects deal with. The arts generally concern themselves with what we might usefully term 'experience-near' concepts, described by Geertz as those that someone 'might naturally and effortlessly use to define what he or his fellows see, feel, think, imagine and so on, and which he would readily understand when similarly applied by others'[2]. 'Experience-distant' concepts, on the other hand, are employed by specialists of one sort or another 'to forward their scientific, philosophical or practical aims'[3]. Love, fear, frustration, embarrassment and other myriad human emotions are 'experience-near' concepts for a child, as are, for instance, family, friendship, honesty, cruelty, kindness and the host of concepts tied to common human experience. Chemical compounds, metamorphosis, photosynthesis, algebra, long division and infinity are by contrast 'experience-distant' concepts. Of course, a strong cultural or class influence is likely to be at play here; if one of my parents is a zoologist or a keen gardener, metamorphosis may not be quite so distant. As Geertz insists, these categories are a matter of degree rather than polar opposition, and, crucially, we should not regard one sort of concept as implicitly preferable to another. In specific subject disciplines, however, we have to, and the differences move beyond the content of the concepts themselves into the means of representation they employ. Whatever the complexities of poetic meter or the intricacies of colour mixing, the poet and the painter work with materials that are in some sense immediate—words, sound and rhythm, light, colour and texture. But the mathematician and the scientist work with abstract concepts well beyond the immediacy of experience and have developed far more difficult, figurative, 'distant' languages to express their ideas succinctly and coherently. I may know nothing about painting or which way up to hold a trumpet, but that need not prevent me from responding deeply to a painting by Vermeer or a tune such as 'It Never Entered My Mind' when played by Miles Davis. A complex algebraic equation, on the other hand, or the account of a revolutionary chemical experiment, is denied such easy access. The abstraction at the heart of mathematical and scientific thinking necessarily compresses concepts into symbolic systems in an attempt to define natural laws; it is not intent to capture nature as it is humanly experienced. If there is beauty in maths and science, then, it is of a different order from that we find in the arts, and the challenges of leading children to experience it are consequently greater.

The fact that I was actually *allowed* to drop science at such a young age in a well-respected and highly successful grammar school could be seen as reflecting cultural dispositions rather than having conceptual causes, as was famously argued by C. P. Snow[4]. Snow claimed, in 1959, that literary intellectuals, on the one hand, and natural scientists, on the other, constituted, in the UK at least, two distinct cultures, deeply mistrustful of each other, sharing neither mutual understanding nor mutual respect. Those with political power and social influence, claimed Snow, tended to belong to the literary culture, knowing little or nothing about science, and seeing it as boring and utilitarian, as uncultured and therefore beneath them; whereas scientists, with little education in the humanities, were characteristically dismissive of literary culture, regarding it as based on an inferior, subjective form of knowledge. The problem was a serious one as the world was on the verge of a new scientific revolution in electronics and automation that would bring about changes more profound than those even of the Industrial Revolution a century and a half earlier. Britain, Snow argued, had the worst record in science education among the world's wealthiest nations, and this would continue unless the prejudice against science was addressed. If not, then the country would find itself in no position to either make policy or successfully administer the new scientific developments necessary to address national and global problems for the benefit of rich and poor alike[5].

Snow's speech proved to be hugely influential and, fifty years on, he has largely been accurate in his predictions about the revolution in electronics and information technology, whilst his concept of 'two cultures' appears to have been vindicated through subsequent responses in education and the media. Considerable efforts have been made by successive governments to promote science and science education, and it is now compulsory for all students in the UK to study science until the age of sixteen. 'Cultured' radio programmes such as the BBC's *In Our Time* have consciously attempted to bridge the two cultures by regularly discussing issues from the world of the sciences as well as those from philosophy, literature and the arts; and these days, we are told, the reading public is far more interested in science than it used to be[6]. There remain, however, reasons for being sceptical of Snow's analysis when we consider the place of beauty within an education in the sciences and F. R. Leavis' famous response to his argument helps us understand why.

Although Leavis' riposte is often recalled principally for the vitriolic, *ad hominem* tone of the attack, many subsequent re-evaluations have argued that his criticisms were fundamentally correct. Leavis dismissed Snow's conceptualisation of culture as simplistic and naïve. For Leavis, culture was not just an intellectual tradition in which people responded alike without thinking about it; a culture provided a society with knowledge that connected it with an organic past, from which it derived its critical capacity to comment on the values of the present[7]. One of the tasks of contemporary culture, therefore, was 'to devise an education whose method and content [would] supply to its recipients sufficient common premises and ideas to give them an effective unity and consequent effective influence on the problems of their time'[8]. As many of these problems would, indeed, continue to emanate from the rapidly expanding fields of science and technology, the challenge was a pressing one, but one that would not be helped simply by a more general teaching of the kind of scientific literacy that Snow was calling for. Instead, it was a challenge rooted in language, one that needed to be addressed at a level more fundamental than the teaching of a set of scientific laws or the reductive language of scientific method. Students needed an education in how those working both in science and in the humanities actually make use of language in order to think. 'Thinking is a difficult art', Leavis wrote, 'and requires training and practice in any given field'[9]. Arthur Stinner has argued that here we find a common and persistent misconception that Snow's position overlooks, namely, the language of 'science-as-an-institution', embedded in scientific papers and text books, is in fact the language with which scientists think. This is not the case: the language that characterises those private aspects of scientific inquiry, what Stinner calls 'science-in-the-making', is imaginative and creative, 'characterized by subjectivity, ambiguity and the need for metaphorical representation'[10]. This creative use of language, integral to the struggle that leads to scientific achievement, is, however, almost always masked from public view.

These criticisms are helpful when we consider where students might find beauty in science—and this is not dependent upon any collaboration with the arts. Such collaborations, quite commonplace these days, tend to be framed in language that accepts the argument of the two cultures as given; that there exist two independent pillars of knowledge in need of bridges to be built between them. Problematically, this can perpetuate muddle-headed assumptions that the arts will bring imagination, enjoyment and creativity to the sciences, which in turn will bring substantive and significant knowledge to work in the arts[11]. Such is to suggest that the sciences, by their very nature, are inherently dull unless given a boost from outside their own conceptual fields and that, in turn, knowledge generated by the arts is by comparison flimsy and insubstantial. As we have seen, the arts are not inherently more creative, imaginative or expressive forms of knowledge than the sciences but deal with concepts that are closer to general human experience. If the arts have something to offer the science teacher, it is not imagination and creativity but a set of practices that can serve to bring the experience-distant concepts of science into more immediate contact with the learner. This is to suggest not so much a role for the arts as a role for artis*try*; more precisely, it proposes that thinking aesthetically about their pedagogy can help teachers bring the beauty of science into their classrooms[12].

These preliminary arguments provide a necessary steer into the issues that this chapter now sets out to address. We begin with an examination of the nature of beauty in science and mathematics as apprehended by those who work in those disciplines. Turning specifically to how scientists make use of language, we then consider the role of metaphor in scientific thinking and how it can help science teachers harness the power of beauty inherent to their subject. Looking specifically at pedagogy and artistry, we then turn to the language and aesthetics of performance in order to re-assert a neglected cultural tradition in popular science education. Finally, bearing in mind Leavis' argument that one of the key roles of culture and education is to help us cast a critical eye on the problems of the present, we consider the Eden Project as an example of how beauty can help conceptualise an ethical pedagogy attuned to the ecological needs of our planet's future. In investigating these issues, we are not being eccentric or working at the margins of science teaching or the culture of science itself. On the contrary, we are addressing questions that Richard Holmes sees as fundamental to a necessary change in our appreciation of how scientists fit into society and the nature of the creativity they bring to it. To borrow his words, this investigation will help us understand 'how science is actually made; how scientists themselves think and feel and speculate'[13]. It will also help us appreciate what he calls 'the three things a scientific culture can sustain: the sense of individual wonder, the power of hope, and the vivid but questing belief in a future for the globe'[14]—principles surely at the heart of any vision for science education in the twenty-first century.

BEAUTY, MYSTERY AND WONDER IN SCIENCE

> *I was like a boy playing on the sea shore and diverting myself in now and then finding a smoother pebble or a prettier shell than ordinary, whilst the great ocean of truth lay undiscovered before me.*
>
> —Isaac Newton[15]

In his short essay 'The Mystery of Science: A Neglected Tool for Science Education', Papacosta claims that science is 'always in contact with an ocean of mystery' but that this is ignored by many science educators, who prefer the security of factual knowledge and thus emphasise certainty and proof in their teaching. He points to how the great scientists were often drawn to science precisely by the mysteries of the natural world. As an example he refers to the sixteen-year-old Einstein who wondered what it might be like to ride upon a beam of light; within ten years, he adds, 'that simple question had given birth to relativity'[16]. This, he argues, illustrates that questions provoked by such a sense of mystery and wonder ought not to be regarded as wasteful fantasy but as nourishment for the creative imagination.

Robert Crease, a philosopher and physicist, is quite precise about how mystery and wonder serve scientific knowledge, seeing them as qualities of beauty evident in scientific experiment. 'Wonder' he defines as 'the desire to explore given and promised profiles of a phenomenon for its own sake— to engage in an adventure of fulfilment'[17]. Scientists, he explains, pursue this adventure through experiments in which they must remain open to the unexpected, to the possibility of surprise; and the excitement and revelation generated by such surprises are what he interprets as Einstein's meaning when he remarked that 'the most beautiful thing we can experience is the mysterious'[18].

There remains a common, persistent cultural belief, however, that science is intent on *solving* mysteries, rather than on finding ways to explain and represent them in formulae and through experimentation; and that it is therefore intent on *destroying* them, in removing our sense of wonder at the beauty of the natural world, on starving our imaginations rather than nourishing them. This underpins the residual prejudice evident in the so-called 'literary culture' and is generally blamed upon the Romantics and their reaction to the grander claims of the Enlightenment. It was during the Enlightenment, in fact, that the division of knowledge between the arts and sciences took root, with philosophers claiming science or 'natural philosophy' as a distinct, more rational and implicitly superior form of knowledge than any practised through poetry and the arts. In their turn, some of the Romantic poets questioned what they saw as the arrogance of scientific rationalism and its inability to capture the complexity of human emotional life with its need for myth, art and beauty. Poets like William Blake tended to blame science for the ugliness and inhuman practices of the Industrial Revolution. The Romantic mission, in Schiller's great phrase, was 'to re-enchant the world' by reaffirming the inner, imaginative life of the individual, a stance seen as morally superior to the cold, narrow, philistine interests of science. In Umberto Eco's words, the Romantics 'opposed the disenchanted Beauty of the day with a concept of the world seen as inexplicable and unpredictable'[19]:

> Our meddling intellect
> Misshapes the beauteous form of things.
> We murder to dissect.[20]

These lines from Wordsworth are often quoted to typify the Romantic suspicion of science and how the figure of Isaac Newton became for them a particular target. In his experiments with prisms, Newton had famously dissected the rainbow and shown it to consist of nothing more than different wavelengths of light. To philosophers and poets of the Enlightenment such as Voltaire, Pope and James Thomson, he had become a hero[21]. But for Keats, Wordsworth and the lesser known Thomas Campbell, Newton—a notoriously arrogant man, who had dismissed poetry as so much 'ingenious nonsense'—had emptied the rainbow of its symbolic resonance and mythical power. It thus became for them a potent symbol for their resistance to what they saw as the delight taken by scientists in 'disenchanting the world'. In 1820 Campbell lamented,

> *When science and Creation's face*
> *Enchantment's veil withdraws,*
> *What lovely visions yield their place*
> *To cold material laws.*[22]

More famously, Keats, in his poem of the same year, 'Lamia', seems to be attacking the cold exactitude of science, the mere touch of which would make 'all charms fly' and empty the universe of its sense of wonder:

> *Philosophy will clip an angel's wings,*
> *Conquer all mysteries by rule and line,*
> *Empty the haunted air and gnomed mine—*
> *Unweave a rainbow . . .*[23]

In casting scientists as the enemies of beauty, the Romantics are thus blamed for initiating the kind of polarised responses to the arts and sciences that typify the worst aspects of the two cultures.

This polarity, however, has been overstated, mythologized even; some relatively brief historical scrutiny readily demonstrates this and also serves to undermine rather than illustrate the argument of the *Two Cultures*. Shelley's poem 'The Cloud', for example, again written in 1820, can be read as a homage to the burgeoning science of meteorology and has been noted for its 'remarkably accurate and scientific understanding of cloud formation and the convection cycle'[24]. The lines from Wordsworth quoted previously are taken from an early poem, whereas in his late version of 'The Prelude', the statue of Newton outside his bedroom window in Cambridge is imagined in terms that portray the great scientist more akin to a Romantic explorer than a soulless villain:

> *. . . Newton, with his prism and silent face,*
> *The marble index of a Mind for ever*
> *Voyaging through strange seas of Thought, alone.*[25]

Keats had been a medical student, and his attitude to science was more complex than the infamous quote seems to imply. At the heart of 'Lamia', in fact, there is a fascination with contemporary scientific debates over vitalism and the existence of the human soul, the same debates that inspired

Mary Shelley's *Frankenstein*, although with a more ambivalent response. In an earlier work, his sonnet 'On First Looking into Chapman's Homer' is revelatory of his enthusiasm for the work of the astronomer, Herschel, as he draws upon his discovery of Uranus to capture his own discovery of Homer's poetry:

> *Then felt I like some watcher of the skies*
> *When a new planet swims into his ken.*[26]

Indeed, the amazing astronomical discoveries of Herschel in the late eighteenth century inspired rather than repelled or dismayed the Romantics. Reflecting on his childhood, Coleridge recalled being taken into his garden one winter evening by his father, a great admirer of Herschel, to be shown the night sky and have the planets named to him. He was then eight years old but never forgot the experience, and many of his mature poems remain diffused with the symbolic presence of the stars and the moon[27]. Indeed, Coleridge retained a great interest in science all of his life. A friend of the chemist Humphrey Davy, he attended his lectures and also corresponded with him. Science, he declared in one of his letters, 'was poetical . . . being necessarily performed with *the passion of Hope*'[28]. The fact that Coleridge also advised Davy on his own poems reminds us that, in their very activity, the great scientists of the Romantic era did not see themselves as culturally separate from the artists of their day. Herschel, in fact, was a professional musician and, initially at least, an amateur astronomer, who likened his reading of the night sky to that of 'a skilled musician sight-reading a musical score'[29]. Davy, meanwhile, published volumes of poetry and philosophical reflection in his lifetime, as well as a highly successful book on the joys of fly-fishing.

Whatever accusations we might hurl at the Romantics, then, we should not accuse them in any simplistic sense of driving a cultural wedge between science and the arts, limiting one to rationality, the other to beauty. This ought to be good news for Richard Dawkins. A famously vocal atheist, he is the scientific rationalist *per se*, intolerant of any claims, such as Evangelical Creationism, that he sees as flying in the face of scientific evidence and any cultural phenomena, from the *X Files* to astrology, that purvey what he labels as superstitious nonsense. However, he insists that he is far from insensitive to the beauty and wonder of the world, which he acknowledges as a deep human need, but denies that we need embrace ignorance or delusion in order to experience it. His book *Unweaving the Rainbow* addresses Keats' famous image literally by examining what he calls the poetry of science and the fascinating knowledge that has emerged as a result of Newton's work—from our understanding of how the eye informs the brain to the theories of relativity and the Big Bang. Surely, he suggests, a poet with Keats' imaginative powers would not fail to be captivated 'by the poetic beauty of what that unweaving has now revealed?'[30] This may well betray a naïve understanding of beauty as the Romantics understood it; after all, 'Beauty is truth and truth is beauty' remains one of Keats' most famous lines[31]. It is nevertheless indicative of how many scientists perceive and appreciate the beauty of the physical world. The solving of one mystery, he suggests, uncovers others, capable of inspiring even greater poetry: 'Mysteries do not lose their poetry when solved. Quite the contrary; the solution often turns out more beautiful than the puzzle'[32]. As an example of this, he offers Isaac Asimov's striking image evoking what we now know about the make-up of the universe. He asks us to imagine it as a room twenty miles long, twenty miles wide and twenty miles high. The room is entirely empty apart from one grain of sand which we now pulverise into a thousand million million million fragments, the approximate number of the stars in the universe, and scatter them through the emptiness. 'These are some of the sober facts of astronomy', comments Dawkins, 'and you can see that they are beautiful'[33]. Neither Keats nor Coleridge would have disagreed.

The beauty that scientists find in their discipline, like all beauty, relates closely to the mysterious, but it is mystery inherent to the knowledge it unearths. If I had been taught science by teachers intent on conveying the excitement and beauty of its mysteries, and not solely the hypothetical representation of its equations and the certainties of its catechism, then my education might have taken a different turn. Mark Girod, a science teacher educator from the US, argues that, still today, many science teachers attend poorly to the beauty of science and are not helped by the textbooks they use. He writes,

> Often in the retelling of a scientific discovery the 'human', 'creative, 'inspired' and 'passionate' sides of scientists and their stories get left out. These are often deemed unimportant or anti-intellectual, pulling readers away from the important details of theory development, research results and solutions to equations.[34]

How can it be possible, however, to tell the remarkable story of Foucault's pendulum without attempting to convey the wonder of its simplicity and the awe-inspiring nature of what it demonstrates? There are now many examples of the pendulum in museums, cathedrals and public buildings around the world, but the first was demonstrated by Jean-Bernard Foucault in the Paris observatory in 1851. It consists of a heavy metal bob suspended at the end of a long wire and, with each swing, it appears to the observer that the plane of the pendulum is slowly but distinctly moving in a clockwise direction. But this is only what we think we see; what we are actually experiencing is the world rotating on its axis, for it is the pendulum's motion that remains constant in relation to the stars. Robert Crease articulates his own response to seeing Foucault's pendulum at the Franklin Institute in Philadelphia when he was a youngster in terms that evoke what he defines as the 'sublime beauty' of the experience. Here a set of four-inch steel pegs were positioned in two semi-circles on the floor, and every twenty minutes or so the swinging bob knocked one of them over. He recalls the excitement he used to feel as he witnessed this:

> Sometimes I'd just stare at the pendulum itself, trying to obey the sign and make myself see that it was I—and the solid floor beneath my feet—that was moving. For reasons I did not understand, I never quite succeeded, though the pendulum did leave me with a feeling of mystery and awe.[35]

He quotes Foucault himself, who commented on the response of those who viewed his early demonstrations: 'Everyone who is in its presence . . . grows thoughtful and silent for a few seconds, and generally takes away a more pressing and intense feeling of our ceaseless mobility in space'[36].

As with Asimov's dramatic image of the universe, such revelations are *sublimely* beautiful—not in terms of the Modernist sublime, with its nihilistic and destructive urges, but within the frame of what Kant described as the 'mathematical sublime', something we experience when confronted with a phenomenon whose magnitude is so vast that we cannot fully grasp it[37]. The beauty of Foucault's pendulum lies in the way that it undermines our common sense understandings—what Crease describes as a sudden and thrilling re-education, alerting us to 'the mismatch between human perception and the workings of nature'[38]. If something as fundamental as our everyday perceptions can be thus challenged, what other mysteries might science open up for us? For science teachers to convey this to their students, they need to be more than competent classroom managers, good organisers of group work and knowledgeable dispensers of scientific fact; they need to be astute and confident demonstrators, performers and storytellers with a keen, aesthetic sense of how to make use of surprise and the unexpected. This is something we return to later, but for now it is enough to suggest that practical work and scientific method will not on their own evoke any appreciation of the beauty of science or a sense of its wonder; after all, as Dawkins points out, one can learn to play the clarinet and still not learn to appreciate the beauty of Mozart's clarinet concerto.

PATTERNS AND PUZZLES: INTELLECTUAL BEAUTY IN MATHEMATICS AND SCIENCE

> *If one observes the whole Natural World as one, one finds everything in the most Beautiful Order; it is my favourite maxim: Tout est dans l'ordre!*[39]

If much of the potential fascination for science lies in the intensity and thrill of sublime beauty, there are also those satisfactions that pertain to our enjoyment of order, harmony and pattern, the more classical beauty that Pythagoras and Plato found in mathematics. This is key to our understanding of how experience-distant concepts can achieve beauty; as the French mathematician Poincaré insisted, such beauty differs from the sensual beauties of quality and appearance inasmuch as it is the intimate product of pure intelligence[40]. The great British mathematician G. H Hardy also thought beauty to be at the heart of mathematics, in its appeal and in the nature of the knowledge it seeks, and shared a vision similar to the idealism of Poincaré. In his *A Mathematician's Apology*, he compares his work to that of a poet and a painter, as all three are weavers of patterns. In Platonic tones, he claims that, if poets weave their patterns out of words and painters out of colour, mathematicians weave theirs from ideas; and, as with the work of poets and painters, the first test of these ideas is their beauty. 'There is no permanent place in the world for ugly mathematics', he quips, asserting that 'the ideas, like the colours or the words, must fit together in a harmonious way'[41]. The more serious a mathematical theorem is, the greater its beauty not because of its usefulness, nor for any instrumental purposes it might serve, but by virtue of its concision, purity, its explanatory and imaginative power and predictive artistry. Hardy summarises these aesthetic characteristics that define a theorem's beauty as three essential qualities: unexpectedness, inevitability and economy, the last of these being particularly important. 'A mathematical proof', he writes, 'should resemble a simple and clear cut constellation, not a scattered cluster in the milky way'[42].

This discussion of Hardy's, locating the appeal of mathematics in its aesthetic processes rather than its instrumental applications, may appear as elitist and detached from social and human concerns, reminiscent of Walter Pater's aesthetics, perhaps, but it is nothing of the sort; it is a reminder to teachers of where the real potential for young people's enjoyment of mathematics may lie. Hardy is quite clear that the most useful maths is actually the dullest and that its real satisfactions address yearnings common to all of us for the beauty we find in order and pattern. Witness, he says, the popularity of chess and number puzzles (and he was writing in the days before *sudoku*). 'Every chess player can appreciate a "beautiful" game or problem', he writes, 'and everyone who calls a problem "beautiful" is applauding mathematical beauty'[43]. The intellectual pleasure that the lover of chess and number puzzles gets from them is, he insists, however rudimentary, inseparable from the experience of mathematical beauty.

The recent work of Stephen Wolfram on cellular automata illustrates admirably how the Pythagorean virtues of harmony, order and simplicity underpin the conceptual beauty of mathematics. The purpose of Wolfram's research has been described by Ed Regis as an attempt to explain 'complexity itself, wherever it might be found, whether in the structure of galaxies or in turbulent fluids, or in the nucleotide sequences of a DNA module'[44]. Wolfram devises simple computer programmes capable of generating their own patterns, some of which lead to chaotic disorder, others to dull, repetitive patterns of no aesthetic interest but others still which self-generate into patterns of extraordinary complexity and beauty, many of which reflect physical systems that already exist in nature. In this sense, Regis defines Wolfram's quest as a search for '[n]ature's own software', but it is one that goes back to the birth of philosophy, responding to Plato's question of 'how to get order out of disorder, complexity out of simplicity'[45].

Wolfram himself describes how one of these patterns was generated. The mathematical formula, to the non-mathematician at least, appears complex and difficult:

(1) $a_i^{(t+1)} = a_{i-1}^{(t)} + a_{i+1}^{(t)} \bmod 2$

However, the idea it expresses is extremely simple. In lay terms, the cellular pattern consists of a series of linear sites, each represented by the boxes in the following table. There are only two values available to each site, 0 or 1. The formula states that the pattern begins with a line on which all values are 0 apart from one. It then self-generates, the value of each particular site on subsequent lines being determined by the values of the neighbours of the site directly above it. If they are the same value, then the new site will have the value 0; if they are different, then the value will be 1. This table demonstrates how this progression works by illustrating the results of the first three steps.

	0	0	1	0	0			
	0	0	1	0	1	0	0	
0	0	1	0	0	0	1	0	
0	1	0	1	0	1	0	1	0

The visual pattern that this formula quickly goes on to generate is strikingly illustrated in the following images. As Regis points out, it is recognisable to any mathematician as Pascal's triangle of binomial coefficients, and to any biologist it will recall the pigmentation patterns of a snakeskin[46]. This is just one example of the many thousands generated by different formulae, some of which have been marketed as postcards, wallpaper patterns and murals; such is their aesthetic appeal[47].

Visual mathematical patterns of varying complexity are ubiquitous, in the beauty of nature and in globally diverse products of culture and art. Simple and complex symmetries, both rotational and reflective, are evident in leaf and flower, in the intricacies of a snail's shell, in architectural and wallpaper designs, in Balinese masks, in Peruvian blankets and in Asian batik. Complex tessellating mosaics are at the very heart of the striking beauty of Islamic art, as are the patterns of Fibonacci number sequences.

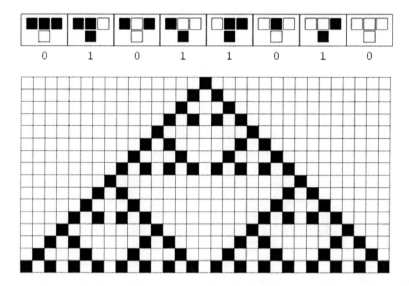

Figure 6.1 Cellular automaton pattern. Copyright Wolframscience (www.wolfram.com).

The sensual pleasures of such visual examples are heightened when we appreciate the mathematical rules that govern their expression, and the mathematics curriculum has long recognised the appeal of practical activities where children are encouraged to explore and copy them and experiment with creating such patterns of their own. The more abstract beauty found in number patterns and theorems, as exemplified in Wolfram's cellular automata and which Hardy places at the heart of mathematical beauty, can be found in more common investigations involving magic squares, tangram puzzles, triangular number sequences and their relationship with square numbers and more complex puzzles, such as Euler and De Moivre's formula for how the knight can move around the chess board, landing on every square only once. If we follow Hardy's argument, it is in activities such as these, pleasurable in themselves, that the real joy of maths can be found. The simple maths we need to get by in everyday life or the advanced knowledge necessary to design complicated bridges may well be socially essential, but utility, even necessity, may not feel insistently relevant for students within the classroom context, whereas the aesthetic play involved in solving puzzles and weaving patterns can be enjoyed for its own sake.

* * * * * * * *

It is a beautiful case—a beautiful case.[48]

The great fictional solver of puzzles, of course, is the detective, and the qualities of unexpectedness, inevitability and economy evoked by Hardy could be equally applied to the aesthetics of classic detective fiction found, for example, in the best stories of Sherlock Holmes and Father Brown. Writers such as Jorge Luis Borges in *Labyrinths* and, more recently, Guillermo Martinez in *The Oxford Murders* have self-consciously explored the link between mathematical puzzles and the fictional detective story. The pleasure we commonly find in such tales can be harnessed by science teachers willing to relate the aesthetics of the genre to the processes of detection in scientific inquiry.

A good example of this is provided in a scheme for nine-year-old children designed by Linda Atherton and Miles Tandy. Entering the classroom, the children find their desks moved back and the outline of a corpse chalked on the floor. They are informed by the teacher (in role as a forensic scientist) that there has been a murder for which there are four suspects, whose details are provided on a worksheet. There are also various pieces of evidence near the body, including samples of fabric, powder and a muddy footprint. Children search for clues in order to correlate data already collected and are then asked to interrogate the evidence, make links and detect patterns in a systematic, safe and fair way as it will be presented to a prosecution lawyer to see if there is enough of it to present a case in court. This is where the activity explores key scientific processes and ideas. Filtering, for example, is a technique that now has a real purpose in order to identify the soils; the white powder samples react in very different ways and allow for a discussion of reversible and irreversible reactions; looking at fibres under a digital microscope, the children explore the differences between those which are natural and those man-made. Once children realise the relationship between size of feet and height, they can confidently use this information to predict the height of someone at the scene. Group talk becomes clearly focussed on scientific principles, and tables are produced to collate evidence. Children have a strong desire to ensure that their methodology is fair and thorough and, of course, an 'expert' (in the form of the teacher) is on hand to support the scientific thinking and processes. The courtroom is then set up with the teacher in a new role as prosecutor, asking tough questions about whether and to what extent the evidence incriminates any of the suspects, thus forcing children to re-evaluate what exactly it is telling them and how valid their interpretations have been. Work of this order recalls the words of Humphrey Davy, one of the greatest of all chemists: 'It may be said of modern chemistry that its beginning is pleasure, its progress knowledge, and its objects truth and utility'[49].

It has been claimed that the modern detective story 'took murder out of the ethical realm and put it into the realm of aesthetics'[50]. This is, however, another misleading example of how aesthetics and ethics have become regarded in polarity, the one with the other. More accurately, we should see the aesthetic appeal of the detective story as serving a deep, human, ethical yearning for justice and order in the world: 'We create worlds of simplicity and clarity in which we can dwell, though perhaps only too briefly'[51].

The fictional world of the detective story and the mathematical world of patterns and puzzles appeal to us precisely because our human organisms and social lives appear to be anything but simple; and so they satisfy those human yearnings for order and harmony, that part of us that aspires to the clarity of Ockham's razor, where the simplest of ontological explanations are regarded as the truest and the best. Sartwell argues that this aesthetic yearning is integral to scientific thinking and uses the Copernican Revolution as a striking example. Ptolemy's cosmology did, after all, account for what astronomers were able to observe in the fifteenth century, but its narrative of cycles, epicycles and epiepicycles lacked the simple elegance of Copernicus' heliocentric explanation for the same observations. The conclusion was as simple as it was revolutionary, but he insists that it was 'aesthetics not observation' that led to a rejection of the Ptolemaic system[52]. As James McAllister has argued, Copernicus' theory did not demonstrate any clear, empirical superiority over Ptolemy's, but its intellectual elegance and appeal to aesthetic preferences ensured its eventual supremacy[53].

METAPHOR AND BEAUTY IN THE LANGUAGE OF SCIENCE

I attended Davy's lectures to enlarge my stock of metaphors.

—Coleridge[54]

This Copernican revolution is a further reminder that science is not the field of absolute certainties that it is often thought to be but rather one whose proofs rely on observable data agreed by communities of scientific specialists. This is the celebrated argument of Thomas Kuhn, who saw the history of science as dependent upon a series of revolutions such as that inspired by Copernicus, in each of which the key foundational principles of scientific discourse had to be re-imagined and redefined, an epistemological position now generally accepted by science educators[55]. Science, like any other discipline of knowledge, is a field of argument, challenge, development, evolution, revolution and critique, in which dominant ideas are open to re-evaluation should observable data demand it. This does not, however, lead us inexorably down the path of absolute relativism taken by the more extreme Postmodernists such as George Levine and Bruno Latour, who have argued that scientific knowledge should not in any sense be privileged; that it is just one of many discourses, 'no more grounded in a foundation of reality that gives special authority to its language than the language of literature'[56]. Of course scientific knowledge is a discourse, but it is not *only* discourse. One has to wonder, with Joseph Carroll, how seriously such theorists take their propositions: 'When they are sick, they do not go to a semiotician for a linguistic consultation; they do not submit their diseased bodies to literary colleagues for rhetorical analysis'[57]. It is tempting to view such theories as the latest manifestation of the literary culture sniping at its adversary. Nevertheless, there is an argument among scientists themselves as to whether there *are* poetic qualities inherent to the language of science, particularly in its use of metaphor, and whether this is a tendency to be fostered or avoided.

Physicists such as Ernst Mach and Pierre Duhem have warned against the use of metaphor in scientific language, arguing from a perspective that can be traced back to the seventeenth-century writings of Thomas Sprat and to William Whewell's *Philosophy of Inductive Science*, which became the standard Victorian text on scientific methodology. 'When our knowledge becomes perfectly exact and purely intellectual', wrote Whewell, 'we require a language which shall also be exact and intellectual; we shall exclude alike vagueness and fancy, imperfection and superfluity, in which each term shall convey a meaning steadily fixed and rigorously limited. Such is the language of science'[58]. Some contemporary physicists, on the other hand, such as John Ziman, are quite clear that metaphors are so deeply a part of our common language use that it is impossible *not* to use them: he insists that we cannot think anything, except by analogy and metaphor[59]. Robert Crease, too, believes that we need to understand how science makes use of metaphor, rather than deny that it should, and that doing this helps us access the beauty of scientific ideas:

> Clarifying the nature of metaphoric usage is important for understanding science and its beauty. One reason is that secondary subjects of metaphors are rooted in culture and history. Scientists always work with culturally and historically transmitted concepts and practices. It is always transforming, not transcending, what it has been given by culture and history.[60]

In this sense, a metaphor can be understood as a testable hypothesis and as one of the key, creative roles of the scientist to be the imagining of new metaphors. Nevertheless, this understanding does not appear to be commonly shared among science teachers, and Clive Sutton sees this as a major problem besetting science pedagogy:

> A good word in science is held to be one which has one meaning only, clear and unambiguous. Scientists and science teachers are aware that in other walks of life words are often ill-defined or used in many different ways, but these features are regarded as 'imperfections of language'—an unfortunate looseness practised by non-scientific people.[61]

In many classrooms, he argues, science teachers regard the vocabulary of science as a form of labelling rather than a language of interpretation. As an example, he quotes the following sentence spoken by a teacher: 'Air contains two gases—nitrogen and oxygen—and there is also some carbon dioxide, some water vapour, and some other gases'. Pupils can note down this information, Sutton comments, and perhaps make some later use of it, but it implies that air just *is*, and that there is no other way to describe it. He goes on,

> There is no hint that coming to a conclusion about what 'air' or 'airs' might be was a problem that absorbed the scientific community for the better part of a century. There is no acknowledgment that the word 'gas' was a triumph of theoretical insight, and no mention that arguments raged about whether it was a good idea to call 'lively air' by a new name: 'oxygen' (acid maker).[62]

Of course labelling has a valid place in scientific activity, but to reduce language to this, the thinnest, most transparent of its functions, is not only to ignore how we use it to construct and process knowledge but also to empty it of those poetic qualities that can add depth and pleasure to our use of it. And this pleasure can be aesthetic as well as intellectual, as the warmth of Sutton's prose very well conveys.

Sutton's book is replete with examples drawn from the history of science that illustrate the hidden histories of some of its key terminologies. Some of these relate to individual words—'titration', for example, developed in nineteenth-century France to find the assay-value of silver and derived from the French word 'titre', or title, as in the title deeds to a property, denoting by analogy the truly reliable content of a precious metal. The word 'gas' is particularly evocative when we understand that it is derived from the Greek 'chaos', intended to capture its wild spirit, shown in its tendency to escape on heating. Harvey's choice of the metaphor of a pump for the heart and Robert Hooke's use of the word *cell* to describe the millions of little cavities he saw in a slice of cork placed under a microscope are further examples of scientific language that arose from excitement and amazement, guided by aesthetic and interpretive choices to capture meaning in terms that have since become conventional. 'An unexpected expression is felt to be apt or insightful', comments Sutton, 'and it is partly that which gives it its beauty'[63]. As a young learner with a literary bent, I, for one, can imagine being drawn into science, and becoming far more able to understand its processes, if my teachers had found ways to make the beauty of its language work on my imagination. And fundamentally, it illustrates how scientists themselves think in ways that render the residual argument of the *Two Cultures* irrelevant by addressing them at base, through language itself, as Leavis implied that we should. Sutton provides a simple pedagogic example with reference to Torricelli's realisation in the nineteenth century that the atmosphere we live in is essentially an 'ocean of air'. By being introduced to a passage written in 1878 by Arabella Buckley, students, he says, can be invited to imagine a being 'whose eyes are so made that he could see gases as we see liquids' and to respond to what they imagine this being would see[64]. This is not an empty exercise in fantasy but is enabling scientific and poetic sensibilities to connect; for getting to know the full significance of words in their historical and cultural contexts is part and parcel of understanding what they represent. It is also a process that can, as George Steiner wrote, 'open doors on "seas of thought" deeper, more richly stocked than any on the globe'[65].

THE WONDER OF SCIENCE IN PEDAGOGY AND PERFORMANCE

If the aesthetic qualities of the language of science are often ignored, so too are the potential artistry of its pedagogy and the learning possibilities inherent to a well-staged, playfully performed scientific demonstration. And yet there is a strong tradition of science being taught and popularised in precisely this way. Humphrey Davy was the great pioneer of this approach and was passionate about educating the general population in science. The series of public lectures and demonstrations he began in the new Albemarle Street lecture theatre in London in the early 1800s proved to be so popular that they led the street to become the first one-way system in London in order to prevent the traffic jams that inevitably built up on his lecture days[66]. A French tourist of the time described his lecture technique as electric, praising the spectacular nature of his chemical demonstrations that produced gasps of amazement and bursts of applause from the audience. As Richard Holmes points out, however, these performances were far from being mere showmanship: 'They were skilfully designed as genuine scientific demonstrations, and Davy believed that surprise and wonder were central to a proper appreciation of science'[67].

Davy began a fashion that spread beyond the UK, to be taken up by scientists less renowned than himself. Eustache Amour Hublin, for example, was a well-known and popular entertainer who could be seen regularly in the fairground of St Germain in nineteenth-century Paris. Science was his field of expertise, he would proclaim, as he addressed the crowds in grand, declamatory tones:

> Ladies and gentlemen, I could have entered an Academy, la Sorbonne, le Collège de France and delivered brilliant lectures. I said no! . . . And if I am here among you, it is because all of you must draw from my demonstrations the true and natural principles of the forces which are above us, these forces which frighten the ignorant but supply the educated with all the moral pleasures of intelligence![68]

The performance he would then conduct was designed to shock, surprise and entertain. A wheel machine would produce lightning; he would bring a member of the audience up to charge a volta pistol which would then be fired to the astonishment of everyone; demonstrations using leyden jars and

Cartesian divers would be met with exclamations and applause. French drama critic Jules Lemaître was impressed by the attention of the crowds, who became far more interested than mere onlookers, and by Hublin's ability to 'educate while entertain'. French science educator Daniel Raichvarg tells this story as a lesson for contemporary science teachers, to remind them that there remains 'a continuous desire for good pedagogy, together with a continuous desire for wonder'[69].

Is he right, however, to draw upon the nineteenth-century tradition of public science demonstrations as a model of good pedagogy, suitable for today's teachers? Helen Nicholson sees such demonstrations as flimsy and seductive, 'more likely to mystify and astonish rather than promote knowledge and understanding'[70]. This mistrust of the manipulative potential of art is well established in our culture and can be traced back as far as Plato and St Augustine, who both saw dangers in the power of art to stimulate the senses and overwhelm reason. For performers like Hublin, of course, these sensational reactions were an essential part of an act that drew in the crowds and thus helped him maintain a meagre living. Mystification and astonishment are powerful and potentially enjoyable emotions, close cousins to wonder and surprise, grabbing our attention, shaking up our thinking and making us want to know more. They would be inimical to learning only if they were the *outcomes* of a lesson, designed to emphasise the authority and superior knowledge of the teacher/performer rather than acting as springboards into inquiry and learning. One of the very few experiments I recall from my own physics education was the teacher demonstrating dramatically how to create a vacuum inside a tin can, which immediately imploded; this initially astonished, me but I was gripped enough to actually want to hear and understand the explanation. This was precisely how Davy made use of surprise and wonder; to grab attention, to foster curiosity and then to offer explanations. He was, as a result, emphatically successful as a teacher as well as a scientist. Jane Marcet's best-selling book *Conversations in Chemistry*, published in 1806, provided narrative accounts of Davy's lectures and was read by the young Michael Faraday who, as a result, began attending Davy's lectures in 1812. As well as going on to invent the electric motor, dynamo and transformer, he began his own *Christmas Lectures for Children* in the 1830s, an institution that continues to this day and that some believe to be his greatest invention of all[71].

Teachers who are good performers need not be charismatic, self-publicists such as Hublin or brilliant scientists such as Davy or Faraday but they do need a keen, aesthetic sense of the lesson as a narrative and a willingness to play with their class as a performer might with an audience. I witnessed a fine example of this in a lesson for Year 1 children, designed to demonstrate that air has physical properties, including force. The teacher had the children sit at her feet and produced two plastic bottles, one almost filled with coloured water, the other empty. 'Is there anything in this bottle?' she asked, holding up the empty one. 'No!' chorused the children. 'Are you sure?' 'Yes!' they cried. Asking for a volunteer, she squeezed the bottle close to the face of one child, who reacted to the jet of air by screwing up her eyes and laughing. Other children then volunteered, reacting similarly and there was now a lively atmosphere in the classroom. 'Is there really nothing coming out of the bottle?' asked the teacher again. 'It was a tickle!' called out one child. 'So what was in the bottle to cause the tickle?' 'Nothing!!' chorused the children. 'Are you sure?' 'Yes!!' This teacher was clearly at home with the conventions of pantomime and of a children's conjuring act, and if she had left things there or had simply told the children the answer, they may well have, indeed, remained mystified. Instead, she turned to the bottle of coloured water and asked what they thought would happen if she squeezed this one. Many were able to predict the outcome and the class watched the water rise and flow over the top, commenting on what they could see. The teacher then placed a small, paper cone over the top of the bottle. 'It's got a hat now', she said—a lovely example of how to use language to bring the concept of this distant experience nearer to children's own understandings—and then asked what would happen to the hat if she squeezed the bottle again. Most seemed confident that it would get wet, and she toyed with their responses, squeezing the bottle gently, watching the water rise and force the hat off its perch accompanied by their increasingly excited commentary. After discussing what had happened, she then took a new cone and placed it over the empty bottle, asking if anything would happen to it if she squeezed *this* bottle. 'No!' 'Why not?' 'Because it's got nothing in it!' 'Are you sure?' 'Yes!!' 'Well let's see, shall we?' The result was truly dramatic. The cone shot high into the air, much higher than I myself had anticipated, to a great chorus of exclamations from the children. Their faces were pictures of wonder—astonished, gripped, inquisitive. It was more than a moment of magic, however; the imaginative power and delightful surprise formally compressed into it made it a moment of *beauty*, and the teacher did not spoil it by offering any immediate explanation. The children of course now wanted to play with plastic bottles, tickle their friends' faces and make paper hats jump high into the air. This they could do in group work. The scientific explanation was not rushed but was planned to connect with further small group activities investigating other ways in which the children could make the air move things. But the main strength of the lesson to me was in the way the teacher had staged a performance, with simple but well-chosen props, to trick the natural world into disclosing one of its secrets to the delight of these young children.

THE SUBLIME, THE BEAUTIFUL AND THE ETHICAL: LEARNING AT THE EDEN PROJECT

We might be tempted to see the beauties of maths and science as value free, providing the pleasures of wonder and the delights of reason and clarity detached from any irrelevant moral considerations. But beauty, as we have seen, is seldom if ever ethically neutral. The beauty of mathematics, for example, with its aesthetic of order, harmony and rationality, is seen by Scarry to underpin a concept of justice, where aesthetic and ethical fairness meet in what she calls 'a symmetry of everyone's relation to one another'[72]. Competitive team games are framed to be fair in essentially mathematical terms—witness the spatial and numerical symmetries of sports pitches and the opposing teams who play on them. When players break the ethical code of a game, the team is punished by arithmetical subtraction, ranging from time out to outright dismissal. Sartwell also makes the connection between mathematical beauty and order and justice through the concept of balance. 'One can find beauty in order or in chaos', he writes, 'but more relevantly and commonly one finds beauty in certain combinations of order and chaos. Perfectly ordered systems are merely boring and perfectly chaotic systems are merely bewildering'[73]. We are reminded once again of Schiller's insistence that beauty is expressed through play, a state where sense and reason are both in balance. At its extreme, an obsession with mathematical pattern and order can be symptomatic of inner *dis*order—emotional, as with the autistic narrator of Mark Haddon's *The Curious Incident of the Dog in the Night Time*, or mental, as with the schizophrenic professor played by Russell Crowe in the film *A Beautiful Mind*. We need a cultural balance of varying types of beauty to allow for the expression of different ethical possibilities and for personal and social happiness to flourish in different ways.

Most scientists, as we have seen, have expressed the beauty of science in terms that align it with definitions of the sublime, but Wendy Steiner's arguments in Chapter 4 remind us that there is an ethical danger in a curriculum dominated by emotions triggered *only* by the sublime, blind as they are to the simpler pleasures of 'the beautiful', pleasures that connect us affectively more directly to the world. Scientists such as Crease and Dawkins insist that the beauty of the sublime brings them closer to nature by provoking a deep appreciation of all its wonders; but the gentler emotions we associate with the beautiful, listed by Scarry as liveliness, gaiety, cheer, compassion and good heartedness, can be experienced through those aspects of a science curriculum that address our domestic pleasures. In some schools, for example, there are mini farms, where children can learn the pleasures of cultivating plant life and attend to the care and welfare of animals. Forest schools, a recent concept developed in Scandinavia, are growing in popularity in the UK and build part of their curriculum around outdoor play and activities in woodland areas. Their specified aims are expressed in terms of the emotional and social development of young people, using the ubiquitous language of skills—the promotion of self-awareness, self-regulation, intrinsic motivation, independence, and good social and communication skills[74]. But they are also an ideal opportunity for children to observe at first hand the delicate ecology of a natural environment and to interact sensitively rather than exploitatively with it. Such a curriculum can integrate the more robust practices of progressive education with clear ecological aims, a significant development now that the sustainability of our planet has become a key global challenge, with scientific and ethical implications.

It was as a response to this challenge that in 2001 the Eden Project was established in Cornwall, UK, both as a commercial tourist venue and as a vast educational resource. Its aims, as summarised by Rob Bowker, are 'to demonstrate environmental best practice and to encapsulate and celebrate the wonder and importance of plants and the vital need to use resources sustainably'[75]. It consists of a series of 'biomes', or geodesic conservatories, built to exhibit thousands of plants from around the world. The largest of these is the Humid Tropic Biome which, individually, is the world's largest greenhouse—240 meters long, 120 meters wide and 50 meters high. Anyone who visits it is able to see and smell the rainforest for themselves and to experience its scale as well as its beauty. Visitors can also see the everyday products that the rainforest provides and how those who live there are able both to survive and sustain its ecological system. It is a remarkable resource for teachers and students and Rob Bowker has been particularly interested in how it is used by schools and what children learn from visiting it. In one piece of research he had three classes of children aged nine to eleven draw pictures of the rainforest before their visit, with the chance to revise them immediately after. The original pictures demonstrate what he calls 'plant blindness', an attitude to vegetation as nothing, just a vague natural backcloth 'pristine and peaceful'[76]. After their visit, however, guided by the Eden Project's educational team, the new pictures demonstrated an awareness of shape, texture, individual fruits and flowers and also a sense of depth, scale and perspective entirely missing in their previous versions. Part of the discussion during the workshop had included reference to the peoples and animals of the rainforest, but the children did not include them. They drew what they had experienced, visually and interactively. Bowker is interested in the cognitive/affective learning that the Eden Project is aiming for and finds clear evidence of it in these drawings. They do, he argues, demonstrate a holistic understanding and capture 'a real sense of being immersed in the rainforest'[77]. His findings recall the analysis of the young girl's painting in the last chapter, in which I argued that its beauty related to the intensity of the experience, which in itself was an experience of beauty. They also emphasise the link between art and nature, beauty and cognition, where the aesthetic qualities of the children's drawings are enhanced by their close attention to detail. This, as the Pre-Raphaelites argued, is itself an ethical response to nature; in attending to the intricacy of its details through art, we come closer to appreciating, understanding and feeling intimately related to it.

The architect of the Eden Project, Tim Smit, writes of it in tones that do indeed recall the visionary ideals of Ruskin as well as the aesthetics of Schiller:

We set out to build a place unlike any other, one that would capture the imagination of all who came upon it. Its landscape and buildings were to bear the hallmarks of a civilisation at one with nature, strangely familiar yet somehow foreign—a place where the future would hold promise and restless discontent would become, for a while, a distant memory.[78]

Elsewhere he writes that the project is 'not just a marvellous piece of science-related architecture; it is also a statement of our passionate belief in an optimistic future for mankind'[79]. Those future-oriented, hopeful energies that we have noted in beauty are self-consciously harnessed by the project's educational agenda, and Smit makes explicit use of artistic approaches as part of its pedagogy:

We knew that traditional scientific interpretation using touch screens and the like was a turn-off, and that passive displays on boards wouldn't hold the attention. But we set our hearts on merging art with science and technology in order to get our message across in as friendly a way as possible.[80]

Friendly is a key word here as it signals, albeit obliquely, the type of morality that frames the optimism of the Eden Project. For Aristotle, friendship was the relationship that best summed up the moral life; for 'great friendship', as Fred Inglis points out, 'brings out, we hope, the best in us'[81]. It provides a stage for moral action that all of us can aspire to perform well on; a domestic and intimate stage, not a stern and dutiful one.

If the biomes approach the dimensions of the sublime in their awesome size and in the way they convey the sheer scale of the rainforest, the Eden experience does not aim to overwhelm and avoids this by introducing a sense of lively gaiety and charm—the pleasures of 'the beautiful'—through its playful and ethical uses of art. Among the many examples there are cork sculptures of pigs, a huge, colourfully sculpted bee called 'Bombus' and the simple but beautifully stylised wall paintings of two Peruvian artists, celebrating the inter-relationship between human, animal and plant life. These are positioned so as to complement and inform the visitor's iterative experience, not merely to decorate it. Paul Bonomoni's WEEE man, for example, is a monster, sculptured entirely from discarded electrical goods. Its educational purpose, as Govan et al. comment, is to provoke an 'act of recognition, enabling visitors to see the wastefulness of disposing of refrigerators, computer mice, cookers and other electrical goods'[82]. Its aesthetic and ethical impact, however, comes from its location as a visual intervention, juxtaposing starkly the ugly, unfriendliness of waste with the beauty of nature.

The integration of art and nature at the Eden Project has been greatly influenced by Smit's friendship with Sue Hill of *Kneehigh* Theatre Company, who has contributed a keen sense of theatricality, pace, rhythm and narrative to its overall design. 'We are not a botanic garden with thousands of little plant labels like tombstones all over the place', writes Smit: 'We don't want to bludgeon people into submission with ridiculous amounts of information, nor do we want to tell all the stories at once'[83]. All the guides at Eden undergo performance training; whether they see their roles as explainers or storytellers, the important thing is for them 'to make Eden come to life'[84]. This principle extends to the educational work with school children; Bowker, for example, describes how the children's two hours spent in the biome was framed by a drama activity, in which they were cast in the role of TV researchers. On summer evenings, performances by musicians, storytellers and theatre groups are features of its programme, and these commonly have an educational agenda. Govan et al. describe one such example, an interactive piece of children's theatre, which used the conventions of the fairy tale to examine issues of deforestation.

All in all, then, the educational outcomes of the Eden Project, in both scientific and ethical terms, are planned with aesthetic as well as rational considerations. The experience it provides, according to Govan et al., troubles a number of oppositions—the local and the global, the natural and the artificial, art and science[85]. It brings this chapter full circle, demonstrating in a grand manner the benefits to pedagogy and learning when the two cultures are transcended in the creation of an educational project driven by beauty. We have journeyed a long way from the acrid smells and deep unpleasantness of the science laboratory I experienced as a schoolboy. Of course, Eden is a utopia, a temporary paradise, as its name suggests. But as such, it embodies principles and practices that can inform how science might be approached in the fallen world in which we must all, alas, teach. This is not to imply a programme of deodorising the chemistry lab or rapping through the periodic table, as the cynic might snidely remark. Rather, it is to recognise the implications for students such as myself when deprived of the wonder and the poetry of science through a narrow and restricted pedagogy, stripped of any artistry and devoid of the ethical energies of beauty.

7 Awakening Beauty in Education

The sense of beauty . . . [is] brought into actual existence by the experience of living in the midst of certain sorts of things to look at, listen to, handle, think about, cope with, and react to.[1]

I do not claim to have exhausted the topic of beauty in education, far from it; there remain many specific issues still to be addressed. The beauty of the humanities or of learning a foreign language I have scarcely touched upon, and the complex relationship between creativity and beauty afforded by new technologies I have rather ignored. The non-Western nuances of beauty, such as we find in Eastern traditions, could inform a study with a more multi-cultural emphasis. Nevertheless, I hope to have established some broad arguments to inform future studies of this kind and, in this final chapter, would like to reflect upon how beauty might find expression in the cultural life of schools, as one of the values that should underpin approaches to teaching and learning. I begin from the premise that values should determine structures, not vice versa, and from the leading principle that, if beauty is to find a place in their thinking, teachers need to begin to talk about it, something they are certainly not used to doing. As a concept, however, it is only sleeping, not dead, and can be awoken, brought again into conscious articulation, if we realise its presence in our own histories as learners and in examples drawn from our professional lives.

We can begin by asking ourselves certain simple questions. Have we ever read a beautiful story, heard a beautiful piece of music or verse, listened to a beautiful idea, seen a beautiful piece of drama, witnessed a beautiful act? Would we consider such experiences as valuable to young people? Why? When in our own lives have we been profoundly affected by beauty, and was this ever connected to learning? In what ways? Has a child ever produced a beautiful piece of work for us? How was it beautiful, and why did this matter? Addressing such questions in the context of professional discussion might help us, as teachers, articulate how beauty already has a tacit place in our thinking. Of equal importance is its relevance to our overall professional lives. When have there been particularly beautiful moments in our lives as teachers? Many of us will here recall quiet, unspectacular responses from individual students, moments that help sustain us through the inevitable periods of difficulty, tension, drudgery and conflict. Such moments remind us why teaching can be a beautiful profession, why we became teachers in the first place.

Throughout the book I have implied that beauty as a concept can provide a necessary counter to the utilitarian values that, due to their overwhelming pre-eminence, are in danger of warping children's overall educational experience. Beauty can soften the technical, find a valued place for the mysterious and the uncertain, remind us that the technically excellent is not always that which we value most in the way of human achievement. It introduces a language of pleasure into education, for teachers and learners, seeing value in the sensuous, more immediate rewards of the aesthetic as well as in those that emanate from sterner, more moralistic values, such as duty, hard work and persistence. Beauty's emphasis on experience and holistic achievement rather than skills and technical progression is particularly significant in the education of the emotions. In the technical-rationalist approach that currently dominates curriculum planning, it would seem to make sense to talk of 'emotional literacy' and to devise a programme of skills-based approaches that attempt to determine and measure affective development. But beauty reminds us that emotion and cognition are inseparably bound together, that the one cannot be dislocated from the other and taught separately and that neither can be learned outside of experience. In Charles Taylor's words, 'To experience fear is to experience some object as terrifying or dangerous; to experience shame is to experience some object as shameful or humiliating, and so on'[2]. Experience teaches us what to know as fearful and shameful, and schools have been traditionally very good at teaching children fear and shame, without any call for emotional literacy. Beauty, by way of contrast, can be an uplifting rather than an oppressive source of cognitive-emotional learning; we enthuse, admire and empathise at the same time as we observe, evaluate, attend and respond. And we experience pleasure in the process, as the mystery at the heart of beauty keeps our intellectual and affective energies alive. The learning is never quite exhausted, and, when it is, we cease to find beauty in whatever the experience is, like the eight-year-old boy who replied to his teacher that he thought he ought to learn to read so that he could stop[3]. In being taught reading as if it were merely a technical, purely cognitive process, this boy had at the same time learned an affective response—possibly frightening and shameful, maybe boring and tiresome, certainly unrelated to the pleasures of beauty that reading can and ought to open up for us.

If we value the power of beauty, we will necessarily want to create spaces where students are likely to find it and are given the time to become immersed in it. Sometimes we need to grab the opportunity when it arises. Recently in the UK we had our first heavy snow falls for eighteen years, which meant that many children of school age had never experienced snow before. It was, therefore, no mere sentimental response for teachers to let their children play in it and make it the centre of their curriculum for the day. But we should not rely on serendipity; such spaces need to be planned for consciously, as integral to the curriculum. If field trips are to provide such spaces, teachers need to plan for them as communal, social events that do far more than service the national curriculum. As a young teacher, I was privileged to work with and learn from a colleague who understood this. When we visited Fort la Latte in Brittany, for example, which features in the film *The Vikings*, we did not just walk in through the gates but crept through the grass on our stomachs before playfully (and noisily) assaulting the drawbridge. Week-long field trips to the Dartmoor National Park were planned consciously to celebrate a certain quality of life as integral to the learning experience. Opportunities to sketch and write poetry complemented visits to disused tin mines and studies of soil erosion and granite rock formations. The treks across moors and over tors during the long, June days were followed in the evenings by treasure hunts, drama events, crazy games, midnight feasts and ghost stories told by candlelight. On our return to school, children would use their sketches to paint pictures, and these, together with their writings, would be mounted in beautifully presented displays of work. Sometimes this would be complemented by an evening of drama, storytelling and music for the rest of the school community to share their experiences and celebrate what they had learned. That these memories persist so vividly in my own mind are more than the sentimental musings that come with age; they are, in large part, a lasting testimony to their beauty as teaching and learning experiences.

As with students, so with their teachers; given the opportunity to be immersed in learning experiences such as these, teachers can renew their energies and find new passions through beauty. The Royal Shakespeare Company has been campaigning for some years now to change how Shakespeare is taught in the classroom. As part of their strategy, groups of teachers have been involved in professionally accredited courses, which begin with an intensive weekend in Stratford-upon-Avon. As well as receiving first-class tuition, they are taught inside the same studios where actors have been recently rehearsing the play they are due to watch that evening. They spend time in the theatre, do workshops with some of the company's actors, have opportunities to visit the town of Stratford and walk along the banks of the river Avon. Unsurprisingly, evaluations show that teachers return to their schools and to the teaching of Shakespeare with greatly enhanced interest and enthusiasm and are pedagogically far more effective as a result.[4]

We cannot coerce students into learning through beauty. We cannot force it upon them in the ways that so much of the curriculum is taught; but we can plan to make it more rather than less likely that they will experience its charms. The school environment can assist in this, as modelled by Reggio Emilia, where light, colour, texture, displays of objects, art work and living plants are part of a conscious design to make the school a beautiful place. And there is, too, as we have seen, the aesthetic potential of the individual lesson. It is common place now for teachers to plan for a range of learning activities, to mix direct instruction with group work and to ensure that the pace of activities does not flag. With the internet and interactive white-boards freely available in most classrooms, they have, too, far greater access to striking visual resources than ever before. Yet teachers are still taught to structure their lessons uniformly, according to narrow rules of logic rather than the rich potential of the aesthetic. No matter how they are conceived, lessons are, in essence, performed narratives and, like all narratives, they have a plot as well as a storyline—in other words, a pattern through which information unfolds in ways that can make them more or less interesting. Surprise, suspense, sudden reversals can all serve to deepen interest, as can a variation of pace, tone and rhythm. The lesson, then, is potentially a far more complex narrative than current practices allow for, where focused objectives must be written on the board at the beginning, effectively con-demning children to the same genre of narrative all day, every day, with no mystery, no suspense, no surprises. This, unfortunately, is of a kind with a national curriculum that reduces the key characteristic of stories to the fact that they have a beginning, a middle and an end.

If the lesson is in itself a narrative, so is the whole school day. How much more pleasurable, more human, might the average school day be, for teachers as well as children, if it were planned as something shapely and complete, with an eye to its patterns and its rhythms, its discords and its harmonies, its textures and its colours, as well as the strictures of curricu-lum content? Various rituals exist in schools to signal that the day is about to end—chairs are placed on desks, children stand behind them waiting for the bell to sound, in religious schools a prayer may be recited. I once super-vised a student in a primary school where the day was brought to an end by class teachers reflecting with their children on what they had done together that day, followed by a short story or a song. These activities brought with them a sense of completion rather than mere cessation, offering children pleasures other than those of a temporary escape.

One of the key claims of this book has been that the moral and the aesthetic cannot be so readily separated, as arguments since Kant have tended to assume, and that the concept of the 'beautiful' helps us articulate a set of educational virtues that might otherwise be sidelined. The quali-ties of grace and charm have moral as well as aesthetic connotations and resonate with the virtues we associate with domesticity at its best. It may be too much to expect our teachers to be assessed for such qualities, to demonstrate saintliness on top of everything else, but this was rather Iris Murdoch's point: that we turn to beauty to bring qualities such as these into our lives, to help us find them within ourselves. And given the stress in schools on what we might call the 'productive' virtues such as competitive-ness, persistence, co-operative and autonomous endeavour, as well as the traditionally liberal virtues of honesty, integrity, resilience and tolerance, beauty can remind us of the softer virtues that we need to create a balanced moral environment. It is all very well our teachers being excellent planners, knowledgeable assessors, subtle behaviour managers, efficient dispensers of justice and skilled to an advanced level in any number of ways; but is it really only white, liberal, middle-class parents who would also want to trust their children to the care of teachers who can find it within themselves to be charming, cheerful, lively, compassionate and good hearted?[5] If the school does not value beauty, if it is not—some times at least—a beautiful place to be, then teachers will be less likely to find the genetic background they need for these qualities to flourish within their practice.

Beauty is fragile, and beauty is uncertain; but one of Elaine Scarry's more striking claims is that, when we come across it, beauty can be life saving. We have seen that, for a time at least, this was the case for Billy Caspar as well as for Odysseus, but these were examples drawn from works of fiction. In June 2006, Luiz Eduardo Soares from Brazil spoke movingly about the street children in his country's cities, in particular the many adolescent boys who fall victim to the drug gangs.[6] Adolescence is a time of confusion, he said, when young people do not know who they are, but for these boys, who feel themselves to be socially invisible, it is potentially devastating. When such a boy is offered a gun by a drug trafficker, he finds that he is no longer invisible, that he can cause powerful emotions in others by pointing the gun at them. His existence is thus acknowledged through their gazes of terror and hatred; in belonging to a gang and killing for them, he can construct an identity for himself that paradoxically serves not a hunger for violence but a need to be loved. Soares believes that this is why the arts can be so important for such boys, as they offer a different dynamic for self-assertion, with languages and forms of expression to help them provoke powerful emotions and hence become visible without the need for a gun. When a boy performs a piece of music or dance or drama and is appreciated for it, he notices that he is being noticed, that he is no longer nothing and thus approaches a normal level of humanity. His bold claim was that such acts of creation touch the strategic nerve of a major social problem more so even than economics. For the boys to whom he was referring, beauty could literally be life saving.

Closer to home and to the every-day experiences of most teachers, I was recently talking to a head teacher in charge of bringing a school out of special measures. Mentioning this project of mine, I asked her if she could recall any moments of beauty in her professional life. Hardly pausing, she told me of an eight-year-old boy—let us call him Billy—at the school where she is currently working. Billy has never known his father. His younger brother died when he was a baby, and his mother's current boyfriend is violent and has been known to assault him. When she started her job at the school six months previously, Billy could neither read nor write his own name. Earlier that week, however, he had come to her office and told her that he had reached reading Level 7, proudly tracking the progress he had made over the past few weeks through the chart on the back of the book. This was her beautiful moment, but she could not isolate it from the narrative of her relationship with Billy. His remarkable progress had been achieved through better management of resources and well-targeted learning, of course, and his need to see the improvements he was making had been clearly recognised. But a range of more intimate moments and personal interventions were at the heart of the story she told me. In the early days, Billy would regularly be disruptive, throwing classroom furniture or running off to hide in the school grounds. Noticing that he loved playing with the clixy building bricks, she had spoken firmly with him but had promised that he could choose a new kit for the school at regular intervals if he could manage to control his behaviour. The agreement was made and, whenever a package arrived, he was invited to her office where he could open it and enjoy being the first child to play with it. This process did not have to go on for long. Now his progress is not only its own reward but also at times his comfort. The day before our conversation had been a bad one for Billy but, when brought to her office, he had not run off or been abusive, or even asked to play with the clixy set; instead, he had wanted to do his phonics work. 'I want to do my sounds', he had said, as if he knew that the gentle rhythm of matching symbol to sound and being quietly praised each time would calm him.

Billy's emotional and social life is fragile, as is his progress towards normal patterns of behaviour and learning, and stable, trusting relationships with adults. This was a brief, intimate moment of happiness shared by Billy and the head teacher that symbolised in a small way the promise of a better future for him. It was a very *domestic* moment, domestic as defined by Stanley Cavell: 'an achievement of the everyday, the ordinary, now, here, again, never again'.[7] Its mix of hope and uncertainty is what makes it beautiful, the kind of beauty whose power, as George Eliot reminds us, lies not in any secret of proportion but in the secret of deep, human sympathy that it conveys. This quality above all else, exceptional but unexceptionally human, can make of education a thing of beauty.

Notes

NOTES TO CHAPTER 1: SEEKING BEAUTY IN EDUCATION

1. See, for example, Francois Matarasso, *Use or Ornament? The Social Impact of the Arts*, Stroud, UK: Comedia, (1997); J. Burton, R. Horowitz and H. Abeles, 'Learning in and Through the Arts: Curriculum Implications', *Champions of Change*, (1999), pp.36–46, available online at http://www.aep@ccsso.org (accessed June 2004); J. Catterall, R. Chapleau and J. Iwanaga, 'Involvement in the Arts and Theatre arts', *Champions of Change*, (1999), pp.1–18, available online at http://www.aep@ccsso.org (accessed June 2004); John Holden, *Capturing Cultural Value*, London: Demos, (2004), available online at http://www.demos.co.uk (accessed May 2005) and *Culture and Learning: Towards a New Agenda*, London: Demos, (2008).
2. John Holden, op. cit., p.23.
3. This was the first in a series of 'Quality of Life' debates organised by the National Trust, UK. It took place on 19 March 2009 and was reported in *The Observer*, 22 March 2009, pp.28–29.
4. See Richard Layard and Judy Dunn, *A Good Childhood: Searching for Values in a Competitive Age*, London: Penguin, (2009), p.59.
5. Euripides, *Orestes*, lines 126–127, cited in Anthony Synnott, *The Body Social: Symbolism, Self and Society*, London: Routledge, (1993), p.79.
6. Naomi Wolf, *The Beauty Myth*, Toronto: Random House, (1990).
7. Pierre Bourdieu, *Distinction: A Social Critique of the Judgment of Taste*, translated by R. Nice, London: Routledge and Kegan Paul, (1984).
8. See John Willett (ed.), *Brecht on Theatre*, London: Eyre Methuen, (1964).
9. Germaine Greer, 'Our Spirits Rose because We Had a Visitation of Spring', *The Observer*, 22 March 2009, p.29.
10. R. G. Collingwood, *Principles of Art*, Oxford: Oxford University Press, (1958), p.40. First published in 1938 by Clarendon Press.
11. In Sappho, *Fragment 16*; she writes, 'I say it (beauty) is what you love'. I have taken this from one of the opening references in Alexander Nehamas, *Only a Promise of Happiness: The Place of Beauty in a World of Art*, Princeton, NJ: Princeton University Press, (2007).
12. See, for example, Elaine Scarry, *On Beauty and Being Just*, London: Duckworth, (2001); Denis Donoghue, *Speaking of Beauty*, New Haven and London: Yale University Press, (2003); and, from a different perspective, Michael Bérubé (ed.), *The Aesthetics of Cultural Studies*, Oxford: Blackwell Publishing, (2005).
13. Janet Wolff, *The Aesthetics of Uncertainty*, New York: Columbia University Press, (2008), p.29.
14. Ibid., p.25.

15. Germaine Greer, op. cit., p.29.
16. Charles Leadbeater, *Personalisation through Participation*, London: Demos, (2003); and *The Shape of Things to Come: Personalised Learning through Collaboration*, London: DfES, (2005).
17. See, for example: R. J. Campbell, W. Robinson, J. Neelands, R. Hewston and L. Mazzoli, 'Personalised Learning: Ambiguities in Theory and Practice', *British Journal of Educational Studies*, vol.5, no.2, (2007), pp.135–154; David Hartley, 'Personalisation: The Emerging "Revised" Code of Education?' *Oxford Review of Education*, vol.33, no.5, (2007), pp.629–642; and A. Pollard and M. James (eds.), *Personalised Learning, a Commentary by the Teaching and Learning Research Programme*, London: Economic and Social Research Council, (2004).
18. David Hargreaves, *Personalising Learning: Next Steps in Working Laterally*, London: Specialists Schools Trust, (2004); and *Deep Leadership: A New Shape for Schooling?* London: Specialist Schools and Academies Trust, (2006).
19. David Hargreaves, op. cit., (2006), p.6.
20. Ibid.
21. This tendency extends beyond Hargreaves. Note how the title of Leadbeater's 2005 paper—*The Shape of Things to Come*—consciously echoes the famous story by H. G. Wells and Alexander Corda's film of the same name. Once again there is irony, however, as the tale was fictional and its predictions wide of the mark.
22. Winifred Nowottny, *The Language Poets Use*, Oxford: Oxford University Press, (1962).
23. Peter Humphries, 'Towards a Personalised Educational Landscape', 2006, http://www.futurelab.org.uk/resources/publications_reports_articles/web_articles/Web_article479 (accessed March 2008).
24. Walter Nash, *Jargon: Its Uses and Abuses*, Oxford: Blackwell, (1993), p.6.
25. Robert Hughes, *The Shock of the New*, London: BBC, (1980), p.366.
26. For an extensive discussion of values, tradition and social practices, see Alasdair McIntyre, *After Virtue: A Study in Moral Theory*, London: Duckworth, (1987), Chapter 15.
27. R. J. Campbell et al., op. cit., p.141.
28. Clifford Geertz, 'Art as a Cultural System', in *Local Knowledge: Further Essays in Interpretive Anthropology*, New York: Basic Books, (1983), p.120.
29. The speech was entitled *Drama and Beauty: Inspiring the desire to learn* and was delivered at the triennial world conference of the International Drama and Theatre Education Association in Hong Kong in July 2007.

NOTES TO CHAPTER 2: THE MEANINGS OF BEAUTY: A BRIEF HISTORY

1. Crispin Sartwell, *Six Names of Beauty*, New York: Routledge, (2004)
2. Paul Kristeller, 'Introduction: Classic Sources', in Steven M. Cahn and Aaron Meskin (eds.), *Aesthetics: A Comprehensive Anthology*, Oxford: Blackwell, (2008), p.4.
3. Cited in J. J O'Connor and E. F Robertson, *Plato*, School of Mathematics and Statistics, University of St Andrews, Scotland, 2003, www-gap.dcs.st-and.ac.uk (accessed March 2008).
4. Quoted in 'The Golden Section of Greek Art', http://milan.milanovic.org/math (accessed 24 April 2008).

5. Alexander Nehamas, *Only a Promise of Happiness: Beauty in a World of Art*, Princeton, NJ: Princeton University Press, (2007), p.2.
6. From Plato's *Symposium*, translated by Alexander Nehamas and Paul Woodruff, Indianapolis, IN / Cambridge: Hackett publishing, (1989), pp. 45–60. This section also appears in Cahn and Meskin, op. cit., pp.34–40.
7. Ibid., p.39.
8. Alexander Nehamas, op. cit., p.7.
9. Plotinus, *Ennead 1, vi*, translated by John Dillon and Lloyd P. Gerson and included in Cahn and Meskin, op. cit., pp.57–63. This quote is taken from p.60
10. George Eliot, *Middlemarch*, London: Penguin Classics, (1994), p.13.
11. John Armstrong, *The Secret Power of Beauty*, London: Penguin, (2005), p.72
12. Ibid., p.72
13. This analysis is greatly influenced by Chapter 9 of Edgar Wind's *Pagan Mysteries in the Renaissance*, London: Faber and Faber, (1968).
14. Plotinus, in Cahn and Meskin, op. cit., p.60.
15. Alexander Nehamas, op. cit., p.24.
16. John Armstrong, *The Intimate Philosophy of Art*, Harmondsworth: Penguin, (2000), p.144.
17. Immanuel Kant, *Critique of Judgment*, originally published in 1790. This translation is by Werner S. Pluhar, Indianapolis, IN / Cambridge: Hackett Publishing, (1987), p.52.
18. Arthur Schopenhauer, *The World as Will and Representation*, translated by R. B. Haldane and J. Kemp in 1883. This quote is taken from Cahn and Meskin, op. cit., p.207.
19. Kant, op. cit., p.173.
20. Alexander Nehamas, op. cit., p.4.
21. From Charles Baudelaire, *Les Fleurs du Mal et autres poèmes*, Paris: Garnier Flammarion, (1964), p.52.
22. William Gaunt, *The Aesthetic Adventure*, London: Jonathan Cape, (1975), p.14.
23. Walter Pater, *The Renaissance: Studies in Art and Poetry*, Oxford: Oxford University Press, (1986). First published in 1877.
24. Cited in William Gaunt, op. cit., p.56.
25. Ibid., p.56.
26. This is Pater as portrayed in the character of Mr Rose in W. H. Mallock's *The New Republic*, published in 1877.
27. William Gaunt, op. cit., p.61.
28. Oscar Wilde, *The Picture of Dorian Gray*, Harmondsworth: Penguin, (1979), p.5.
29. Wilde, of course, was a complex character, a socialist as well as a dandy, and *Dorian Gray* is hardly an amoral book in the manner of Huysman's *A Rebours*, the classic novel of Aestheticism.
30. John Armstrong, op. cit., (2005), pp.59–61.
31. Reported in *The Daily Telegraph*, 14 May 2007, p.7.
32. Mary Devereux, 'Beauty and Evil: The Case of Leni Riefenstahl's Triumph of the Will', in J. Levinson (ed.), *Aesthetics and Ethics: Essays at the Intersection*, Cambridge: Cambridge University Press, (1998), pp.205–223.
33. Philip Alperson and Noel Carroll, 'Music, Mind and Morality: Arousing the Body Politic', *Journal of Aesthetic Education*, vol.42, no.1, (2008), pp.1–15, p.4.
34. Ronald Paulson in the preface to William Hogarth's *The Analysis of Beauty*, New Haven, CT / London: Yale University Press, (1997), p.xxiii.

35. Amelia Jones, '"Every man knows where and how beauty gives him pleasure": Beauty Discourse and the Logic of Aesthetics', in E. Elliott, L. Freitas Caton and J. Rhyne (eds.), *Aesthetics in a Multicultural Age*, Oxford: Oxford University Press, (2002), pp.215–239, p.220.
36. Alexander Nehamas, op. cit., (2007), p.10.
37. Clifford Geertz, 'Art as a Cultural System', in *Local Knowledge: Further Essays in Interpretive Anthropology*, New York: Basic Books, (1983), p.98.
38. Alexander Nehamas, op. cit., (2007), p.44.
39. Steve Strand (University of Warwick), *Attitude to Shakespeare among Y10 Students: Report to the Royal Shakespeare Company on the Learning and Performance Network Baseline survey 2007/08*.
40. Rob Pope, *Creativity: Theory, History, Practice*, London: Routledge, (2005), p.119.
41. John Armstrong, op. cit., (2000), p.148.
42. Austin Harrington, *Art and Social Theory: Sociological Arguments in Aesthetics*, Cambridge: Polity Press, (2004), p.101.
43. See Christopher Ricks, *Dylan's Visions of Sin*, New York: Harper Collins, (2003).
44. David Shumway, 'Cultural Studies and Questions of Pleasure and Value', in Michael Bérubé (ed.), *The Aesthetics of Cultural Studies*, Oxford: Blackwell, (2005), pp.103–116, p.110.
45. Elaine Scarry, *On Beauty and Being Just*, London: Duckworth, (2001), p.83.
46. Ibid., p.84.
47. From 'Auguries of Innocence' in *The Selected Poems of William Blake*, Ware Herts: Wordsworth Press, (1994), p.135.
48. John Ruskin, *Collected Writings*, vol.3, p.130; cited in Denis Donoghue, *Speaking of Beauty*, New Haven, CT / London: Yale University Press, (2003), p.159.
49. From William Butler Yeats, 'Easter 1916', in *W.B Yeats Selected Poems*, London: Penguin, (2000), p.119.
50. Robert Hughes, *The Shock of the New*, London: British Broadcasting Association, (1980), p.15.
51. 'One evening I sat Beauty on my knee—and I found her bitter—and I abused her.' Arthur Rimbaud, *Poésies complètes*, edited by Pascal Pia, Paris: Gallimard Livre de Poche, (1963), p.107.
52. These quotes are taken from Marinetti's 'Futurist Manifesto' (1909) and 'Pride in Ugliness' (1912) in Umberto Eco *On Ugliness*, London: Harvill Secker, (2007), p.370.
53. The quote is from Tony Pinkney's introduction to Raymond Williams *Politics of Modernism*, London: Verso Radical Thinkers series, (2007), p.19.
54. Georges Bataille, *Eroticism*, translated by Mary Dalwood, London: Boyars, (1987), p.143.
55. Crispin Sartwell, op. cit., (2004), p.16.
56. T. S. Eliot, 'The Metaphysical Poets', *Times Literary Supplement*, 20 October 1921, p.670; cited in Alexander Nehamas, op. cit., (2007), p.34.
57. T. S. Eliot, 'The Waste Land', in *Selected Poems*, London: Faber and Faber, (1961), p.61.
58. Cited in Arthur Danto, *The Abuse of Beauty: Aesthetics and the Concept of Art*, Chicago / La Salle, IL: Open Court, (2003), p.145.
59. Wendy Steiner, *The Trouble with Beauty*, London: Heinemann, (2001), p.xvi.
60. Ibid., p.xxi.
61. Ibid., p.xxi.

62. Ibid., p.xxiii.
63. Ibid., p.6.
64. Ibid., p.236.
65. Many of these have been core sources for this book and have been already cited. Apart from Steiner, see Scarry (2001), Danto (2003), Eco (2004), Armstrong (2005), Nehamas (2007), Woolf (2008).
66. T. J. Clark, *Farewell to an Idea: Episodes from a History of Modernism*, New Haven, CT / London: Yale University Press, (1999), p. 2–3.
67. Ibid., p.7.
68. Fred Inglis, *Culture*, Cambridge: Polity Press, (2004), p.52.
69. Crispin Sartwell, op. cit., (2004), p.16.
70. Frederic Jameson, *Signatures of the Visible*, London: Routledge, (1990), p.1; cited in Denis Donoghue, op. cit., (2003), p.85.
71. Umberto Eco, op. cit., (2007), p.396.
72. Herman Broch, *Kitsch*, (1933), cited in Eco, op. cit., p.403.
73. Fred Inglis, op. cit., (2004), pp.55–56.
74. Ibid., p.52.
75. This full-page feature on Claxton was published in the *Times Educational Supplement*, 1 August 2008, p.17.
76. Guy Claxton, *Building Learning Power*, Bristol: TLO Ltd, (2005), pp.9–11. All quotes in this summary are taken from these three pages. 'Building Learning Power' (BLP) has been adopted as a strategy by several local authorities in England and is timetabled as a discrete subject in some schools. Latest publications as I write include *Infusing BLP into KS2 core subjects* and two BLP activity banks aimed at children aged four to six years old. Interestingly, authors are not named on the publicity—it's the movement that counts. See www.buildinglearningpower.co.uk.
77. Ibid., p.63.
78. One of the new publications, aimed at very young pupils, is titled *Learning Power Heroes* and features on the cover a fair-haired boy of about five years old, dressed in a superhero costume flexing his muscles, arms raised in the air in triumph.
79. Denis Donoghue, op. cit., (2003), p.86.

NOTES TO CHAPTER 3: BEAUTY AS EDUCATIONAL EXPERIENCE

1. William Butler Yeats, 'Vacillation', in *W.B. Yeats Selected Poems*, Harmondsworth: Penguin, p.176, lines 42–44.
2. John Armstrong, *The Secret Power of Beauty*, Harmondsworth: Penguin, (2005), p.136.
3. From the Greek word *epipheneion* meaning 'to manifest', the term was first given its modern, secular meaning by James Joyce who used it to describe moments in our lives which are sudden and dramatic, with heightened significance.
4. At a keynote to teachers of English, organised by Warwickshire Educational Development Service in 1999.
5. In R. G. Collingwood, *An Autobiography*, Oxford: Oxford University Press, (1939), pp.3–4.
6. This is taken from the short author's note, written in 1958, that precedes each of the novels in the *Swallowdale* series, London: Puffin Books, (1962).
7. Robert Gibson, *The Land without a Name: Alain-Fournier and His World*, London: Elek, (1975), p.34.

8. John Ruskin, 'The Two Boyhoods', in *Modern Painters*, vol.5, cited in John Armstrong, *The Intimate Philosophy of Art*, London: Penguin, (2000), p.37.
9. John Armstrong, op. cit., (2000), p.37.
10. Michael Oakeshott, *Experience and Its Modes*, London: Cambridge University Press, (1978), p.19. First published in 1933.
11. Ibid., p.27.
12. Ibid., p.54.
13. Ibid., pp.40–41.
14. Ibid., p.41.
15. Elaine Scarry, *On Beauty and Being Just*, London: Duckworth, (2001), p.22.
16. Hans-Georg Gadamer, *Truth and Method*, London: Continuum, (2004), p.58.
17. Ibid., p.61.
18. Elaine Scarry, op. cit., p. 24.
19. Hans-Georg Gadamer, op. cit., p.58.
20. John Dewey, *Art as Experience*, New York: Perigree Books, (2005), p.42. First published in 1934.
21. Ibid., Chapter 3, 'Having an Experience'.
22. See Donald Schon, *Educating the Reflective Practitioner: Toward a new design for Teaching and Learning in the Profession*, San Francisco: Jossey Bass, (1987). See Chapter 1, in particular.
23. Michael Oakeshott, op. cit., p.259.
24. Ibid., p.290.
25. Ibid., p.261.
26. R. G. Collingwood, *Principles of Art*, Oxford: Oxford University Press, (1958), pp.115–117.
27. Richard Sennett, *The Craftsman*, London: Allen Lane, (2008), p.28.
28. John Milton, *Paradise Lost*, London: Penguin Classics, (2000), Book 9, lines 469–470, p.197.
29. Kathleen Gallagher, *The Theatre of Urban: Youth and Schooling in Dangerous Times*, Toronto: University of Toronto Press, (2007), p.92.
30. Ibid., p.95.
31. Iris Murdoch, 'The Sovereignty of Good over Other Concepts', in *The Sovereignty of Good*, London: Routledge, (1991), pp.84–85. First published 1970.
32. Ibid., p.84.
33. John Carey, *What Good Are the Arts?* London: Faber and Faber, (2005), p.42.
34. Michael Apple, *Official Knowledge: Democratic Education in a Conservative Age*, 2nd ed., New York: Routledge, (2000).
35. Ibid., Chapter 3, pp.42–60.
36. Alexander Nehamas, *Only a Promise of Happiness: The Place of Beauty in a World of Art*, Princeton, NJ: Princeton University Press, (2007), p.57.
37. This argument is not unlike the one made by Germaine Greer on behalf of women in her book *The Boy*, London: Thames and Hudson, (2003).
38. John Berger, 'The Field', in *About Looking*, London: Writers and Readers Publishing Co-operative, (1980), pp.197–198.
39. This definition is taken from Fred Inglis, *Popular Culture and Political Power*, London: Harvester, (1988), p.78.
40. Keats defined his theory of negative capability in his letter to George and Thomas Keats in 1817.

41. Piet Mondrian's painting *The Red Tree* is exhibited at the Haags Gee-mensmuseum, the Hague. Sean Tan's picture book *The Red Tree* is published by Simply Read, Vancouver (2003).
42. Elaine Scarry, op. cit., p.6.
43. John Ruskin, *The Stones of Venice*, London: Faber, (1981). First published in 1853. This edition edited and introduced by Jan Morris.
44. John Ruskin, 'The Nature of Gothic', from *The Stones of Venice*, vol.2, *Selected Writings*, Oxford: Oxford University Press, (2004), p.41.
45. Ibid., p.49.
46. Richard Sennett, *The Craftsman*, London: Allen Lane, (2008), p.116.
47. In the Channel 4 series *This Is Civilisation*, broadcast on 8 December 2007.
48. R. G. Collingwood, op. cit., (1958), p.111.
49. For an examination of this tendency, see David Hartley, 'The Instrumentali-sation of the Expressive in Education', *British Journal of Educational Studies*, vol.51, no.1, (2003), pp.6–19.
50. Germaine Greer, 'Our Spirits Rose because We Had a Visitation of Spring', *The Observer*, 22 March 2009, p.29.
51. Crispin Sartwell, *Six Names of Beauty*, New York: Routledge, (2004), p.150.
52. Barry Hines, *A Kestrel for a Knave*, Harmondsworth: Penguin, (1969).
53. Elaine Scarry, op. cit., p.21.
54. Ibid., p.22.
55. Ibid., p.24.
56. Ibid., p.8.
57. Alan Bennett, *The History Boys*, London: Faber and Faber, (2004), p.48.
58. Ibid., p.38.
59. Ibid., p.48.
60. Ibid., p.67.
61. See Alasdair MacIntyre, *After Virtue: A Study in Moral theory*, London: Duckworth, (1985), Chapter 8 for a critique of contemporary management theory.
62. Alan Bennett, op. cit., p.55.
63. Ibid., p.56.
64. I take this metaphor of conversation from Michael Oakeshott's essay 'The Voice of Poetry in the Conversation of Mankind', in *Rationalism in Politics and Other Essays*, London: Methuen, (1962), and from Alasdair MacIntyre, op. cit., pp.210–211.
65. Alan Bennett, op. cit., p.108.
66. Ibid., p.109.
67. In an interview with Melvyn Bragg on *The South Bank Show*, screened in the UK on the Sky Arts Channel in February 2008.

NOTES TO CHAPTER 4: BEAUTY, EDUCATION AND THE GOOD SOCIETY

1. From George Eliot *Adam Bede*, London: Penguin Classics, (2008), p.196.
2. Iris Murdoch, 'The Sovereignty of Good over Other Concepts', in *The Sovereignty of Good*, London: Routledge, (1991), p.83.
3. Ibid., p.83.
4. Ibid., p.83.
5. Ibid., p.86.

6. Annette Baier, *Moral Prejudice: Essays on Ethics*, Cambridge, MA: Harvard University Press, (1994); Nancy Chodorow, *The Reproduction of Mothering*, Berkeley: University of California Press, (1978); Martha Nussbaum, *Love's Knowledge*, Oxford: Oxford University Press, (1990); Martha Nussbaum, *Upheavals of Thought: The Intelligence of the Emotions*, Cambridge: Cambridge University Press, (2001).
7. Carol Gilligan, *In a Different Voice: Psychological Theory and Women's Development*, Cambridge, MA: Harvard University Press, (1982).
8. Lawrence Kohlberg, *The Philosophy of Moral Development: Moral Stages and the Idea of Justice*, New York: HarperCollins, (1981); John Rawls, *A Theory of Justice*, Cambridge, MA: Harvard University Press, (1971).
9. Annette Baier, op. cit., p.32.
10. Wendy Steiner, *The Trouble with Beauty*, London: Heinemann, (2001), p.6.
11. Ibid., p.xxiii.
12. Francis Hodgson Burnett, *The Secret Garden*, London: Wordsworth Classics, (1993), pp.210–211.
13. Michelle Magorian, *Goodnight Mr Tom*, London: Kestrel, (1981).
14. Fred Inglis, *The Promise of Happiness: Value and Meaning in Children's Fiction*, Cambridge: Cambridge University Press, (1982), p.112.
15. There are many published versions of this tale. My personal favourite is a picture book version, illustrated by S. Saelig Gallagher and published by Hove, East Sussex: Macdonald Young Books, (1995).
16. See Jarlath Killeen, *The Tales of Oscar Wilde*, Bristol: Ashgate, (2007), pp.61–78.
17. Oscar Wilde, 'The Soul of Man under Socialism', in *Selected Essays and Poems*, London: Penguin, (1954), p.27.
18. I heard him tell this story in an address given to teachers in Exeter, UK, in October 2003.
19. Jarlath Killeen, op. cit., p.61.
20. Gordon Lidstone, 'Education and the Arts: Evaluating Arts Education Programmes', in John Cowling (ed.), *For Art's Sake?* London: Institute for Public Policy Research, (2004), p.42.
21. Ibid., p.51.
22. Ibid., p.58.
23. Alasdair MacIntyre, *After Virtue: A Study in Moral Theory*, London: Duckworth, (1985), p.29.
24. *Sure Start* is the name of the UK's Labour government initiative that brought different educational, welfare and social agencies together in identified areas of social deprivation to improve the life chances of very young children.
25. Iris Murdoch, op. cit., p.6.
26. Wendy Steiner, op. cit., p.26. See also Adorno's commentary on the power of ornament in *Minima Moralia*, London: Verso, (2005), p.224. Like Steiner, he identified the lingering aftermath of magic and charm in our relationship to beauty but also saw it as a positive force for good.
27. Terry Eagleton, *The Ideology of the Aesthetic*, Oxford: Blackwell, (1990), p.38.
28. For a full discussion of *orexis* see Martha Nussbaum, *The Fragility of Goodness: Luck and Ethics in Greek Tragedy and Philosophy*, Cambridge: Cambridge University Press, (1986), pp. 273–280.
29. Elaine Scarry, *On Beauty and Being Just*, London: Duckworth, (2001), p.47.
30. Ibid., p.90.
31. Wendy Steiner, op. cit., p.xix.
32. Elaine Scarry, op. cit., p.92.
33. Theodor Adorno, op. cit., p.224.
34. Fred Inglis, op. cit., (1982), p.111.

35. Oscar Wilde, op. cit., (1954), p.34.
36. Walter Lippmann, *The Good Society*, London: Allen and Unwin, (1937); cited in Anthony Arblaster and Steven Lukes (eds.), *The Good Society: A Book of Readings*, London: Methuen, (1971), p.342.
37. Oliver Bennett, *Cultural Pessimism: Narratives of Decline in the Post-modern World*, Edinburgh: Edinburgh University Press, (2001), p.181.
38. Zygmunt Bauman, *Socialism: The Active Utopia*, London: George Allen and Unwin, (1976); cited in David Halpin, *Hope and Education: The Role of the Utopian Imagination*, London: RoutledgeFalmer, (2003), p.31.
39. Friedrich Schiller, *On the Aesthetic Education of Man, in a Series of Letters*, edited and translated by Elizabeth M. Wilkinson and L. A Willoughby, Oxford: Clarendon Press, (1967), p.xv.
40. John Armstrong, *The Intimate Philosophy of Art*, Harmondsworth: Penguin, (2000), p.163.
41. John Armstrong, *The Secret Power of Beauty*, Harmondsworth: Penguin, (2005), p.83.
42. Friedrich Schiller, op. cit., p.217.
43. Elaine Scarry, op. cit., pp. 106–107; John Berger, *A Painter of Our Time*, Harmondsworth: Penguin, (1965).
44. John Berger, op. cit., p.96
45. See the quote from 'The Field', for full reference, note 38 in the last chapter.
46. I am using the word 'football' as the term used in the UK for soccer.
47. All the quotes here are taken from John Berger, op. cit., p.122.
48. Alasdair MacIntyre, op. cit., pp.188–194.
49. Peter Arnold, 'Sport and Moral Education', in *The Journal of Moral Education*, vol.23, no.1, (1994), p.85.
50. In Berger's novel, op. cit., p.22, Lavin comments, 'Capitalism has finally destroyed the traditions of art it once inherited or created'. The words resound somewhat prophetically with regard to the effects of globalised capitalism on the UK's Football Premier League.
51. Peter Arnold, op. cit., p.80.
52. Alasdair MacIntyre, op. cit., p.187.
53. See, for example, David L. L. Sheilds and Brenda J. L. Bredemeier, *Character Development and Physical Activity*, Champaign, IL: Human Kinetics Publishers, (1995) who point to the central importance of the teacher or coach in influencing the socio-moral behaviour in the young players in their charge. Carwyn Jones emphasises the importance of the context and the character of the teacher if children are to learn virtuous behaviour in sport in 'Teaching Virtue through Physical Education: Some Comments and Reflections', *Sport, Education and Society*, vol.13, no.3, (August 2008). Jarvis, in observing boys in the early years playing soccer at lunchtime in the school playground, noted the complexity of social development that it inspired, including the creation and development of rules, the mediation of fair play and also the care shown for those who were injured See Pam Jarvis, 'Monsters, Magic and Mr Psycho: A Biocultural Approach to Rough and Tumble Play in the Early Years of Primary School', *Early Years*, vol.27, no.2, (July 2007).
54. Richard Sennett, *The Craftsman*, London: Allen Lane, (2008), p.272.
55. Ibid., p.270.
56. Julian Bell 'Back to Basics: The Craftsman by Richard Sennett', in *The New York Review of Books*, vol.55, no.16, (23 October 2008), p.29.
57. Richard Sennett, op. cit., p.277.
58. This is exemplified in his story of the journey of critical understanding inspired by his love for Manet's 'Olympia'. See Alexander Nehamas, *Only a Promise of Happiness: The Place of Beauty in a World of Art*, Princeton, NJ: Princeton University Press, (2007), pp.105–120.

59. Julian Bell, op. cit., p.30.
60. The phrase is taken from Michael Kimmelman. See his *The Accidental Master-piece: On the Art of Life and Vice Versa*, New York: Penguin, (2005), p.32.
61. W. B. Yeats, 'Among School Children' in *The Collected Poems of W.B. Yeats*, Princetion: Scribner (1996).
62. John Varley, *The Persistence of Vision*, New York: Dial Press, (1978); referenced in Lennard J. Davis, *Enforcing Normalcy: Disability, Deafness and the Body*, London: Verso, (1995), p.22.
63. Lennard J. Davis, op. cit., p.35.
64. Quetelet, cited in Lennard J. Davis, op. cit., p.27.
65. Michael Kimmelman, op. cit., p.55.
66. Ibid., p.55.
67. Lennard J. Davis, op. cit., p.149.
68. Ibid., p.149.
69. Interestingly, Alison Lapper also exhibited a photograph of herself as Venus de Milo as a more ironic but similarly political statement. In an interview with the *Disability Arts in London Magazine* in 2007 she said, 'I wanted to recreate this because it's such a classic image. It was quite a tongue in cheek kind of thing for a disabled person to put herself up as the Venus de Milo because she is looked upon as being the most beautiful sculpture, and because her arms fell off she's kind of allowed to be disabled. Nobody ever says at all that she is disabled, but they look at me and say "oh she's disabled!". Where's the difference? I have no arms either. I'm more beautiful than she is because I'm alive, I'm living flesh and blood. But I'm labelled something else. Why? So really it was to challenge people's perceptions of the Venus de Milo. And it did. It was ten years ago now and still people remember'.
70. For an interview with Bill Shannon, see http://www.villagevoice.com/ issues/0302/mattingly.php (accessed June 2004).
71. Petra Kuppers, *Disability and Contemporary Performance: Bodies on Edge*, London: Routledge, (2003), p.62.
72. The programme was entitled *Dancers and Their Bodies* and was broadcast by the BBC in 2003.
73. Dani Kasrel, *Crutchmaster Bill Shannon: The Art of Weightlessness*, (1999), http://www.citypaper.net/articles/111199/ae.dance.crutch.shtml (accessed June 2004).
74. Ibid.
75. Elaine Scarry, op. cit., p.66.
76. Ibid., p.66.
77. Ibid., p.67.
78. Alexander Nehamas, op. cit., p.127.
79. Ibid., p.127.
80. For a passionate account of how this can be realised, see Sally Mackey, 'Emotion and Cognition in Arts Education', *Curriculum Studies*, vol.1, no.2, (1993).
81. I am grateful to Colette Conroy of Royal Holloway, University of London, for this observation.

NOTES TO CHAPTER 5: BEAUTY AND CREATIVITY: EXAMPLES FROM AN ARTS CURRICULUM

1. William Morris, *Political Writings of William Morris*, edited by A. L.Morton, London: Lawrence and Wishart, (1979), p.121.

2. John Ruskin, *Selected Writings*, edited by Dinah Birch, Oxford: Oxford University Press, (2004), p.42.
3. Ibid., p.53.
4. In an episode of the Channel 4 series *This Is Civilisation*, broadcast on 8 December 2007
5. Ibid.
6. William Morris, op. cit., p.91. I trust that we can readily agree to substitute 'human' for 'man' here, as doubtlessly would Morris himself if he were writing today.
7. John Armstrong, *The Secret Power of Beauty*, London: Penguin, (2005), p.161.
8. NACCCE, *All Our Futures: Creativity, Culture and Education*, London: Department for Education and Employment, (1999), p.29.
9. S. Banaji, A. Burn and D. Buckingham, *The Rhetorics of Creativity: A Review of the Literature. A Report for Creative Partnerships*, London: Arts Council England, (2006).
10. See Raymond Williams, *Keywords: A Vocabulary of Culture and Society*, London: Fontana, (1983), p.82.
11. See John Hope Mason, *The Value of Creativity: The Origins and Emergence of an Idea*, Hampshire: Ashgate, (2003).
12. For a succinct examination of these, see Jonothan Neelands and Boyun Choe, 'The English Model of Creativity: Cultural Politics of an Idea', *International Journal of Cultural Policy*, vol.15, no.3, (2009).
13. Wendy Steiner, *The Trouble with Beauty*, London: Heinemann, (2001), p.13.
14. John Hope Mason, op. cit., p.4.
15. Peter Conrad, *Creation: Artists, Gods and Origins*, London: Thames and Hudson, (2007), p.582.
16. John Hope Mason, op. cit., p.236.
17. In a keynote delivered to National Drama, UK, at Durham in April 2008.
18. *Creativity Research Journal*, vol.20, no.2, (April–June 2008).
19. Anna Craft, 'Fostering Creativity with Wisdom', *Cambridge Journal of Education*, vol.36, no.3, (September 2006).
20. Jenny Frost, *Creativity in Primary Science*, Buckingham: Open University Press, (1996). Note also the glib comment from D. P Newton and L. D Newton: 'It is of course possible for children to be creative in other ways in a science lesson. They may, for instance, create a poem or a painting to express their feelings about what people are doing to their world'. See 'Some Student Teachers' Conceptions of Creativity in Science', *Research in Science and Technology Education*, vol.27, no.1, (April 2009), p.48.
21. Michael Fleming, *Arts in Education and Creativity: A Review of the Literature. A Report for Creative Partnerships*, London: Arts Council England, (2008), p.25.
22. This was something I observed on my visits to schools during this project.
23. Iona Opie, *New Yorker*, 7 November 1988; cited in John Hope Mason, op. cit., p.231.
24. Richard Shusterman, *Performing Live: Aesthetic Alternatives for the Ends of Art*, Ithaca, NY: Cornell University Press, (2000), p.5.
25. See Michael Morpurgo and Christina Balit, *Blodin the Beast*, London: Frances Lincoln, (1995). For details of this project, see Joe Winston, *Drama and English at the Heart of the Curriculum*, London: David Fulton Press, (2004).
26. Kit Wright, *Cat among the Pigeons*, London: Viking, (1987).
27. K. Negus and M. Pickering, *Creativity, Communication and Cultural Value*, London / Thousand Oaks, CA / New Delhi: SAGE, (2004), p.68.

28. Ron Carter, *Language and Creativity: The Art of Common Talk*, London: Routledge, (2004), pp.18–21.
29. Friedrich Schiller, *On the Aesthetic Education of Man, in a Series of Letters*, edited and translated by Elizabeth M. Wilkinson and L. A Willoughby, Oxford: Clarendon Press, (1967), p.cxciii.
30. William Morris, op. cit., p.41.
31. Elaine Scarry, *On Beauty and Being Just*, London: Duckworth, (2001), p.4.
32. Ibid., p.8.
33. This arose, in England, during the famous quarrel between the Ancients and Moderns. See Noel Carroll's 'Art, Creativity and Tradition', in Berys Gaut and Paisley Livingston (eds.), *The Creation of Art: New Essays in Philosophical Aesthetics*, Cambridge: Cambridge University Press, (2003), pp.209–210.
34. As well as the previous definition provided by the NACCCE report, Berys Gaut suggests that '[o]riginality, value and flair are the vital ingredients to creative making'. Margaret Boden suggests that 'creativity is the ability to come up with ideas that are new, surprising and valuable', whereas John Hope Mason defines it as 'to act in the world, or on the world, in a new and significant way'. See Berys Gaut, 'Creativity and Imagination' in Gaut and Livingston (eds.), op. cit., p.151; Margaret Boden, *The Creative Mind: Myths and Mechanisms*, London: Wiedenfeld and Nicolson, (1990), p.1; John Hope Mason, op. cit., p.7.
35. Noel Carroll, op. cit., p.211.
36. Ibid.
37. Ibid., p.218.
38. Susan Fraser and Carol Gestwicki, *Authentic Childhood: Exploring Reggio Emilia in the Classroom*, New York: Delmar, (2002), p.221.
39. Ibid., p.217.
40. Ibid., p.220.
41. See, for example, the numerous examples in C. Edwards, L. Gandini and G. Forman, *The Hundred Languages of Children: the Reggio Emilia Approach—Advanced Reflections*, London, JAI Press, (1998).
42. Raymond Williams, *The Long Revolution*, Harmondsworth: Pelican, (1965), p.34.
43. Ibid., p.46.
44. Ibid., p.42.
45. Noel Carroll, op. cit., p.216.
46. To appreciate this painting and the later analysis, it needs to be seen in colour. This can be done by accessing the following Web site: http://www2.warwick.ac.uk/fac/soc/wie/staff/teaching-research/joe_winston/beauty_and_education.
47. Mihaly Csikszentmihaly, *Creativity: Flow and the Psychology of Discovery and Invention*, New York: Harper Collins, (1997), p.347.
48. Cropley in Mark Runco (ed.), *The Creativity Research Handbook*, vol. 1, Cresskill, NJ: Hampton Press, (1997), p.98.
49. Ibid., p.93.
50. I am particularly influenced by Alasdair MacIntyre's definition of a conversation as a dramatic work 'in which the participants are not only the actors but also the joint authors, working out in agreement or disagreement the mode of their production'. See *After Virtue: A Study in Moral Theory*, London: Duckworth, (1987), p.211. For the analogous relationship between conversation and tradition, see also Michael Oakeshott's 'The Voice of Poetry and the Conversation of Mankind', in *Rationalism in Politics and Other Essays*, London: Methuen, (1962).

51. Noel Carroll, op. cit., p. 217. This concept of filtration he credits to Jon Elster, *Ulysses Unbound*, Cambridge: Cambridge University Press, (2000).
52. F.R. Leavis, *Two Cultures? The Significance of C. P. Snow*, London: Chatto and Windus, (1962), p.28.
53. Richard Eyre, *Utopia and Other Places: Memoir of a Young Director*, London: Bloomsbury (1993), p.176.
54. John Gingell and E. P. Brandon, 'Special Issue: In Defence of High Culture', *Journal of Philosophy of Education*, vol.34, no.3, (2000), p.526.
55. S. Banaji et al,. op. cit.
56. Wolfgang Iser, *The Act of Reading: A Theory of Aesthetic Response*, London: Routledge and Kegan Paul, (1972).
57. Stanley Fish, *Is there a text in this class? The Authority of Interpretive Communities*, Cambridge, MA: Harvard University Press, (1980).
58. R. G. Collingwood, *The Principles of Art*, Oxford: Oxford University Press, (1958), pp.128–129.
59. Ron Carter, op. cit.; Anna Craft, *Creativity across the Primary Curriculum: Framing and Developing Practice*, London: Routledge, (2000).
60. Anna Craft, op. cit.; Margaret Boden, op. cit.
61. Rob Pope, *Creativity: Theory, History, Practice*, London: Routledge, (2005).
62. Pope traces this to Edward Young's *Conjectures on Original Composition*, published in 1759. John Hope Mason suggests we should look even earlier to the first Copyright Act of 1710.
63. Rob Pope, op. cit., p.88
64. Ibid.
65. These examples are taken from a workshop I attended, led by Cicely Berry at the RSC in 2007.
66. Cicely Berry, *The Actor and the Text*, London: Virgin Publishing Ltd, (1993), p.199.
67. John Dewey, *Art as Experience*, New York: Perigree Books, (2005), p.58.
68. Ibid., p.40.
69. Ibid., p.58.
70. The following scheme of work is drawn from a workshop led by myself and Helen Lloyd of the RSC Education Department in January 2009.
71. John Hope Mason, op. cit., Chapter 11.
72. Peter Conrad, op. cit., p.584.
73. The political aspirations and revolutionary aesthetics of such artists still have great appeal for many secondary teachers. The plays of Brecht, the art of Picasso, the music of Schoenberg, the poetry of Eliot.
74. John Hope Mason, op. cit., p.236.
75. Elaine Scarry, op. cit., p.46.

NOTES TO CHAPTER 6: BEAUTY IN SCIENCE AND MATHS EDUCATION

1. Alfred North Whitehead, *The Aims of Education*, Presidential address to the Mathematical Association of England, 1916, available at http://www.eco.utexas.edu/facstaff/Cleaver (accessed December 2008).
2. Clifford Geertz, '"From the Native's Point of View": On the Nature of Anthropological Understanding', in *Local Knowledge: Further Essays in Interpretive Anthropology*, New York: Basic Books, (1983), p.57.
3. Ibid.

4. C. P. Snow, *The Two Cultures*, Cambridge: Cambridge University Press, (1959).
5. For a useful summary of Snow's argument and the resultant controversy it sparked, see Peter Watson, *A Terrible Beauty: The People and Ideas that Shaped the Twentieth Century*, London: Phoenix Press, (2001), pp.468–470.
6. Peter Watson, op. cit., p.470.
7. See Arthur Stinner, 'Science, Humanities and Society—The Snow-Leavis Controversy', *Interchange*, vol.20, no.2, (Summer 1989).
8. Ibid., p.20.
9. F. R. Leavis, *Two Cultures? The Significance of C. P. Snow*, London: Chatto and Windus, (1962), p.17. Later in the essay he wrote, 'There is a prior human achievement of collaborative creation . . . one without which the triumphant erection of the scientific edifice would not have been possible: that is, the creation of the human world, including language' (p.27).
10. Arthur Stinner, op. cit., p.21. The categories he attributes to Holton. See D. Holton, *Thematic Origins of Scientific Thought: Kepler to Einstein*, Cambridge, MA: Harvard University Press, (1975).
11. This is implied as a common misconception in Per Morten Kind and Vanessa Kind, 'Creativity in Science Education: Perspectives and Challenges for Developing School Science', *Studies in Science Education*, vol.43, (2007).
12. The arts—notably drama—often explore how science impacts on human lives. Plays such as *Hapgood* by Tom Stoppard and *Copenhagen* by Michael Frayn have their parallels in educational projects with children. As a particularly subtle example, see, Anna Ledgard, '*Visiting Time* and *Boychild*: Site Specific Pedagogical Experiments on the Boundaries of Theatre and Science', in Ralph Levinson, Helen Nicholson and Simon Parry (eds.), *Creative Encounters: New Conversations in Science, Education and the Arts*, London: Wellcome Trust, (2008), pp.110–129. This is, however, a relationship distinct from the central concerns of this chapter.
13. Richard Holmes, *The Age of Wonder: How the Romantic Generation Discovered the Terror and Wonder of Science*, London: Harper Press, (2008), p.469.
14. Ibid.
15. In Brewster, *Memoirs of Newton*, vol.2, Chapter 27, (1855). Cited by Pangratios Papacosta, 'The Mystery in Science: A Neglected Tool for Science Education', *Science Education International*, vol.19, no.1, (March 2008), p.5.
16. Pangratios Papacosta, op. cit., p.7.
17. Robert P. Crease, *The Prism and the Pendulum: The Ten Most Beautiful Experiments in Science*, New York: Random House, (2003), p.165.
18. Ibid., p.166.
19. Umberto Eco (ed.), *On Beauty: A History of a Western Idea*, translated by Alistair McEwan, London: Secker and Warburg, (2004), p. 314.
20. William Wordsworth, 'The Tables Turned', *The Poems*, vol.1, Harmondsworth: Penguin (1977), p.357, lines 26–28.
21. See Marjorie Nicolson, *Newton Demands the Muse: Newton's Opticks and the Eighteenth Century Poets*, Hamden, CT: Archon, (1963).
22. From Thomas Campbell, *To the Rainbow*, cited in Robert Crease, op. cit., p.79.
23. John Keats, 'Lamia', *The Poems of John Keats*, London: Tiger Books, (1991), p.228, lines 235–238. These lines are cited by both Robert Crease, op. cit., p.79 and Richard Dawkins as evidence of the Romantics' hostility to scientific thought. See Richard Dawkins, *Unweaving the Rainbow*, London: Penguin, (2006), p.39.

24. Richard Homes, op. cit., p.160.
25. William Wordsworth, *The Prelude, 1850,* London: Norton, (1979), p.95, Book 3, lines 61–64.
26. John Keats, op. cit., (1991), p.91. See also Richard Holmes, op. cit., p.113.
27. Richard Holmes, op. cit., p.112.
28. Ibid., p.268.
29. Ibid., p.115.
30. Richard Dawkins, op. cit., p.63.
31. John Keats, *Ode on a Grecian Urn,* op. cit., p.259.
32. Richard Dawkins, op. cit., p.41.
33. Ibid., p.118.
34. Mark Girod, 'A Conceptual Overview of the Role of Beauty and Aesthetics in Science and Science Education', *Studies in Science Education,* vol.43, (2006), p.39.
35. Robert Crease, op. cit., p.126.
36. Ibid., p.130.
37. Thomas Hardy captured the experience of stellar observation thus in his 1882 novel *Two on a Tower:* 'At night . . . there is nothing to moderate the blow that the infinitely great, the stellar universe, strikes down upon the infinitely little, the mind of the beholder'. Cited in Richard Homes, op. cit., p.118n.
38. Robert Crease, op. cit., p.142.
39. William Herschel; cited in Richard Holmes, op. cit., p.73.
40. Henri Poincaré, *Science and Method,* translated by Francis Maitland and Bertrand Russell, London: Nelson, (1914), p.22.
41. G. H. Hardy, *A Mathematician's Apology, with a Foreword by C. P. Snow,* Cambridge: Cambridge University Press Canto edition, (1992), p.85.
42. Ibid., p.113.
43. Ibid., p.87.
44. Ed Regis, *Who Got Einstein's Office? Eccentricity and Genius at the Princeton Institute for Advanced Study,* London: Penguin, (1989), p.229.
45. Ibid., p.232.
46. Ibid., p.244.
47. Ibid., p.250. See also the official Stephen Wolfram Web site: www.stephen-wolfram.com.
48. The words of Inspector Buckett in Charles Dickens, *Bleak House,* Oxford: Oxford University Press, (1996), p.749.
49. Humphrey Davy, 'The Chemical Philosopher', Dialogue 5 of his *Consolations;* cited in Richard Holmes, op. cit., p.429.
50. The quote is from David Lehman, *The Perfect Murder: A Study in Detection,* Ann Arbor: University of Michigan Press, (1998); cited in Kate Summerscale, *The Suspicions of Mr Whicher or the Murder at Road Hill House,* London: Bloomsbury, (2009), p.331.
51. Crispin Sartwell, *Six Names of Beauty,* New York: Routledge, (2004), p.87.
52. Ibid., p.20.
53. James W. McAllister, *Beauty and Revolution in Science,* Ithaca, NY / London: Cornell University Press, (1996), pp.172–174.
54. Samuel Taylor Coleridge, *Letters,* (1802); cited in Richard Holmes, op. cit., p.288.
55. Thomas Kuhn, *The Structure of Scientific Revolutions,* Chicago: University of Chicago Press, (1970).
56. George Levine, *Darwin and the Novelists: Patterns of Science in Victorian Fiction,* Chicago: University of Chicago Press, (1988), p.25. See also Gillian Beer, *Darwin's Plots: Evolutionary Narratives in Darwin George Eliot and Nineteenth Century Fiction,* London: Routledge, (1983) and Bruno Latour,

Pandora's Hope: Essays on the Reality of Science Studies, Cambridge, MA: Harvard University Press, (1999).

57. Joseph Carroll, *Evolution and Literary Theory*, Columbia / London: University of Missouri Press, (1995), p.81.

58. William Whewell, cited in Clive Sutton, *Words, Science and Learning*, Buckingham: Open University Press, (1992), p.52.

59. See John Ziman, *Reliable Knowledge: An Exploration of the Grounds for Belief in Science*, New York: Cambridge University Press, (1978).

60. Robert Crease, op. cit., p.122

61. Clive Sutton, op. cit., p.52.

62. Ibid., p.51.

63. Ibid., p.30.

64. Ibid., p.41.

65. Richard Holmes, op. cit., p.469.

66. Ibid., p.291.

67. Ibid., p.292.

68. Daniel Raichvarg, 'Science in the Fairgrounds: From Black to White Magic', *Science and Education*, vol.16, no.6, (June 2007), p.587.

69. Ibid., p.587.

70. Helen Nicholson, 'Introducing Wonder', in Ralph Levinson, Helen Nicholson and Simon Parry (eds.), *Creative Encounters: New Conversations in Science, Education and the Arts*, London: Wellcome Trust, (2008), p.26.

71. See Richard Homes, op. cit., p.454.

72. Elaine Scarry, *On Beauty and Being Just*, London: Duckworth, (2001), p.93.

73. Crispin Sartwell, op. cit., p.99.

74. See www.forestschools.com.

75. Rob Bowker, 'Children's Perceptions and Learning about Tropical Rainforests: An Analysis of Their Drawings', *Environmental Education Research*, vol.31, no.1 (February 2007), p.76.

76. Ibid., p.78.

77. Ibid., p.93.

78. Tim Smit, *Eden*, London: Corgi Books, (2001), p.255.

79. Rob Bowker, 'Evaluating Teaching and Learning Projects in the Eden Project', *Evaluation and Research in Education*, vol.16, no.3, (2002), p.123.

80. Tim Smit, op. cit., p.257.

81. Fred Inglis, *Culture*, Cambridge: Polity Press, p.165.

82. Emma Govan, Helen Nicholson and Katie Normington, *Making a Performance: Devising Histories and Contemporary Practices*, London: Routledge, (2007), p.146.

83. Tim Smit, op. cit., p.257.

84. Ibid., p.259.

85. Emma Govan et al., op. cit., p.146.

NOTES TO CHAPTER 7: AWAKENING BEAUTY IN EDUCATION

1. Clifford Geertz, 'Art as a Cultural System', in *Local Knowledge: Further Essays in Interpretive Anthropology*, New York: Basic Books, (1983), p.118.

2. Charles Taylor, 'Self-interpreting Animals', in *Human Agency and Language: Philosophical Papers 1*, Cambridge: Cambridge University Press, (1985), p.47. For a recent critique of emotional intelligence, see Sophie Rietti,

'Emotional Intelligence as an Educational Goal: A Case for Caution', *Journal of Philosophy of Education*, vol.42, nos.3–4, (2008).
3. Helen Arnold, *Listening to Children Reading*, Sevenoaks: Hodder and Stoughton, (1982), p.16.
4. An official evaluation of the RSC's :earning and Performance Network 2006–2009 is available from the company's head of school partnerships. Contact Rob Ellkington at rob.elkington@rsc.org.uk
5. I take these from Elaine Scarry's summary of what constitutes the qualities of the beautiful as opposed to those of the sublime.
6. At an international conference on Performance Studies held in Queen Mary College, University of London, in June 2006. Luiz Eduardo Soares is Municipal Secretary for the Valorization of Life and the Prevention of Violence in Nova Iguaçu (Rio de Janeiro). Formerly he was National Secretary of Public Security (2003) and Sub-Secretary of Security and Co-ordinator of Security, Justice and Citizenship for the State of Rio de Janeiro (1999–2000).
7. Stanley Cavell, *Conditions Handsome and Unhandsome*, Chicago: University of Chicago Press, (1990), p.61.

Bibliography

Adorno, T. (2005) *Minima Moralia*, London: Verso.

Alperson, P. and Carroll, N. (2008) 'Music, Mind and Morality: Arousing the Body Politic', *Journal of Aesthetic Education*, vol.42, no.1, pp.1–15.

Apple, M. (2000) *Official Knowledge: Democratic Education in a Conservative Age* (2nd ed.) New York: Routledge.

Arblaster, A. and Lukes, S. (eds.) (1971) *The Good Society: A Book of Readings*, London: Methuen.

Armstrong, J. (2000) *The Intimate Philosophy of Art*, London: Penguin.

——(2005) *The Secret Power of Beauty*, London: Penguin.

Arnold, H. (1982) *Listening to Children Reading*, Sevenoaks: Hodder and Stoughton.

Arnold, P. (1994) 'Sport and Moral Education', *The Journal of Moral Education*, vol.23, no.1, pp.75–89.

Baier, A. (1994) *Moral Prejudice: Essays on Ethics*, Cambridge, MA: Harvard University Press.

Banaji, S., Burn, A. and Buckingham, D. (2006) *The Rhetorics of Creativity: A Review of the Literature* (A Report for Creative Partnerships) London: Arts Council England.

Bataille, G. (1987) *Eroticism*, trans. M. Dalwood, London: Boyars.

Baudelaire, C. (1964) *Les Fleurs du Mal et autres poèmes*, Paris: Garnier Flammarion.

Bauman, Z. (1976) *Socialism: The Active Utopia*, London: George Allen and Unwin.

Beer, G. (1983) *Darwin's Plots: Evolutionary Narratives in Darwin George Eliot and Nineteenth Century Fiction*, London: Routledge.

Bell, J. (2008) 'Back to Basics: The Craftsman by Richard Sennett', *The New York Review of Books*, vol.55, no.16.

Bennett, A. (2004) *The History Boys*, London: Faber and Faber.

Bennett, O. (2001) *Cultural Pessimism: Narratives of Decline in the Post-modern World*, Edinburgh: Edinburgh University Press.

Berger, J. (1965) *A Painter of Our Time*, Harmondsworth: Penguin.

——(1980) *About Looking*, London: Writers and Readers Publishing Co-operative.

Berry, C. (1993) *The Actor and the Text*, London: Virgin Publishing Ltd.

Bérubé, M. (ed.) (2005) *The Aesthetics of Cultural Studies*, Oxford: Blackwell Publishing.

Blake, W. (1994) *The Selected Poems of William Blake*, Ware Herts: Wordsworth Press.

Boden, M. (1990) *The Creative Mind: Myths and Mechanisms*, London: Wiedenfeld and Nicolson.

Borges, J. L. (1970) *Labyrinths*, Harmondsworth: Penguin.

Bourdieu, P. (1984) *Distinction: A Social Critique of the Judgment of Taste*, trans. R. Nice, London: Routledge and Kegan Paul.

Bowker, R. (2002) 'Evaluating Teaching and Learning Projects in the Eden Project', *Evaluation and Research in Education*, vol.16, no.3, pp.123–135.

———(2007) 'Children's Perceptions and Learning about Tropical Rainforests: An Analysis of Their Drawings', *Environmental Education Research*, vol.31, no.1, pp.75–96.

Burton, J., Horowitz, R. and Abeles, H. (1999) *Learning in and through the Arts: Curriculum Implications*, New York: Centre for Arts Education Research, Columbia University.

Cahn, S. M. and Meskin, A. (eds.) (2008) *Aesthetics: A Comprehensive Anthology*, Oxford: Blackwell.

Campbell, R. J, Robinson, W., Neelands, J., Hewston, R. and Mazzoli L. (2007) 'Personalised Learning: Ambiguities in Theory and Practice', *British Journal of Educational Studies*, vol.5, no.2, pp.135–154.

Carey, J. (2005) *What Good Are the Arts?* London: Faber and Faber.

Carroll, J. (1995) *Evolution and Literary Theory*, Columbia / London: University of Missouri Press.

Carroll, N. (2003) 'Art, Creativity and Tradition', in B. Gaut and P. Livingston (eds.), *The Creation of Art: New Essays in Philosophical Aesthetics*, Cambridge: Cambridge University Press.

Carter, R. (2004) *Language and Creativity: The Art of Common Talk*, London: Routledge.

Catterall, J. S., Chapleau, R. and Iwanaga, J. (1999) *Involvement in the Arts and Human Development: General Involvement and Intensive Involvement in Music and Theatre Arts*, The Imagination Project at UCLA Graduate School of Education and Information Studies, University of California in Los Angeles.

Cavell, S. (1990) *Conditions Handsome and Unhandsome: The Constitution of Emersonian Perfectionism*, Chicago: University of Chicago Press.

Chodorow, N. (1978) *The Reproduction of Mothering*, Berkeley: University of California Press.

Clark, T. J. (1999) *Farewell to an Idea: Episodes from a History of Modernism*, New Haven, CT / London: Yale University Press.

Claxton, G. (2005) *Building Learning Power*, Bristol: TLO Ltd.

Collingwood, R. G. (1939) *An Autobiography*, Oxford: Oxford University Press.

———(1958) *Principles of Art*, Oxford: Oxford University Press.

Conrad, P. (2007) *Creation: Artists, Gods and Origins*, London: Thames and Hudson.

Cowling, J. (ed.) (2004) *For Art's Sake? Society and the Arts in the 21st Century*, London, Institute for Public Policy Research.

Craft, A. (2000) *Creativity across the Primary Curriculum: Framing and Developing Practice*, London: RoutledgeFalmer.

———(2006) 'Fostering Creativity with Wisdom', *Cambridge Journal of Education*, vol.36, no.3, pp.337–350.

Crease, R. P. (2003) *The Prism and the Pendulum: The Ten Most Beautiful Experiments in Science*, New York: Random House.

Csikszentmihaly, M. (1997) *Creativity: Flow and the Psychology of Discovery and Invention*, New York: Harper Collins.

Danto, A. (2003) *The Abuse of Beauty: Aesthetics and the Concept of Art*, Chicago / La Salle, IL: Open Court.

Davis, L. J. (1995) *Enforcing Normalcy: Disability, Deafness and the Body*, London: Verso.

Dawkins, R. (2006) *Unweaving the Rainbow*, London: Penguin.

Devereux, M. (1998) 'Beauty and Evil: The Case of Leni Riefenstahl's Triumph of the Will', in J. Levinson (ed.), *Aesthetics and Ethics: Essays at the Intersection*, Cambridge: Cambridge University Press.

Dewey, J. (1997) *Experience and Education*, New York: Touchstone.

———(2005) *Art as Experience*, New York: Perigree Books.

Dickens, C. (1996) *Bleak House*, Oxford: Oxford University Press.

Donoghue, D. (2003) *Speaking of Beauty*, New Haven, CT / London: Yale University Press.

Eagleton, T. (1990) *The Ideology of the Aesthetic*, Oxford: Blackwell.

Eco, U. (2004) *On Beauty: A History of a Western Idea*, trans. A. McEwen, London: Secker and Warburg.

———(2007) *On Ugliness*, trans. A. McEwen London: Harvill Secker.

Edwards, C., Gandini, L. and Forman, G. (1998) *The Hundred Languages of Children: The Reggio Emilia Approach—Advanced Reflections*, London: JAI Press.

Eliot, G. (1994) *Middlemarch*, London: Penguin Classics. First published, 1872.

———(2008) *Adam Bede*, London: Penguin Classics. First published 1859.

Eliot, T. S. (1961) *Selected Poems*, London: Faber and Faber.

Elliott, E., Freitas Caton, L. and Rhyne, J. (eds.) (2002) *Aesthetics in a Multicultural Age*, Oxford: Oxford University Press.

Elster, J. (2000) *Ulysses Unbound*, Cambridge: Cambridge University Press.

Eyre, R. (1993) *Utopia and Other Places: Memoir of a Young Director*, London: Bloomsbury.

Fish, S. (1980) *Is There a Text in This Class? The Authority of Interpretive Communities*, Cambridge, MA: Harvard University Press.

Fleming, M. (2008) *Arts in Education and Creativity: a Review of the Literature* (A report for Creative Partnerships), London: Arts Council England.

Fraser, S. and Gestwicki, C. (2002) *Authentic Childhood: Exploring Reggio Emilia in the Classroom*, New York: Delmar.

Frayn, M. (2003) *Copenhagen*, London: Methuen Drama.

Frost, J. (1996) *Creativity in Primary Science*, Buckingham: Open University Press.

Gadamer, H. G. (2004) *Truth and Method*, London: Continuum.

Gallagher, K. (2007) *The Theatre of Urban: Youth and Schooling in Dangerous Times*, Toronto: University of Toronto Press.

Gaunt, W. (1975) *The Aesthetic Adventure*, London: Jonathan Cape.

Gaut, B. and Livingston, P. (eds.) (2003) *The Creation of Art: New Essays in Philosophical Aesthetics*, Cambridge: Cambridge University Press.

Geertz, C. (1983) *Local Knowledge: Further Essays in Interpretive Anthropology*, New York: Basic Books.

Gibson, R. (1975) *The Land without a Name: Alain-Fournier and His World*, London: Elek.

Gilligan, C. (1982) *In a Different Voice: Psychological Theory and Women's Development*, Cambridge, MA: Harvard University Press.

Gingell, J. and Brandon, E. P. (2000) 'Special Issue: In Defence of High Culture', *Journal of Philosophy of Education*, vol.34, no.3.

Girod, M. (2006) 'A Conceptual Overview of the Role of Beauty and Aesthetics in Science and Science Education', *Studies in Science Education*, vol.43, pp.38–61.

Govan, E., Nicholson, H. and Normington, K. (2007) *Making a Performance: Devising Histories and Contemporary Practices*, London: Routledge.

Greer, G. (2003) *The Boy*, London: Thames and Hudson.

Halpin, D. (2003) *Hope and Education: The Role of the Utopian Imagination*, London: RoutledgeFalmer.

Hardy, G. H. (1992) *A Mathematician's Apology, with a Foreword by C. P. Snow,* Cambridge: Cambridge University Press Canto edition.

Hargreaves, D. (2004) *Personalising Learning: Next Steps in Working Laterally,* London: Specialists Schools Trust

——(2006) *Deep Leadership: A New Shape for Schooling?* London: Specialist Schools and Academies Trust

Harrington, A. (2004) *Art and Social Theory: Sociological Arguments in Aesthetics,* Cambridge: Polity Press.

Hartley, D. (2003) 'The Instrumentalisation of the Expressive in Education', *British Journal of Educational Studies,* vol.51, no.1, pp.6–19.

——(2007) 'Personalisation: The Emerging "Revised" Code of Education?' *Oxford Review of Education,* vol.33, no.5, pp.629–642.

Hayward, G., Hodgson, A., Johnson, J., Oancea, A., Pring, R., Spours, K., Wilde, S. and Wright, S. (2005) *Annual Report of the Nuffield Review of 14–19 Education and Training,* Oxford: University of Oxford Department of Educational Studies.

Hines, B. (1969) *A Kestrel for a Knave,* Harmondsworth: Penguin.

Hodgson Burnett, F. (1993) *The Secret Garden,* London: Wordsworth Classics.

Hogarth, W. (1997) *The Analysis of Beauty,* New Haven, CT / London: Yale University Press.

Holden, J. (2004) *Capturing Cultural Value,* London: Demos

——(2008) *Culture and Learning: Towards a New Agenda,* London: Demos.

Holmes, R. (2008) *The Age of Wonder: How the Romantic Generation Discovered the Terror and Wonder of Science,* London: Harper Press.

Holton, D. (1975) *Thematic Origins of Scientific Thought: Kepler to Einstein,* Cambridge, MA: Harvard University Press.

Hood, C. (2000) *The Arts of the State: Culture, Rhetoric and Public Management,* Oxford: Oxford University Press.

Hope Mason, J. (2003) *The Value of Creativity: The Origins and Emergence of an Idea,* Hampshire: Ashgate.

Hughes, R. (1980) *The Shock of the New: Art and the Century of Change,* London: BBC Publications.

Humphries, P. (2006) 'Towards a Personalised Educational Landscape', http://www.futurelab.org.uk/resources/publications_reports_articles/web_articles/Web_article479. Accessed March 2008.

Inglis, F. (1982) *The Promise of Happiness: Value and Meaning in Children's Fiction,* Cambridge: Cambridge University Press.

——(1988) *Popular Culture and Political Power,* London: Harvester.

——(2004) *Culture,* Cambridge: Polity Press.

Iser, W. (1972) *The Act of Reading: A Theory of Aesthetic Response,* London: Routledge and Kegan Paul.

Jarvis, P. (2007) 'Monsters, Magic and Mr Psycho: A Biocultural Approach to Rough and Tumble Play in the Early Years of Primary School', *Early Years,* vol.27, no.2, pp.171–188.

Jones, A. (2002) '"Every man knows where and how beauty gives him pleasure": Beauty Discourse and the Logic of Aesthetics', in E. Elliott, L. Freitas Caton and J. Rhyne (eds.), *Aesthetics in a Multicultural Age,* Oxford: Oxford University Press, pp. 215–239.

Jones, C. (2008) 'Teaching Virtue through Physical Education: Some Comments and Reflections', *Sport, Education and Society,* vol.13, no.3, pp.337–349.

Kant, I. (1987) *Critique of Judgment,* trans. W. S. Pluhar, Indianapolis, IN / Cambridge: Hackett Publishing.

Kasrel, D. (1999) *Crutchmaster Bill Shannon: The Art of Weightlessness,* http://www.citypaper.net/articles/111199/ae.dance.crutch.shtml. Accessed July 2004.

Keats, J. (1991) *The Poems of John Keats*, London: Tiger Books.
Killeen, J. (2007) *The Tales of Oscar Wilde*, Bristol: Ashgate.
Kimmelman, M. (2005) *The Accidental Masterpiece: On the Art of Life and Vice Versa*, New York: Penguin.
Kind, P. M. and Kind, V. (2007) 'Creativity in Science Education: Perspectives and Challenges for Developing School Science', *Studies in Science Education*, vol. 43, pp.1–37.
Kohlberg, L. (1981) *The Philosophy of Moral Development: Moral Stages and the Idea of Justice*, New York: HarperCollins.
Kristeller, P. (2008) 'Introduction: Classic Sources', in S. M. Cahn and A. Meskin (eds.), *Aesthetics: A Comprehensive Anthology*, Oxford: Blackwell.
Kuhn, T. (1970) *The Structure of Scientific Revolutions*, Chicago: University of Chicago Press.
Kuppers, P. (2003) *Disability and Contemporary Performance: Bodies on Edge*, London: Routledge.
Latour, B. (1999) *Pandora's Hope: Essays on the Reality of Science Studies*, Cambridge, MA: Harvard University Press.
Layard, R. and Dunn, J. (2009) *A Good Childhood: Searching for Values in a Competitive Age*, London: Penguin.
Leadbeater, C. (2003) *Personalisation through Participation*, London: Demos
——(2005) *The Shape of Things to Come: Personalised Learning through Collaboration*, London: DfES.
Leavis, F. R. (1962) *Two Cultures? The Significance of C. P. Snow*, London: Chatto and Windus.
Ledgard, A. (2008) '*Visiting Time* and *Boychild*: Site Specific Pedagogical Experiments on the Boundaries of Theatre and Science', in R. Levinson, H. Nicholson and S. Parry (eds.), *Creative Encounters: New Conversations in Science, Education and the Arts*, London: Wellcome Trust, pp.110–129.
Lehman, D. (1998) *The Perfect Murder: A Study in Detection*, Ann Arbor: University of Michigan Press.
Levine, G. (1988) *Darwin and the Novelists: Patterns of Science in Victorian Fiction*, Chicago: University of Chicago Press.
Levinson, J. (ed.) (1998) *Aesthetics and Ethics: Essays at the Intersection*, Cambridge: Cambridge University Press.
Levinson, R., Nicholson, H. and Parry, S. (eds.), (2008) *Creative Encounters: New Conversations in Science, Education and the Arts*, London: Wellcome Trust.
Lidstone, G. (2004) 'Education and the Arts: Evaluating Arts Education Programmes', in J. Cowling (ed.), *For Art's Sake?* London: Institute for Public Policy Research.
Lippmann, W. (1937) *The Good Society*, London: Allen and Unwin.
MacIntyre, A. (1987) *After Virtue: A Study in Moral Theory*, London: Duckworth.
McAllister, J. W. (1996) *Beauty and Revolution in Science*, Ithaca, NY / London: Cornell University Press.
Mackey, S. (1993) 'Emotion and Cognition in Arts Education', *Curriculum Studies*, vol.1, no.2.
Magorian, M. (1981) *Goodnight Mr Tom*, London: Kestrel.
Martinez, G. (2005) *The Oxford Murders*, trans. S. Sotio, London: Abacus.
Matarasso, F. (1997) *Use or Ornament? The Social Impact of Participation in the Arts*, Stroud Glos: Comedia.
Milton, J. (2000) *Paradise Lost*, London: Penguin Classics.
Morpurgo, M. and Balit, B. (1995) *Blodin the Beast*, London: Frances Lincoln.
Morris, W. (1979) *Political Writings of William Morris*, ed. A. L.Morton, London: Lawrence and Wishart.

Murdoch, I. (1991) *The Sovereignty of Good*, London: Routledge.

National Advisory Committee for Culture and Creativity in Education (1999) *All Our Futures: Creativity, Culture and Education*, London: Department for Education and Employment.

Nash, W. (1993) *Jargon: Its Uses and Abuses*, Oxford: Blackwell.

Neelands, J. and Choe, B. (2009) 'The English Model of Creativity: Cultural Politics of an Idea', *International Journal of Cultural Policy*, vol.15, no.3.

Negus, K. and Pickering, M. (2004) *Creativity, Communication and Cultural Value*, London / Thousand Oaks, CA / New Delhi: SAGE.

Nehamas, A. (2007) *Only a Promise of Happiness: The Place of Beauty in a World of Art*, Princeton, NJ: Princeton University Press.

Newton, D. P. and Newton, L. D. (2009) 'Some Student Teachers' Conceptions of Creativity in Science', *Research in Science and Technology Education*, vol. 27, no. 1.

Nicolson, M. (1963) *Newton Demands the Muse: Newton's Opticks and the Eighteenth Century Poets*, Hamden, CT: Archon.

Nowottny, W. (1962) *The Language Poets Use*, Oxford: Oxford University Press.

Nussbaum, M. (1986) *The Fragility of Goodness: Luck and Ethics in Greek Tragedy and Philosophy*, Cambridge: Cambridge University Press.

——(1990) *Love's Knowledge*, Oxford: Oxford University Press.

——(2001) *Upheavals of Thought: The Intelligence of the Emotions*, Cambridge: Cambridge University Press.

O'Connor, J. J. and Robertson, E. F. (2003) *Plato*, School of Mathematics and Statistics, University of St Andrews, Scotland, www-gap.dcs.st-and.ac.uk. Accessed March 2008.

Oakeshott, M. (1978) *Experience and Its Modes*, London: Cambridge University Press. First published 1933.

——(1962) 'The Voice of Poetry in the Conversation of Mankind', in *Rationalism in Politics and Other Essays*, London: Methuen.

——(1989) *The Voice of Liberal Learning*, New Haven, CT: Yale University Press.

Papacosta, P. (2008) 'The Mystery in Science: A Neglected Tool for Science Education', *Science Education International*, vol.19, no.1, pp.5–8.

Pater, W. (1986) *The Renaissance: Studies in Art and Poetry*, Oxford: Oxford University Press.

Poincaré, H. (1914) *Science and Method*, trans. F. Maitland and B. Russell, London: Nelson.

Pollard, A. and James, M. (eds.) (2004) *Personalised Learning, a Commentary by the Teaching and Learning Research Programme*, London: Economic and Social Research Council (ESRC).

Pope, R. (2005) *Creativity: Theory, History, Practice*, London: Routledge.

Plato (1989) *Symposium*, trans. A. Nehamas and P. Woodruff, Indianapolis, IN / Cambridge: Hackett Publishing.

Raichvarg, D. (2007) 'Science in the Fairgrounds: From Black to White Magic', *Science and Education*, vol.16, no.6, pp.585–591.

Ransome, A. (1962) *Swallows and Amazons*, Harmondsworth: Puffin books.

Rawls, J. (1971) *A Theory of Justice*, Cambridge, MA: Harvard University Press.

Regis, E. (1989) *Who Got Einstein's Office? Eccentricity and Genius at the Princeton Institute for Advanced Study*, London: Penguin.

Ricks, C. (2003) *Dylan's Visions of Sin*, New York: Harper Collins.

Rietti, S. (2008) 'Emotional Intelligence as an Educational Goal: A Case for Caution', *Journal of Philosophy of Education*, vol.42, nos.3–4, pp.631–643.

Rimbaud, A. (1963) *Poésies complètes*, ed. P. Pia, Paris: Gallimard Livre de Poche.

Runco. M. (ed.) (1997) *The Creativity Research Handbook*, vol. 1, Cresskill, NJ: Hampton Press.

Ruskin, J. (2004) *Selected Writings*, ed. D. Birch, Oxford: Oxford University Press.

Sartwell, C. (2004) *Six Names of Beauty*, New York: Routledge.

Scarry, E. (2001) *On Beauty and Being Just*, London: Duckworth.

Schiller, F. (1967) *On the Aesthetic Education of Man, in a Series of Letters*, ed. and trans. E. M. Wilkinson and L. A. Willoughby, Oxford: Clarendon Press.

Schon, D. (1987) *Educating the Reflective Practitioner: Toward a New Design for Teaching and Learning in the Profession*, San Francisco: Jossey Bass.

Sennett, R. (2008) *The Craftsman*, London: Allen Lane.

Sheilds, D. L. L. and Bredemeier, B. J. L. (1995) *Character Development and Physical Activity*, Champaign, IL: Human Kinetics Publishers.

Shelley, P. B. (1993) *Ode to the West Wind and Other Poems*, Mineola / New York: Dover Publications, Inc.

Shumway, D. (2005) 'Cultural Studies and Questions of Pleasure and Value', in M. Bérubé (ed.), *The Aesthetics of Cultural Studies*, Oxford: Blackwell, pp.103–116.

Shusterman, R. (1992) *Pragmatist Aesthetics: Living Beauty, Rethinking Art*, Oxford: Blackwell.

——(2000) *Performing Live: Aesthetic Alternatives for the Ends of Art*, Ithaca, NY: Cornell University Press.

Smit, T. (2001) *Eden*, London: Corgi Books.

Snow, C. P. (1959) *The Two Cultures*, Cambridge: Cambridge University Press.

Steiner, W. (2001) *The Trouble with Beauty*, London: Heinemann.

Stinner, A. (1989) 'Science, Humanities and Society—The Snow-Leavis Controversy', *Interchange*, vol.20, no.2, pp.16–23.

Stoppard, T. (1999) 'Hapgood' in *Tom Stoppard Plays: 5*, London: Faber and Faber.

Summerscale, K. (2009) *The Suspicions of Mr Whicher or the Murder at Road Hill House*, London: Bloomsbury.

Sutton, C. (1992) *Words, Science and Learning*, Buckingham: Open University Press.

Synnott, A. (1993) *The Body Social: Symbolism, Self and Society*, London: Routledge.

Tan S. (2003) *The Red Tree* Vancouver: Simply Read.

Taylor, C. (1985) *Human Agency and Language: Philosophical Papers 1*, Cambridge: Cambridge University Press.

Varley, J. (1978) *The Persistence of Vision*, New York: Dial Press.

Watson, P. (2001) *A Terrible Beauty: The People and Ideas that Shaped the Twentieth Century*, London: Phoenix Press.

Whitehead, A. N. (1916) *The Aims of Education*, Presidential address to the Mathematical Association of England, http://www.eco.utexas.edu/facstaff/Cleaver. Accessed December 2008.

Wilde, O. (1954) *Selected Essays and Poems*, London: Penguin.

——(1979) *The Picture of Dorian Gray*, Harmondsworth: Penguin.

——(1995) *The Selfish Giant*, illustr. Saelig Gallagher, Hove, East Sussex: Macdonald Young Books.

Williams, R. (1965) *The Long Revolution*, Harmondsworth: Pelican.

——(1983) *Keywords: A Vocabulary of Culture and Society*, London: Fontana.

——(2007) *Politics of Modernism*, London: Verso Radical Thinkers series.

Willett, J. (ed.) (1964) *Brecht on Theatre*, London: Eyre Methuen.

Wind, E. (1968) *Pagan Mysteries in the Renaissance*, London: Faber and Faber.

Winston, J. (2004) *Drama and English at the Heart of the Curriculum*, London: David Fulton Press.

Wolf, N. (1990) *The Beauty Myth*, Toronto: Random House.
Wolff, J. (2008) *The Aesthetics of Uncertainty*, New York: Columbia University Press.
Wordsworth, W. (1977) *The Poems*, vol.1, ed. J. O. Hayden, Harmondsworth: Penguin.
——(1979) *The Prelude: 1799, 1805, 1850*, ed. J. Wordsworth, M. H. Abrams, S. Gill, London: Norton.
Wright, K. (1987) *Cat Among the Pigeons*, London: Viking.
Yeats, W. B. (2000) *W.B Yeats Selected Poems*, London: Penguin.
Ziman, J. (1978) *Reliable Knowledge: An Exploration of the Grounds for Belief in Science*, New York: Cambridge University Press.

Index

Note: Page references in bold are to figures.

Lightning Source UK Ltd.
Milton Keynes UK
174030UK00002B/15/P